Bloomsbury Christening.

PHILADELPHIA.

The Winglebury Duel.

SKETCHES BY BOZ

BY

CHARLES DICKENS.
(BOZ.)

WITH TWENTY ILLUSTRATIONS.

FROM DESIGNS BY GEORGE CRUIKSHANK.

IN TWO VOLUMES.

VOL. II

Philadelphia:
T. B. PETERSON, NO. 306 CHESTNUT STREET,
GIRARD BUILDINGS, ABOVE THIRD.

CHAPTER XI.

MAKING A NIGHT OF IT.

DAMON and Pythias were undoubtedly very good fellows in their way: the former for his extreme readiness to put in special bail for a friend, and the latter for a certain trump-like punctuality in turning up just in the very nick of time, scarcely less remarkable. Many points in their character have however grown obsolete. Damons are rather hard to find in these days of imprisonment for debt (except the sham ones, and they cost half-a-crown); and, as to the Pythiases, the few that have existed in these degenerate times have had an unfortunate knack of making themselves scarce at the very moment when their appearance would have been strictly classical. If the actions of these heroes, however, can find no parallel in modern times, their friendship can. We have Damon and Pythias on the one hand—Potter and Smithers on the other; and lest the two last-mentioned names should never have reached the ears of our unenlightened readers, we can do no better than make them acquainted with the owners thereof.

Mr. Thomas Potter, then, was a clerk in the city, and Mr. Robert Smithers was a ditto in the same; their incomes were limited, but their friendship was unbounded. They lived in the same street, walked into town every morning at the same hour, dined at the same slap-bang every day, and reveled in each other's company every night. They were knit together by the closest ties of intimacy and friendship; or, as Mr. Thomas Potter touchingly observed, they were "thick-and-thin pals, and nothing but it." There was a spice of romance in Mr. Smithers's disposition, a ray of poetry, a gleam of misery, a sort of consciousness of he didn't exactly know what, coming across him, he didn't precisely know why—which stood out in fine relief against the off hand, dashing amateur pickpocket-sort-of-manner, which distinguished Mr. Potter in an eminent degree.

The peculiarity of their respective dispositions extended itself to their individual costume. Mr. Smithers generally appeared in public in a surtout and shoes, with a narrow black neckerchief and a brown hat, very much turned up at the sides —peculiarities which Mr. Potter wholly eschewed, for it was his ambition to do something in the celebrated "kiddy" or stage-coach way, and he had even gone so far as to invest capital in the purchase of a rough blue coat with wooden buttons, made upon the fireman's principle, in which, with the addition of a low-crowned, flowerpot-saucer-shaped hat, he had created no inconsiderable sensation at the Albion in Little Russel-street, and divers other places of public and fashionable resort.

Mr. Potter and Mr. Smithers had mutually agreed that on the receipt of their quarter's salary, they would jointly and in company "spend the evening"—an evident misnomer—the spending applying, as every body knows, not to the evening itself, but to all the money the individual may chance to be possessed of on the occasion to which reference is made; and they had further agreed that, on the evening aforesaid, they would "make a night of it"—an expressive term, implying the borrowing of several hours from to-morrow morning, adding them to the night before, and manufacturing a compound night of the whole.

The quarter-day arrived at last—we say at last, because quarter days are as eccentric as comets, moving wonderfully quick when you have a good deal to pay, and marvelously slow when you have a little to receive. Mr. Thomas Potter and Mr. Robert Smithers met by appointment to begin the evening with a dinner; and a nice, snug, comfortable dinner they had, consisting of a little procession of four chops and four kidneys following each other, supported on either side by a pot of the real draught stout, and attended by divers cushions of bread and wedges of cheese.

When the cloth was removed, Mr. Thomas Potter ordered the waiter to bring in two goes of his best Scotch whisky, with warm water and sugar, and a couple of his "very mildest" Havannahs, which the waiter did. Mr. Thomas Potter mixed his grog, and lit his cigar; Mr. Robert Smithers did the same; and then Mr. Thomas Potter jocularly proposed as the first toast, "the abolition of all offices whatever" (not sinecures, but counting-houses), which was immediately drunk by Mr. Robert Smithers, with enthusiastic applause. So they went on talking politics, puffing cigars, and sipping whisky-and-water, till the "goes"—most appropriately so called—were both gone, which Mr. Robert Smithers perceiving, immediately ordered in two more goes of the best Scotch whisky and two more of the very mildest Havannahs; and the goes kept coming in, and the mild Havannahs kept going out, until what with the drinking, and lighting, and puffing, and the stale ashes on the table, and the tallow-grease on the cigars, Mr. Robert Smithers began to doubt the mildness of the Havannahs, and to feel very much as if he had been sitting in a hackney-coach with his back to the horses.

As to Mr. Thomas Potter, he would keep laughing out loud, and volunteering inarticulate declarations that he was "all right," in proof of which, he feebly bespoke the evening paper after the next gentleman, but finding it a matter of some difficulty to discover any news in its columns or to ascertain distinctly whether it had any columns at all, he walked slowly out to look for the moon, and after coming back quite pale with looking up at the sky so long, and attempting to express mirth at Mr. Robert Smithers having fallen asleep, by various galvanic chuckles, he laid his head on his arm, and went to sleep also. When he woke again, Mr. Robert Smithers woke too, and they both very gravely agreed that it was extremely unwise to eat so many pickled walnuts with the chops, as it was a notorious fact that they always made people queer and sleepy; indeed, if it had not been for the whisky and cigars, there was no knowing what harm they mightn't have done 'em. So they took some coffee, and after paying the bill, twelve and twopence the dinner, and the odd tenpence for the waiter—thirteen shillings in all—started out on their expedition to manufacture a night.

It was just half-past eight, so they thought they couldn't do better than go half-price to the slips at the City Theatre, which they did accordingly. Mr. Robert Smithers, who had become extremely poetical after the settlement of the bill, enlivening the walk by informing Mr. Thomas Potter in confidence that he felt an inward presentiment of approaching dissolution and subsequently embellishing the threatre, by falling asleep, with his head and both arms gracefully drooping over the front of the boxes.

Such was the quiet demeanor of the unassuming Smithers, and such was the happy effects of Scotch whisky and Havannahs on that interesting person; but Mr. Thomas Potter, whose great aim it was to be considered as a "knowing card," a "fast goer," and so forth, conducted himself in a very different manner, and commenced going very fast indeed—rather too fast at last, for the patience of his audience to keep pace with him. On his first entry, he contented himself by earnestly calling upon the gentlemen in the gallery to "flare up," accompanying the demand with another request, expressive of his wish that they would instantaneously "form a union," both which requisitions were responded to, in the manner most in vogue on such occasions.

"Give that dog a bone!" cried one gentleman in his shirt-sleeves.

"Where have you been a having half a pint of intermediate beer?" cried a second. "Tailor!" screamed a third. "Barber's clerk!" shouted a fourth. "Throw him o—ver!" roared a fifth; while numerous voices concurred in desiring Mr. Thomas Potter to return to the arms of his maternal parent or in common parlance, "to go home to his mother!" All these taunts Mr. Thomas Potter received with supreme contempt, cocking the low-crowned hat a little more on one side whenever any reference was made to his personal appearance, and standing up with his arms a-kimbo, expressing defiance most melodramatically.

The overture—to which these various sounds had been an *ad libitum* accompaniment—concluded, the second piece began, and Mr. Thomas Potter, emboldened by importunity, proceeded to behave in a most unprecedented outrageous manner. First of all, he imitated the shake of the principal female singer; then groaned at the blue fire, then affected to be frightened into convulsions of terror at the appearance of the ghost; and lastly not only made a running commentary in an audible voice, upon the dialogue on the stage, but actually awoke Mr. Robert Smithers, who hearing his companion making a noise, and having a very indistinct notion of where he was, or what was required of him, immediately, by way of imitating a good example, set up the most unearthly, unremitting, and appalling howling that ever audience heard. It was too much. "Turn them out!" was the general cry. A noise as of shuffling of feet, and men being knocked up with violence against wainscoting was heard : a hurried dialogue of "Come out!"—"I won't!"—"You shall!"—"I shan't!"—"Give me your card, sir,"—"You're a scoundrel, sir," and so forth, succeeded. A round of applause betokened the approbation of the audience, and Mr. Robert Smithers and Mr. Thomas Potter found themselves shot with astonishing swiftness into the road, without having had the trouble of once putting foot to ground during the whole progress of their rapid descent.

Mr. Robert Smithers being constitutionally one of the slow-goers, and having had quite enough of fast-going, in the course of his recent expulsion, to last to the quarter-day then next ensuing at the very least, had no sooner emerged with his companion from the precincts of Milton-street, than he proceeded to indulge in circuitous references to the beauties of sleep, mingled with distant allusions to the propriety of returning to Islington, and testing the influence of their patent Bramahs over the street-door locks to which they respectively belonged. Mr. Thomas Potter, however, was valorous and peremptory. They had come out to make a night of it : and a night must be made. So Mr. Robert Smithers, who was three parts dull and the other dismal, despairingly assented ; and they went into a wine-vault to get materials for assisting them in making a night, where they found a good many young ladies, and various old gentlemen, and a plentiful sprinkling of hackney-coachmen and cab-drivers, all drinking and talking together; and Mr. Thomas Potter and Mr. Robert Smithers drank small glasses of brandy, and large glasses of soda, till they began to have a very confused idea, either of things in general, or any thing in particular ; and when they had done treating themselves, they began treating every body else ; and the rest of the entertainment was a confused mixture of heads and heels, black eyes and blue uniforms, mud and gas-lights, thick doors and a stone paving.

Then, as standard novelists expressly inform us—"all was blank!" and in the morning the blank was filled with the words "STATION-HOUSE," and the station-house was filled up with Mr. Thomas Potter, Mr. Robert Smithers, and the major part of their wine-vault companions of the preceding night, with a comparatively small portion of clothing of any kind. And it was disclosed at the Police-office, to the indignation of the Bench, and the astonishment of the spectators, how one Robert Smithers, aided and abetted by one Thomas Potter, had knocked down and beaten, in divers streets, at different times, five men, four boys, and three women; how the said Thomas Potter had feloniously obtained possession of five door-knockers, two bell-handles, and a bonnet; how Robert Smithers, his friend, had sworn at least forty pound's worth of oaths, at the rate of five shillings apiece; terrified whole streets full of Her Majesty's subjects with awful shrieks and alarms of fire; destroyed the uniforms of five policemen, and committed various other atrocities too numerous to recapitulate. And the magistrate, after an appropriate reprimand, fined Mr. Thomas Potter and Mr. Robert Smithers five shillings each, for being what the law vulgarly terms drunk, with the trifling addition of thirty-four pounds for seventeen assaults at forty shillings a-head with liberty to speak to the prosecutors.

The prosecutors *were* spoken to, and Messrs. Potter and Smithers lived on credit for a quarter as best they might; and, although the prosecutors expressed their readiness to be assaulted twice a-week on the same terms, they have never since been detected in "making a night of it."

CHAPTER XII.

THE PRISONERS' VAN.

We were passing the corner of Bow-street, on our return from a lounging excursion the other afternoon, when a crowd, assembled around the door of the Police Office, attracted our attention, and we turned up the street accordingly. There were thirty or forty people standing on the pavement and half across the road, and a few stragglers were patiently stationed on the opposite side of the way—all evidently waiting in expectation of some arrival. We waited too, a few minutes, but nothing occurred; so we turned round to an unshaven sallow-looking cobbler, who was standing next us with his hands under the bib of his apron, and put the usual question of "What's the matter?" The cobbler eyed us from head to foot with superlative contempt, and laconically replied "Nuffin."

Now, we were perfectly aware that if two men stop in the street to look at any given object, or even to gaze in the air, two hundred men will be assembled in no time: but as we knew very well that no crowd of people could by possibility remain in a street for five minutes without getting up a little amusement among themselves, unless they had some absorbing object in view, the natural inquiry next in order was, "What are all these people waiting here for?"—"Her Majesty's carriage," replied the cobbler. This was still more extraordinary. We could not imagine what earthly business Her Majesty's carriage could have at the Public Office, Bow-street, and we were beginning to ruminate on the possible causes of such an uncommon appearance, when a general exclamation from all the boys in the crowd of "Here's the wan!" caused us to raise our heads and look up the street.

The covered vehicle, in which prisoners are conveyed from the police-offices to the different prisons, was coming along at full speed, and it then occurred to us for the first time that Her

Majesty's carriage was merely another name for the prisoners' van, conferred upon it, not only by reason of the superior gentility of the term, but because the aforesaid van is maintained at Her Majesty's expense, having been originally started for the exclusive accommodation of ladies and gentlemen under the necessity of visiting the various houses of call known by the general denomination of "Her Majesty's Gaols."

The van drew up at the office-door, and the people thronged round the steps, just leaving a little alley for the prisoners to pass through. Our friend the cobbler and the other stragglers crossed over, and we followed their example. The driver, and another man who had been seated by his side in front of the vehicle, dismounted, and were admitted into the office. The office-door was closed after them, and the crowd were on the tiptoe of expectation.

After a few minutes delay the door again opened, and the two first prisoners appeared. They were a couple of girls, of whom the elder could not be more than sixteen, and the younger of whom had certainly not attained her fourteenth year. That they were sisters was evident from the resemblance which still subsisted between them, though two additional years of depravity had fixed their brand upon the elder girl's features as legibly as if a red-hot iron had seared them. They were both gaudily dressed, the younger one especially; and although there was a strong similarity between them in both respects, which was rendered the more obvious by their being handcuffed together, it is impossible to conceive a greater contrast than the demeanor of the two presented. The younger girl was weeping bitterly—not for display or in the hope of producing effect, but for very shame; her face was buried in her handkerchief, and her whole manner was but too expressive of bitter and unavailing sorrow.

"How long are you for, Emily?" screamed a red-faced woman in the crowd. "Six weeks and labor," replied the elder girl with a flaunting laugh; "and that's better than the stone jug any how; the mill's a deal better than the Sessions, and here's Bella a-going too for the first time. Hold up your head, you chicken," she continued, boisterously tearing the other girl's handkerchief away; "Hold up your head, and show 'em your face; I an't jealous, but I'm blessed if I an't game."—"That's right, old gal," exclaimed a man in a paper cap, who, in common with the greater part of the crowd, had been inexpressibly delighted with this little incident.—"Right!" replied the girl; "ah to be sure; what's the odds, eh?"—"Come in with you," interrupted the driver.—"Don't you be in a hurry, coachman," replied the girl, "and recollect I want to be set down in Cold-Bath Fields—large house with a high garden-wall in front; you can't mistake it. Hallo, Bella, where are you going to—you'll pull my precious arm off?" This was addressed to the younger girl, who, in her anxiety to hide herself in the caravan, had ascended the steps first, and forgotten the strain upon the handcuff; "Come down, and let's show you the way." And after jerking the miserable girl down with a force which made her stagger on the pavement, she got into the vehicle, and was followed by her wretched companion.

These two girls had been thrown upon London streets, their vices and debauchery, by a sordid and rapacious mother. What the younger girl was then, the elder had been once; and what the elder then was, she must soon become. A melancholy prospect, but how surely to be realized: a tragic drama, but how often acted! Turn to the prisons and police-offices of London—nay look into the very streets themselves. These things pass before our eyes day after day, and hour after hour—they have become such matters of course, that they are utterly disregarded. The progress of these girls in crime will be as rapid as the flight of a pestilence, resembling it too in its baneful influence and wide-spreading infection. Step by step how many wretched females, within the sphere of every man's observation, have become involved in a career of vice frightful to contemplate; hopeless at its commencement, loathsome and repulsive in its course, friendless, forlorn, and unpitied, at its miserable conclusion!

There were other prisoners—boys of ten, as hardened in vice as men of fifty—a houseless vagrant going joyfully to prison as a place of food and shelter, handcuffed to a man whose prospects were ruined, character lost, and family rendered destitute by his first offense.—Our curiosity, however, was satisfied. The first group had left an impression on our mind we would gladly have avoided, and would willingly have effaced.

The crowd dispersed; the vehicle rolled away with its load of guilt and misfortune, and we saw no more of the Prisoners' Van.

TALES.

CHAPTER I.

THE BOARDING-HOUSE.

CHAPTER THE FIRST.

MRS. TIBBS was, beyond all dispute, the most tidy, fidgety, thrifty little personage that ever inhaled the smoke of London ; and the house of Mrs. Tibbs was decidedly the neatest in all Great Coram-street. The area and the area-steps, and the street-door and the street-door steps, and the brass handle, and the door-plate, and the knocker, and the fan-light, were all as clean and bright as indefatigable white-washing, and hearth-stoning, and scrubbing and rubbing could make them. The wonder was, that the brass door-plate, with the interesting inscription "MRS. TIBBS," had never caught fire from constant friction, so perseveringly was it polished. There were meat-safe-looking blinds in the parlor windows, blue and gold curtains in the drawing-room, and spring-roller blinds, as Mrs. Tibbs was wont in the pride of her heart to boast, "all the way up." The bell-lamp in the passage looked as clear as a soap-bubble ; you could see yourself in all the tables, and French-polish yourself on any one of the chairs. The banisters were bees'-waxed, and the very stair-wires made your eyes wink, they were so glittering.

Mrs. Tibbs was somewhat short of stature, and Mr. Tibbs was by no means a large man. He had, moreover, very short legs, but, by way of indemnification, his face was peculiarly long. He was to his wife what the 0 is in 90—he was of some importance *with* her—he was nothing without her. Mrs. Tibbs was always talking. Mr. Tibbs rarely spoke ; but if it were at any time possible to put in a word just when he should have said nothing at all, he did it. Mrs. Tibbs detested long stories, and Mr. Tibbs had one, the conclusion of which had never been heard by his most intimate friends. It always began, "I recollect when I was in the volunteer corps, in eighteen hundred and six,"—but as he spoke very slowly and softly and his better half very quickly and loudly, he rarely got beyond the introductory sentence. He was a melancholy specimen of the story-teller. He was the wandering Jew of Joe Millerism.

Mr. Tibbs enjoyed a small independence from the pension-list—about 43*l.* 15*s.* 10*d.* a-year. His father, mother, and five interesting scions from the same stock, drew a like sum from the revenue of a grateful country, though for what particular service was never distinctly known. But as this said independence was not quite sufficient to furnish two people with *all* the luxuries of this life, it had occurred to the busy little spouse of Tibbs, that the best thing she could do with a legacy of 700*l.*, would be to take and furnish a tolerable house, some where in that partially-explored tract of country which lies between the British Museum, and a remote village called Somers Town, for the reception of boarders. Great Coram-street was the spot pitched upon. The house had been furnished accordingly; two female servants and a boy engaged, and an advertisement inserted in the morning papers, informing the public that "Six individuals would meet with all the comforts of a cheerful musical home in a select private family, residing within ten minutes' walk of every where." Answers out of number were received, with all sorts of initials; all the letters of the alphabet seemed to be seized with a sudden wish to go out boarding and lodging; voluminous was the correspondence between Mrs. Tibbs and the applicants, and most profound was the secrecy which was to be observed. "E." didn't like this, and "I." couldn't think of putting up with that; "I. O. U." didn't think the terms would suit him; and "G. R." had never slept in a French bed. The result, however, was, that three gentlemen became inmates of Mrs. Tibbs's house, on terms which were "agreeable to all parties." In went the advertisement again, and a lady with her two daughters, proposed to increase—not their families, but Mrs. Tibbs's.

"Charming woman, that Mrs. Maplesone!" said Mrs. Tibbs, as she and her spouse were sitting by the fire after breakfast; the gentlemen having gone out on their several avocations "Charming woman, indeed!" repeated little Mrs. Tibbs, more by way of soliloquy than any thing else, for she never thought of consulting her husband. "And the two daughters are delightful. We must have some fish to-day; they'll join us at dinner for the first time."

Mr. Tibbs placed the poker at right angles with the fire-shovel, and essayed to speak, but recollected he had nothing to say.

"The young ladies," continued Mrs. T., "have kindly volunteered to bring thir own piano."

Tibbs thought of the volunteer story, but did not venture it. A bright thought struck him—

"It's very likely," said he.

"Pray don't lean your head against the paper," interrupted Mrs. Tibbs—"and don't put your feet on the steel fender; that's worse."

Tibbs took his head from the paper, and his feet from the fender, and proceeded. "It's very likely one of the young ladies may set her cap at young Mr. Simpson, and you know a marriage"——

"A what!" shrieked Mrs. Tibbs. Tibbs modestly repeated his former suggestion.

"I beg you won't mention such a thing," said Mrs. T. "A marriage, indeed!—to rob me of my boarders—no, not for the world."

Tibbs thought in his own mind that the event was by no means unlikely, but as he never argued with his wife, he put a stop to the dialogue, by observing it was "time to go to business." He always went out at ten o'clock in the morning, and returned at five in the afternoon, with an exceedingly dirty face, and smelling very mouldy. Nobody knew what he was, or where he went to; but Mrs. Tibbs used to say with an air of great importance, that he was engaged in the City.

The Miss Maplesones and their accomplished parent arrived in the course of the afternoon in a hackney-coach, and accompanied by a most astonishing number of packages. Trunks, bonnet-boxes, muff-boxes and parasols, guitar-cases, and parcels of all imaginable shapes, done up in brown paper, and fastened with pins, filled the passage. Then, there was such a running up and down with the luggage, such scampering for warm water for the ladies to wash in, and such a bustle, and confusion, and beating of servants and curling-irons, as had never been known in Great Coram-street before. Little Mrs. Tibbs was quite in her element, bustling about, talking incessantly, and distributing towels and soap, and all the *et ceteras*, like a head nurse in a hospital. The house was not restored to its usual state of quiet repose until the ladies were safely shut up in their respective bedrooms, engaged in the important occupation of dressing for dinner.

"Are these gals 'andsome?" inquired Mr. Simpson of Mr. Septimus Hicks, another of the boarders, as they were amusing themselves in the drawing-room before dinner, by lolling on sofas, and contemplating their pumps.

"Don't know," replied Mr. Septimus Hicks, who was a tallish, white-faced young man, with spectacles, and a black ribbon round his neck instead of a neckerchief—a most interesting person; a poetical walker of the hospitals and a "very talented young man." He was fond of "lugging" into conversation all sorts of quotations from Don Juan, without fettering himself by the propriety of their application, in which particular he was remarkably independent. The other, Mr. Simpson, was one of those young men, who are in society what walking gentlemen are upon the stage, only infinitely worse skilled in his vocation than the most indifferent artist. He was emptyheaded as the great bell of St. Paul's; always dressed according to the caricatures published in the monthly fashions, and spelt Character with a K.

"I saw a devilish number of parcels in the passage when I came home," simpered Simpson.

"Materials for the toilet, no doubt," rejoined the Don Juan reader

———"Much linen, lace, and several pair
Of stockings, slippers, brushes, combs, complete;
With other articles of ladies' fair,
To keep them beautiful or leave them neat."

"Is that from Milton?" inquired Mr. Simpson.

"No—from Byron," returned Mr. Hicks, with a look of profound contempt. He was quite sure of his author, beaause he had never read any other.—"Hush!" said the sapient hospital walker, "Here come the gals," and they both commenced talking in a very loud key.

"Mrs. Maplesone and the Miss Maplesones, Mr. Hicks. Mr. Hicks—Mrs. Maplesones and the Miss Maplesones," said Mrs. Tibbs with a very red face, for she had been superintending the cooking operations below stairs, and looked like a wax-doll on a sunny day. "Mr. Simpson, I beg your pardon—Mr. Simpson—Mrs. Maplesone and the Miss Maplesones"—and *vice versa.* The gentlemen immediately began to slide about with much politeness, and to look as if they wished their arms had been legs, so little did they know what to do with them. The ladies smiled, courtesied, and glided into chairs, and dived for dropped pocket-handkerchiefs: the gentlemen leant against two of the curtain pegs; and Mrs. Tibbs went through an admirable bit of serious pantomime with a servant who had come up to ask some question about the fish-sauce, and then the two young ladies looked at each other; and every body else appeared to discover something very attractive in the pattern of the fender.

"Julia, my love," said Mrs. Maplesone to her youngest daughter, in a tone just loud enough for the remainder of the company to hear,—"Julia."

"Yes Ma."

"Don't stoop."—This was said for the purpose of directing general attention to Miss Julia's figure, which was undeniable. Every body looked at her accordingly, and there was another pause.

"We had the most uncivil hackney-coachman to-day, you can imagine," said Mrs. Maplesone to Mrs. Tibbs, in a confidential tone.

"Dear me!" replied the hostess, with an air of great commiseration. She couldn't say more, for the servant again appeared at the door, and commenced telegraphing most earnestly to her "Missis."

"I think hackney-coachmen generally are uncivil," said Mr. Hicks in his most insinuating tone.

"Positively I think they are," replied Mrs. Maplesone, as if the idea had never struck her before.

"And cabmen, too," said Mr. Simpson. This remark was a

failure, for no one intimated by word or sign the slightest knowledge of the manners and customs of cabmen.

"Robinson, what *do* you want?" said Mrs. Tibbs to the servant, who, by way of making her presence known to her mistress, had been giving sundry hems and sniffs outside the door during the preceding five minutes.

"Please, ma'am, master wants his clean things," replied the servant, completely taken off her guard. There was no resisting this: the two young men turned their faces to the window, and "went off" like a couple of bottles of ginger beer; the ladies put their handkerchiefs to their mouths, and little Mrs. Tibbs bustled out of the room to give Tibbs his clean linen,—and the servant warning.

Mr. Calton, the remaining boarder, shortly afterward made his appearance, and proved a surprising promoter of the conversation. Mr. Calton was a superannuated beau—an old boy. He used to say of himself that although his features were not regularly handsome they were striking. They certainly were: it was impossible to look at his face without being forcibly reminded of a chubby street-door knocker, half-lion, half-monkey; and the comparison might be extended to his whole character and conversation. He had stood still while every thing else had been moving. He never originated a conversation, or started a new idea; but if any commonplace topic were broached, or, to pursue the comparison, if any body *lifted him up*, he would hammer away with surprising rapidity. He had the tic-douloureux occasionally, and then he might be said to be muffled, because he did not make quite as much noise as at other times, when he would go on prosing, rat-tat-tat the same thing over and over again. He had never been married; but he was still on the look-out for a wife with money. He had a life-interest worth about 300*l.* a year—he was exceedingly vain and inordinately selfish. He had acquired the reputation of being the very pink of politeness, and he walked round the park, and up Regent-street every day.

This respectable personage had made up his mind to render himself exceedingly agreeable to Mrs. Maplesone—indeed, the desire of being as amiable as possible extended itself to the whole party; Mrs. Tibbs having considered it an admirable little bit of management to represent to the gentlemen that she had *some* reason to believe the ladies were fortunes, and to hint to the ladies, that all the gentlemen were "eligible." A little flirtation, she thought, might keep her house full, without leading to any other result.

Mrs. Maplesone was an enterprising woman of about fifty: shrewd, scheming, and good-looking. She was amiably anxious on behalf of her daughters; in proof whereof she used to remark, that she would have no objection to marry again, if it would benefit her dear girls—she could have no other motive. The "dear girls" themselves were not at all insensible to the merits of "a good establishment." One of them was twenty-five, the other three years younger. They had been at different watering-places for four seasons; they had gambled at libraries, read books in balconies, sold at fancy fairs, danced at assemblies, talked sentiment—in short, they had done all that industrious girls could do—and all to no purpose.

"What a magnificent dresser Mr. Simpson is!" whispered Matilda Maplesone to her sister Julia.

"Splendid!" returned the youngest. The magnificent individual alluded to wore a sort of maroon-colored dress-coat, with a velvet collar and cuffs of the same tint—very like that which usually invests the form of the distinguished unknown who condescends to play the "swell" in the pantomime at "Richardson's Show."

"What whiskers!" said Miss Julia.

"Charming!" responded her sister; "and what hair!" His hair was like a wig, and distinguished by that insinuating wave which graces the shining locks of those *chef-d'œuvres* of peruquerian art surrounding the waxen images in Bartellot's window, in Regent-street; his whiskers meeting beneath his chin, seemed strings wherewith to tie it on, ere science had rendered them unnecessary by her patent invisible springs.

"Dinner's on the table, ma'am, if you please," said the boy, who now appeared for the first time, in a revived black coat of his master's.

"Oh! Mr. Calton, will you lead Mrs. Maplesone?—Thank you." Mr. Simpson offered his arm to Miss Julia; Mr. Septimus Hicks escorted the lovely Matilda; and the procession proceeded to the dining-room. Mr. Tibbs was introduced, and Mr. Tibbs bobbed up and down to the three ladies like a figure in a Dutch clock with a powerful spring in the middle of his body, and then dived rapidly into his seat at the bottom of the table, delighted to screen himself behind a soup-tureen, which he could just see over, and that was all. The boarders were seated, a lady and gentleman alternately, like the layers of bread and meat in a plate of sandwiches; and then Mrs. Tibbs directed James to take off the covers. Salmon, lobster-sauce, giblet-soup, and the usual accompaniments were *dis*-covered; potatoes like petrifactions, and bits of toasted bread, the shape and size of blank dice.

"Soup for Mrs. Maplesone, my dear," said the bustling Mrs. Tibbs. She always called her husband "my dear" before company. Tibbs, who had been eating his bread, and calculating how long it would be before he should get any fish, helped the soup in a hurry, made a small island on the tablecloth, and put his glass upon it, to hide it from his wife.

"Miss Julia, shall I assist you to some fish?"

"If you please—very little—oh! plenty, thank you" (a bit about the size of a walnut put upon the plate).

"Julia is a *very* little eater," said Mrs. Maplesone to Mr. Calton.

The knocker gave a single rap He was busy eating the fish with his eyes: so he only ejaculated, "Ah!"

"My dear," said Mrs. Tibbs, to her spouse after every one else had been helped, "What do *you* take?" The inquiry was accompanied with a look intimating that he musn't say fish, because there was not much left. Tibbs thought the frown referred to the island on the tablecloth; he therefore coolly replied, "Why—I'll take a little—fish, I think."

"Did you say fish, my dear?" (another frown.)

"Yes, dear," replied the villain, with an expression of acute hunger depicted in his countenance. The tears almost started to Mrs. Tibbs's eyes, as she helped her "wretch of a husband," as she inwardly called him, to the last eatable bit of salmon on the table.

"James, take this to your master, and take away your master's knife." This was deliberate revenge, as Tibbs never could eat fish without one. He was, however, constrained to chase small particles of salmon round and round his plate with a piece of bread and a fork, occasionally securing a bit; the number of successful attempts being about one in seventeen.

"Take away, James," said Mrs. Tibbs, just as Tibbs had swallowed the fourth mouthful—and away went the plates like lightning.

"I'll take a bit of bread, James," said the poor "*master* of the house," more hungry than ever.

"Never mind your master now, James," said Mrs. Tibbs, "see about the meat."—This was conveyed in the tone in which ladies usually give admonitions to servants in company, that is to say, a low one; but which, like a stage whisper, from it's peculiar emphasis, is most distinctly heard by every body present.

A pause ensued before the table was replenished—a sort of parenthesis in which Mr. Simpson, Mr. Carlton, and Mr. Hicks produced respectively a bottle of sauterne, bucellas, and sherry, and took wine with every body—except Tibbs: no one ever thought of him.

Between the fish and an intimated sirloin there was a prolonged interval.

Here was an opportunity for Mr. Hicks. He could not resist the singularly appropriate quotation—

"But beef is rare within these oxless isles;
Goat's flesh there is, no doubt, and kid and mutton;
And, when a holiday upon them smiles,
A joint upon their barbarous spits they put on."

"Very ungentlemanly behavior," thought little Mrs. Tibbs, 'to talk in that way."

"Ah," said Mr. Calton, filling his glass, "Tom Moore is my poet."

"And mine," said Mrs. Maplesone.

"And mine," said Miss Julia.

"And mine," added Mr. Simpson.

"Look at his compositions," resumed the knocker.

"To be sure," said Simpson, with confidence.

"Look at Don Juan," replied Mr. Septimus Hicks.

"Julia's letter," suggested Miss Matilda.

"Can any thing be grander than the Fire Worshipers!" inquired Miss Julia.

"To be sure," said Simpson.

"Or Paradise and the Peri," said the old beau.

"Yes; or Paridise and the Peer," repeated Simpson, who thought he was getting through it capitally.

"It's all very well," replied Mr. Septimus Hicks, who, as we have before hinted, never had read any thing but Don Juan "Where will you find any thing finer than the description of the siege, at the commencement of the seventh canto?"

"Talking of a siege," said Tibbs, with a mouthful of bread—"when I was in the volunteer corps, in eighteen hundred and six, our commanding officer was Sir Charles Rampart; and one day, when we were exercising on the ground on which the London University now stands, he says, says he, Tibbs (calling me from the ranks) Tibbs——'"

"Tell your master, James," interrupted Mrs. Tibbs, in an awfully distinct tone, "tell your master if he *won't* carve those fowls, to send them to me." The discomfited volunteer instantly set to work, and carved the fowls almost as expeditiously as his wife operated on the haunch of mutton. Whether he ever finished the story is not exactly known, but if he did nobody heard it.

As the ice was now broken, and the new inmates more at home, every member of the company felt more at ease. Tibbs himself most certainly did, because he went to sleep, immediately after dinner. Mr. Hicks and the ladies discoursed most eloquently about poetry, and the theatres, and Lord Chesterfield's Letters; and Mr. Calton followed up what every body said, with continuous double-knocks. Mrs. Tibbs highly approved of every observation that fell from Mrs. Maplesone; and as Mr. Simpson sat with a smile upon his face and said "Yes," or "Certainly," at intervals of about four minutes each, he received fnll credit for understanding what was going forward. The gentlemen rejoined the ladies in the drawing-room very shortly after they had left the dining-parlor. Mrs. Maplesone and Mr. Calton played cribbage, and the "young people" amused themselves with music and conversation. The Miss Maplesones sang the most fascinating duets, and accompanied themselves on guitars, ornamented with bits of ethereal blue ribbon. Mr. Simpson put on a pink waistcoat, and said he was in raptures: and Mr. Hicks felt in the seventh heaven of poetry, or the seventh canto of Don Juan—it was the same thing to him.

Mrs. Tibbs was quite charmed with the new comers, and Mr. Tibbs spent the evening in his usual way—he went to sleep, and woke up, and went to sleep again, and woke at supper-time.

* * * * * * *

We are not about to adopt the license of novel-writers, and to "let years roll on;" but we will take the liberty of requesting the reader to suppose that six months have elapsed since the dinner we have just described, and that Mrs. Tibbs's boarders have, during that period, sang, and danced, and gone to theatres and exhibitions together, as ladies and gentlemen, wherever they board, often do; and we will beg them, the period we have mentioned having elapsed, to imagine further, that Mr. Septimus Hicks received, in his own bedroom (a front attic), at an early hour one morning, a note from Mr. Calton, requesting the favor of seeing him, as soon as convenient to himself, in his (Calton's) dressing-room on the second floor back.

"Tell Mr. Calton I'll come down directly," said Mr. Septimus to the boy. "Stop—is Mr. Calton unwell?" inquired the excited walker of hospitals, as he put on a bed-furniture-looking dressing-gown.

"Not as I know on, sir," replied the boy. "Please sir, he looked rather rum, as it might be."

"Ah, that's no proof of his being ill," returned Hicks, unconsciously. "Very well: I'll be down directly." Down stairs went the boy with the message, and down went the excited Hicks himself, almost as soon as the message was delivered. "Tap, tap." "Come in."—Door opens, and discovers Mr. Calton sitting in an easy chair, and looking more like a knocker than ever. Mutual shakes of the hand exchanged, and Mr. Septimus Hicks motioned to a seat. A short pause. Mr. Hicks coughed, and Mr. Calton took a pinch of snuff. It was just one of those interviews where neither party knows what to say. Mr. Septimus Hicks broke silence.

"I received a note—" he said, very tremulously, in a voice like a Punch with a cold.

"Yes," returned the other, "you did."

"Exactly."

"Yes."

Now, although this dialogue must have been satisfactory, both gentlemen felt there was something more important to be said; and so they did as many in such a situation would have done—they looked at the table with a most determined aspect. The conversation had been opened, however, and Mr. Calton had made up his mind to continue it, with a regular double-knock. He always spoke very pompously.

"Hicks," said he, "I have sent for you in consequence of certain arrangements which are pending in this house, connected with a marriage."

"With a marriage!" gasped Hicks, compared with whose expression of countenance, Hamlet's, when he sees his father's ghost, is pleasing and composed.

"With a marriage," returned the knocker. "I have sent for you to prove the great confidence I can repose in you."

"And will you betray me?" eagerly inquired Hicks, who in his alarm had even forgotten to quote.

"*I* betray *you!* Won't *you* betray *me?*"

"Never: no one shall know to my dying day that you had a hand in the business," responded the agitated Hicks, with an inflamed countenance, and his hair standing on end as if he were on the stool of an electrifying machine in full operation.

"People must know that, some time or other—within a year, I imagine," said Mr. Calton, with an air of great self-complacency—"We *may* have a family you know."

"*We!*—That won't affect you, surely?"

"The devil it won't!"

"No! how can it?" said the bewildered Hicks. Calton was too much inwrapped in the contemplation of happiness to see the equivoque between Hicks and himself; and threw himself back in his chair. "Oh, Matilda!" sighed the antique beau, in a lack-a-daisical voice, and applying his right hand a little to the left of the fourth button of his waistcoat, counting from the bottom. This was meant to be pathetic—"Oh, Matilda!"

'What Matilda ?" inquired Hicks, starting up.

"Matilda Maplesone," responded the other, doing the same.

"I marry her to-morrow morning," said Hicks, furiously.

"It's false," rejoined his companion: "I marry her!"

'You marry her!"

"I marry her!"

"You marry Matilda Maplesone?"

"Matilda Maplesone."

"*Miss* Maplesone marry *you*?"

"Miss Maplesone! No: Mrs. Maplesone."

"Good God!" said Hicks, falling into his chair: "You marry the mother, and I the daughter!"

"Most extraordinary circumstance!" replied Mr. Calton, "and rather inconvenient too; for the fact is, that owing to Matilda's wishing to keep her intention secret from her daughters until the ceremony had taken place, she dosen't like applying to any of her friends to give her away. I entertain an objection to making the affair known to my acquaintance just now; and the consequence is, that I sent to you to know whether you'd oblige me by acting as father."

"I should have been most happy, I assure you," said Hicks, in a tone of condolence; "but you see I shall be acting as bridegroom. One character is frequently a consequence of the other; but it is not usual to act in both at the same time. There's Simpson—I have no doubt he'll do it for you."

"I don't like to ask him," replied Calton; "he's such a donkey."

Mr. Septimus Hicks looked up at the ceiling, and down at the floor; at last an idea struck him—"Let the man of the house, Tibbs, be the father," he suggested; and then he quoted, as peculiarly applicable to Tibbs and the pair—

> "Oh Powers of Heaven! what dark eyes meets she there?
> 'Tis—'tis her father's—fixed upon the pair."

"The idea has struck me already," said Mr. Calton: "but, you see, Matilda, for what reason I know not, is very anxious that Mrs. Tibbs should know nothing about it till it's all over. It's a natural delicacy, after all, you know."

"He's the best-natured little man in existence, if you manage him properly," said Mr. Septimus Hicks. "Tell him not to mention it to his wife, and assure him she won't mind it, and he'll do it directly. My marriage is to be a secret one, on account of the mother and *my* father: therefore he must be enjoined to secrecy."

A small double-knock, like a presumptuous single one, was that instant heard at the street-door. It was Tibbs; it could be no one else, for no one else occupied five minutes in rubbing their shoes. He had been out to pay the baker's bill.

"Mr. Tibbs," called Mr. Calton in a very bland tone, looking over the banisters.

"Sir!" replied he of the dirty face.

"Will you have the kindness to step up stairs for a moment?"

"Certainly, sir," said Tibbs, delighted to be taken notice of. The bedroom-door was carefully closed, and Tibbs, having put his hat on the floor (as all timid men do), and been accommodated with a seat, looked as astounded as if he were suddenly summoned before the familiars of the Inquisition.

"A rather unpleasant occurrence, Mr. Tibbs," said Calton, in a very portentous manner, "obliges me to consult you, and to beg you will not communicate what I am about to say to your wife."

Tibbs acquiesced, wondering in his own mind what the deuce the other could have done, and imagining that at least he must have broken the best decanters.

Mr. Calton resumed; "I am placed, Mr. Tibbs, in rather an unpleasant situation."

Tibbs looked at Mr. Septimus Hicks, as if he thought his being in the immediate vicinity of his fellow-boarder might constitute the unpleasantness of his situation; but as he did not exactly know what to say, he merely ejaculated the monosyllable "Lor!"

"Now," continued the knocker, "let me beg you will exhibit no manifestations of surprise, which may be overheard by the domestics, when I tell you—command your feelings of astonishment—that two inmates of this house intend to be married to-morrow morning,"—and he drew back his chair several feet to perceive the effect of the unlooked-for announcement.

If Tibbs had rushed from the room, staggered down stairs,

The Boarding House.

T. B. PETERSON, PHILADELPHIA.

and fainted in the passage—if he had instantaneously jumped out of the window into the mews behind the house, in an agony of surprise—his behavior would have been much less inexplicable to Mr. Calton than it was, when he put his hands into his inexpressible-pockets, and said with a half-chuckle, "Just so."

"You are not surprised, Mr. Tibbs?" inquired Mr. Calton.

"Bless you, no, sir," returned Tibbs; "after all it's very natural. When two young people get together, you know——"

"Certainly, certainly," said Calton, with an indescribable air of self-satisfaction.

"You don't think it's at all an out-of-the-way affair then?" asked Mr. Septimus Hicks, who had watched the countenance of Tibbs in mute astonishment.

"No, sir," replied Tibbs; "I was just the same at his age." He actually smiled when he said this.

"How devilish well I must carry my years!" thought the delighted old beau, knowing that he was at least ten years older than Tibbs at that moment.

"Well, then, to come to the point at once," he continued, "I have to ask you whether you will object to act as father on the occasion?"

"Certainly not," replied Tibbs; still without evincing an atom of surprise.

"You will not?"

"Decidedly not," reiterated Tibbs, who appeared as calm as a pot of porter with the head off.

Mr. Calton seized the hand of petticoat-governed little man, and vowed eternal friendship from that hour. Hicks, who was all admiration and surprise, did the same.

"Now confess," asked Mr. Calton of Tibbs, as he picked up his hat, "were you not a little surprised?"

"I b'lieve you!" replied that illustrious person, holding up one hand; "I b'lieve you! when I first heard of it."

"So sudden," said Septimus Hicks.

"So strange to ask *me*, you know," said Tibbs.

"So odd altogether," said the superannuated love-maker; and then all three laughed.

"I say" said Tibbs, shutting the door which he had previously opened, and giving full vent to a hitherto corked-up giggle, "what bothers me is, what *will* his father say?"

Mr. Septimus Hicks looked at Mr. Calton.

"Yes; but the best of it is," said the latter, giggling in his turn, "I haven't got a father—he! he! he!"

"*You* haven't got a father. No; but *he* has," said Tibbs.

"*Who* has?" inquired Septimus Hicks, almost rabid.

"Why *him*."

"Him, who? Do you know my secret? Do you mean me?"

"You! No; you know who I mean," returned Tibbs, with a knowing wink.

"For Heaven's sake whom *do* you mean?" inquired Mr. Calton, who, like Septimus Hicks, was all but out of his senses at the strange confusion.

"Why, Mr. Simpson, of course," replied Tibbs; "who else could I mean?"

"I see it all," said the Byron-quoter; "Simpson marries Julia Maplesone to-morrow morning!"

"Undoubtedly," replied Tibbs, thoroughly satisfied; "of course he does."

It would require the pencil of Hogarth to illustrate—our feeble pen is inadequate to describe—the expression which the countenances of Mr. Calton and Mr. Septimus Hicks respectively assumed at this unexpected announcement. Equally impossible is it to describe, although it is much easier for our lady readers to imagine, what arts the three ladies could have used, so completely to entangle their separate partners. Whatever they were, however, they were successful. The mother was perfectly aware of the intended marriage of both daughters: and the young ladies were equally acquainted with the intention of their estimable parent. They agreed, however, that it would have a much better appearance if each feigned ignorance of the other's engagement; and it was equally desirable that all the marriages should take place on the same day, to prevent the discovery of one clandestine alliance, operating prejudicially on the others. Hence the mystification of Mr. Calton and Mr. Septimus Hicks, and the pre-engagement of the unwary Tibbs.

On the following morning Mr. Septimus Hicks was united

to Miss Matilda Maplesone. Mr. Simpson also entered into a "holy alliance" with Miss Julia: Tibbs acting as father, "his first appearance in that character." Mr. Calton, not being quite so eager as the two young men, was rather struck by the double discovery; and as he had found some difficulty in getting any one to give the lady away, it occurred to him that the best mode of obviating the inconvenience would be not to take her at all. The lady, however, "appealed," as her counsel said on the trial of the cause, *Maplesone* v. *Calton*, for a breach of promise, "with a broken heart, to the outraged laws of her country." She recovered damages to the amount of 1000*l.*, which the unfortunate knocker was compelled to pay. Mr. Septimus Hicks having walked the hospitals, took it into his head to walk off altogether. His injured wife is at present residing with her mother at Boulogne. Mr. Simpson, having the misfortune to lose his wife six weeks after marriage (by her eloping with an officer during his temporary sojourn in the Fleet Prison, in consequence of his inability to discharge her little mantua-maker's bill), and being disinherited by his father, who died soon afterward, was fortunate enough to obtain a permanent engagement at a fashionable hair-cutter's; hair-dressing being a science to which he had frequently directed his attention. In this situation he had necessarily many opportunities of making himself acquainted with the habits and style of thinking of the exclusive portion of the nobility of this kingdom. To this fortunate circumstance are we indebted for the production of those brilliant efforts of genius, his fashionable novels, which so long as good taste, unsullied by exaggeration, cant, and maudlin quackery continues to exist, can not fail to instruct and amuse the thinking portion of the community.

It only remains to add, that this complication of disorders completely deprived poor Mrs. Tibbs of all her inmates, except the one whom it would have afforded her the greatest pleasure to lose—her husband. That wretched little man returned home on the day of the wedding in a state of partial intoxication; and under the influence of wine, excitement, and despair, actually dared to brave the anger of his wife. Since that ill-fated hour he has constantly taken his meals in the kitchen, to which apartment it is understood his witticisms will be in future confined: a turn-up beadstead having been conveyed there by Mrs. Tibbs's order for his exclusive accommodation. It is very likely that he will be enabled to finish there his story of the volunteers.

The advertisement has again appeared in the morning papers. Results must be reserved for another chapter.

CHAPTER THE SECOND.

"WELL," said little Mrs. Tibbs to herself, as she sat in the front parlor of the Coram-street mansion one morning, mending a piece of stair-carpet off the first landing;—"well! things have not turned out so badly either, and if I only get a favorable answer to the advertisement, we shall be full again."

Mrs. Tibbs resumed her occupation of making worsted lattice-work in the carpet, anxiously listening to the twopenny postman, who was hammering his way down the street at the rate of a penny a knock. The house was as quiet as possible. There was only one low sound to be heard—it was the unhappy Tibbs cleaning the gentlemen's boots in the back kitchen, and accompanying himself with a buzzing noise, in wretched mockery of humming a tune.

The postman drew near the house. He paused—so did Mrs. Tibbs—a knock—a bustle—a letter—post-paid.

"T. I. presents compt. to I. T. and T. I. begs To say that i see the advertisement And she will Do Herself the pleasure of calling On you at 12 o'clock to-morrow morning.

"T. I. as To apologize to I. T. for the shortness Of the notice But i hope it will not unconvenience you.

"I remain

"yours Truly

"Wednesday evening."

Little Mrs. Tibbs perused the document over and over again; and the more she read it, the more she was confused by the mixture of the first and third person; the substitution of the "I" for the "T. I." and the transition from the "I. T." to the "you." The writing looked like a skein of thread in a tangle, and the note was ingeniously folded into a perfect square, with the direction squeezed up into the right-hand corner, as if it were ashamed of itself. The back of the epistle was pleasingly ornamented with a large red wafer, which, with the addition of divers ink-stains, bore a marvelous resemblance to a black beetle trodden upon. One thing, however, was perfectly clear to the perplexed Mrs. Tibbs. Somebody was to call at twelve. The drawing-room was forthwith dusted for the third time that morning; three or four chairs were pulled out of their places, and a corresponding number of books carefully upset, in order that there might be a due absence of formality. Down went the piece of stair-carpet before noticed, and up ran Mrs. Tibbs "to make herself tidy."

The clock of New Saint Pancras Church struck twelve, and the Foundling, with laudable politeness, did the same ten minutes afterward. Saint something else struck the quarter, and then there arrived a single lady with a double knock, in a pelisse the color of the interior of a damson pie; a bonnet of the same, with a regular conservatory of artificial flowers; a white vail, and a green parasol, with a cobweb border.

The visitor (who was very fat and red-faced) was shown into the drawing-room; Mrs. Tibbs presented herself, and the negotiation commenced.

"I called in consequence of an advertisement," said the stranger, in a voice as if she had been playing a set of Pan's pipes for a fortnight without leaving off.

"Yes!" said Mrs. Tibbs, rubbing her hands very slowly, and looking the applicant full in the face—two things she always did on such occasions.

"Money isn't no object whatever to me," said the *lady*, "so much as living in a state of retirement and obtrusion."

Mrs. Tibbs, as a matter of course, acquiesced in such an exceedingly natural desire.

"I am constantly attended by a medical man," resumed the pelisse wearer; "I have been a shocking unitarian for some time—I, indeed, have had very little peace since the death of Mr. Bloss."

Mrs. Tibbs looked at the relict of the departed Bloss, and thought he must have had very little peace in his time. Of course she should not say so; so she looked very sympathizing.

"I shall be a good deal of trouble to you," said Mrs. Bloss; "but for that trouble I am willing to pay. I am going through a course of treatment which renders attention necessary. I have one mutton chop in bed at half-past eight, and another at ten, every morning."

Mrs. Tibbs, as in duty bound, expressed the pity she felt for any body placed in such a distressing situation; and the carnivorous Mrs. Bloss proceeded to arrange the various preliminaries with wonderful dispatch. "Now mind," said that lady, after terms were arranged; "I am to have the second floor for my bedroom?"

"Yes, ma'am."

"And you'll find room for my little servant, Agnes?"

"Oh! certainly."

"And I can have one of the cellars in the area for my bottled porter?"

"With the greatest pleasure; James shall get it ready for you by Saturday."

"And I'll join the company at the breakfast-table on Sunday morning," said Mrs. Bloss. "I shall get up on purpose."

"Very well," returned Mrs. Tibbs, in her most amiable tone; for satisfactory references had been "given and required," and it was quite certain that the new-comer had plenty of money. "It's rather singular," continued Mrs. Tibbs, with what was meant for a most bewitching smile, "that we have a gentleman now with us, who is in a very delicate state of health—a Mr. Gobler. His apartment is the back drawing-room."

"The next room?" inquired Mrs. Bloss.

"The next room," repeated the hostess.

"How very promiscuous!" ejaculated the widow.

"He hardly ever gets up," said Mrs. Tibbs in a whisper.

"Lor!" cried Mrs. Bloss, in an equally low tone.

"And when he is up," said Mrs. Tibbs, "we never can persuade him to go to bed again."

"Dear me!" said the astonished Mrs. Bloss, drawing her chair nearer Mrs. Tibbs. "What is his complaint?"

"Why, the fact is," replied Mrs. Tibbs, with a most communicative air, "he has no stomach, whatever."

"No what?" inquired Mrs. Bloss, with a look of the most indescribable alarm.

"No stomach," repeated Mrs. Tibbs, with a shake of the head.

"Lord bless us! what an extraordinary case!" gasped Mrs. Bloss, as if she understood the communication in its literal sense, and was astonished at a gentleman without a stomach finding it necessary to board anywhere.

"When I say he has no stomach," explained the chatty little Mrs. Tibbs, "I mean that his digestion is so much impaired, and his interior so deranged, that his stomach is not of the least use to him;—in fact, it's rather an inconvenience than otherwise."

"Never heard such a case in my life!" exclaimed Mrs. Bloss. "Why he's worse than I am."

"Oh, yes!" replied Mrs. Tibbs; "certainly." She said this with great confidence, for the damson pelisse satisfactorily proved that Mrs. Bloss, at all events, was not suffering under Mr. Gobler's complaint.

"You have quite incited my curiosity," said Mrs. Bloss, as she rose to depart. "How I long to see him!"

"He generally comes down once a week," replied Mrs. Tibbs; "I dare say you'll see him on Sunday." With this consolatory promise Mrs. Bloss was obliged to be contented. She accordingly walked slowly down the stairs, detailing her complaints all the way; and Mrs. Tibbs followed her, uttering an exclamation of compassion at every step. James (who looked very gritty, for he was cleaning the knives) fell up the kitchen stairs, and opened the street-door; and, after mutual farewells, Mrs. Bloss slowly departed down the shady side of the street.

It is almost superfluous to say, that the lady whom we have just shown out at the street-door (and whom the two female servants are now inspecting from the second-floor windows) was exceedingly vulgar, ignorant, and selfish. Her deceased better-half had been an eminent cork-cutter, in which trade he had amassed a decent fortune. He had no relative but his nephew, and no friend but his cook. The former had the insolence one morning to ask for the loan of fifteen pounds, and by way of retaliation he married the latter next day; he made a will immediately afterward, containing a burst of honest indignation against his nephew (who supported himself and two sisters on 100*l.* a year), and a bequest of his whole property to his wife. He felt ill at breakfast, and died after dinner. There is a mantlepiece-looking tablet in a civic parish church, setting forth his virtues and deploring his loss. He never dishonored a bill, or gave away a halfpenny!

The relict and sole executrix of this noble-minded man was an odd mixture of shrewdness and simplicity, liberality and meanness. Bred up as she had been, she knew no mode of living so agreeable as a boarding-house; and having nothing to do, and nothing to wish for, she naturally imagined she must be very ill—an impression which was most assiduously promoted by her medical attendant, Dr. Wosky, and her handmaid, Agnes, both of whom, doubtless for excellent reasons, encouraged all her extravagant notions.

Since the catastrophe recorded in the last chapter, Mrs. Tibbs had been very shy of young-lady boarders. Her present inmates were all lords of the creation, and she availed herself of the opportunity of their assemblage at the dinner-table, to announce the expected arrival of Mrs. Bloss. The gentlemen received the communication with stoical indifference, and Mrs. Tibbs devoted all her energies to prepare for the reception of the valetudinarian. The second-floor front was scrubbed, and washed, and flanneled, till the wet went through to the drawing-room ceiling. Clean white counterpanes, and curtains and napkins; water-bottles as clear as crystal, blue jugs and mahogany furniture, added to the splendor and increased the comfort of the apartment. The warming pan was in constant requisition, and a fire lighted in the room every day. The chattels of Mrs. Bloss were forwarded by installments. First there came a large hamper of Guinness's stout and an umbrella; then a train of trunks; then a pair of clogs and a bandbox; then an easy chair with an air-cushion, then a variety of suspicious-looking packages; and—"though last not least"—Mrs. Bloss and Agnes, the latter in a cherry-colored merino dress, open-work stockings, and shoes with sandals; looking like a disguised Columbine.

The installation of the Duke of Wellington, as Chancellor of the University of Oxford, was nothing in point of bustle and turmoil to the installation of Mrs. Bloss in her new quarters. True, there was no bright doctor of civil law to deliver a classical address on the occasion; but there were several other old women present, who spoke quite as much to the purpose, and understood themselves equally well. The chop-eater was so fatigued with the process of removal that she declined leaving her room until the following morning; so a mutton-chop, pickle, a two-grain calomel pill, a pint bottle of stout, and other medicines, were carried up stairs for her consumption.

"Why, what *do* you think, ma'am?" inquired the inquisitive Agnes of her mistress, after they had been in the house some three hours; "what *do* you think, ma'am? the lady of the house is married."

"Married!" said Mrs. Bloss, taking the pill and a draught of Guinness—"married! Unpossible!"

"She is indeed, ma'am," returned the Columbine; "and her husband, ma'am, lives—he—he—he—lives in the kitchen, ma'am."

"In the kitchen!"

"Yes, ma'am: and he—he—he—the housemaid says, he never goes into the parlor except on Sundays; and that Mrs. Tibbs makes him clean the gentlemen's boots; and that he cleans the windows, too, sometimes; and that one morning early, when he was in the front balcony cleaning the drawing-room windows, he called out to a gentleman on the opposite side of the way, who used to live here—'Ah! Mr. Calton, sir, how are you?'" Here the attendant laughed till Mrs. Bloss was in serious apprehension of her chuckling herself into a fit.

"Well, I never!" said Mrs. Bloss.

"Yes, and please, ma'am, the servants give him gin-and-water sometimes; and then he cries and says he hates his wife and the boarders, and wants to tickle them."

"Tickle the boarders!" exclaimed Mrs. Bloss seriously alarmed.

"No, ma'am, not the boarders, the servants."

"Oh, is that all!" said Mrs. Bloss, quite satisfied.

"He wanted to kiss me as I came up the kitchen-stairs, just now," said Agnes, indignantly: "but I gave it him—a little wretch!"

This intelligence was but too true. A long course of snubbing and neglect; his days spent in the kitchen, and his nights in the turn-up bedstead, had completely broken the little spirit that the unfortunate volunteer had ever possessed. He had no one to whom he could detail his injuries but the servants, and they were almost of necessity his chosen confidents. It is no less strange than true, however, that the little weaknesses which he had incurred, most probably during his military career, seemed to increase as his comforts diminished. He was actually a sort of journeyman Giovanni in the basement story.

The next morning, being Sunday, breakfast was laid in the front parlor at ten o'clock. Nine was the usual time, but the family always breakfasted an hour later on Sabbath. Tibbs enrobed himself in his Sunday costume—a black coat, and exceedingly short, thin trousers, with a very large white waistcoat, white stockings and cravat, and Blucher boots—and mounted to the parlor aforesaid. Nobody had come down, and he amused himself by drinking the contents of the milkpot with a teaspoon.

A pair of slippers were heard descending the stairs; Tibbs flew to a chair, and a stern-looking man, of about fifty, with very little hair on his head, and a Sunday paper in his hand, entered the room.

"Good morning, Mr. Evenson," said Tibbs, very humbly, with something between a nod and a bow.

"How do you, Mr. Tibbs?" replied he of the slippers, as he sat himself down, and began to read his paper without saying another word.

"Is Mr. Wisbottle in town to-day, do you know, sir?" inquired Tibbs, just for the sake of saying something.

"I should think he was," replied the stern gentleman. "He was whistling 'The Light Guitar,' in the next room to mine, at five o'clock this morning."

"He's very fond of whistling," said Tibbs with a slight smirk.

"Yes—I ain't," was the laconic reply.

Mr. John Evenson was in the receipt of an independent income, arising chiefly from various houses he owned in the different suburbs. He was very morose and discontented. He was a thorough radical, and used to attend a great variety of public meetings, for the express purpose of finding fault with every thing that was proposed. Mr. Wisbottle, on the other hand, was a high Tory. He was a clerk in the Woods and Forests Office, which he considered rather an aristocratic employment; he knew the peerage by heart, and could tell you off-hand where any illustrious personage lived. He had a good set of teeth, and a capital tailor. Mr. Evenson looked on all these qualifications with profound contempt; and the consequence was that the two were always disputing, much to the edification of the rest of the house. It should be added, that, in addition to his partiality for whistling, Mr. Wisbottle had a great idea of his singing powers. There were two other boarders besides the gentleman in the back drawing-room—Mr. Alfred Tomkins and Mr. Frederick O'Bleary. Mr. Tomkins was a clerk in a wine-house; he was a connoisseur in paintings, and had a wonderful eye for the picturesque. Mr. O'Bleary was an Irishman, recently imported; he was in a perfectly wild state, and had come over to England to be an apothecary, a clerk in a government office, an actor, a reporter, or any thing else that turned up—he was not particular. He was on familiar terms with two small Irish members, and got franks for every body in the house. He felt convinced that his intrinsic merits must procure him a high destiny. He wore shepherd's-plaid inexpressibles, and used to look under all the ladies' bonnets as he walked along the streets. His manners and appearance always forcibly reminded one of Orson.

"Here comes Mr. Wisbottle," said Tibbs; and Mr. Wisbottle forthwith appeared in blue slippers, and a shawl dressing-gown, whistling "*Di piacer.*"

"Good morning, sir," said Tibbs again. It was about the only thing he ever said to any body.

"How are you, Tibbs?" condescendingly replied the amateur; and he walked to the window, and whistled louder than ever.

"Pretty air, that?" said Evenson with a snarl, and without taking his eyes off the paper.

"Glad you like it," replied Wisbottle, highly gratified.

"Don't you think it would sound better, if you whistled it a little louder?" inquired the mastiff.

"No; I don't think it would," rejoined the unconscious Wisbottle.

"I'll tell you what, Wisbottle," said Evenson, who had been bottleing up his anger for some hours—"the next time you feel disposed to whistle 'The Light Guitar' at five o'clock in the morning, I'll trouble you to whistle it with your head out o'window. If you don't, I'll learn the triangle—I will, by ———."

The entrance of Mrs. Tibbs (with the keys in a little basket) interrupted the threat, and prevented its conclusion.

Mrs. Tibbs apologized for being down rather late; the bell was rung; James brought up the urn, and received an unlimited order for dry toast and bacon. Tibbs sat down at the bottom of the table, and began eating water-cresses like a second Nebuchadnezzar. Mr. O'Bleary appeared, and Mr. Alfred Tomkins. The compliments of the morning were exchanged, and the tea was made.

"God bless me!" exclaimed Tomkins, who had been looking out at the window. "Here—Wisbottle—pray come here: make haste."

Mr. Wisbottle started from the table, and every one looked up.

"Do you see," said the connoisseur, placing Wisbottle in the right position—"a little more this way: there—do you see how splendidly the light falls upon the left side of that broken chimney-pot at No. 48?"

"Dear me! I see," replied Wisbottle, in a tone of admiration.

"I never saw an object stand out so beautifully against the clear sky in my life," ejaculated Alfred. Every body (except John Evenson) echoed the sentiment, for Mr. Tomkins had a great character for finding out beauties which no one else could discover—he certainly deserved it.

"I have frequently observed a chimney-pot in College-green, Dublin, which has a much better effect," said the patriotic O'Bleary, who never allowed Ireland to be outdone on any point.

The assertion was received with obvious incredulity, for Mr. Tomkins declared that no other chimney-pot in the United

Kingdom, broken or unbroken, could be so beautiful as the one at No. 48.

The room-door was suddenly thrown open, and Agnes appeared leading in Mrs. Bloss, who was dressed in a geranium-colored muslin gown, and displayed a gold watch of huge dimensions; a chain to match, and a splendid assortment of rings, with enormous stones. A general rush was made for a chair, and a regular introduction took place. Mr. John Evenson made a slight inclination of the head; Mr. Frederick O'Bleary, Mr. Alfred Tomkins, and Mr. Wisbottle bowed like the mandarins in a grocer's shop; Tibbs rubbed hands, and went round in circles. He was observed to close one eye, and to assume a clock-work sort of expression with the other; this has been considered as a wink, and it has been reported that Agnes was its object. We repel the calumny, and challenge contradiction.

Mrs. Tibbs inquired after Mrs. Bloss's health in a low tone. Mrs. Bloss, with a supreme contempt for the memory of Lindley Murray, answered the various questions in a most satisfactory manner; and a pause ensued, during which the eatables disappeared with awful rapidity.

"You must have been very much pleased with the appearance of the ladies going to the drawing-room the other day, Mr O'Bleary?" said Mrs. Tibbs, hoping to start a topic.

"Yes," replied Orson, with a mouthful of toast.

"Never saw any thing like it before, I suppose?" suggested Wisbottle.

"No—except the Lord Lieutenant's levees," replied O'Bleary.

"Are they at all equal to our drawing-rooms?"

"Oh, infinitely superior!"

"'Gad! I don't know," said the aristocratic Wisbottle, "the Dowager Marchioness of Publiccash was most magnificently dressed, and so was the Baron Slappenbachenhausen."

"What was he presented on?" inquired Evenson.

"On his arrival in England."

"I thought so," growled the radical; "you never hear of these fellows being presented on their going away again. They know better than that."

"Unless somebody pervades them with an apintment," said Mrs. Bloss, joining in the conversation in a faint voice.

"Well," said Wisbottle, evading the point, "it's a splendid sight."

"And did it never occur to you," inquired the radical, who never would be quiet—"did it never occur to you, that you pay for these precious ornaments of society?"

"It certainly *has* occurred to me," said Wisbottle, who thought this answer was a poser; "it *has* occurred to me, and I am willing to pay for them."

"Well, and it has occurred to me too," replied John Evenson, "and I ain't willing to pay for 'em. Then why should I? —I say, why should I?" continued the politician, laying down the paper, and knocking his knuckles on the table. "There are two great principles—demand—"

"A cup of tea, if you please, dear," interrupted Tibbs.

"And supply—"

"May I trouble you to hand this tea to Mr. Tibbs?" said Mrs. Tibbs, interrupting the argument, and unconsciously illustrating it.

The thread of the orator's discourse was broken. He drank his tea and resumed the paper.

"If it's very fine," said Mr. Alfred Tomkins, addressing the company in general, "I shall ride down to Richmond to-day, and come back by the steamer. There are some splendid effects of light and shade on the Thames; the contrast between the blueness of the sky and the yellow water is frequently exceedingly beautiful." Mr. Wisbottle hummed, "Flow on, thou shining river."

"We have some splendid steam-vessels in Ireland," said O'Bleary.

"Certainly," said Mrs. Bloss, delighted to find a subject broached in which she could take part.

"The accommodations are extraordinary," said O'Bleary.

"Extraordinary indeed," returned Mrs. Bloss. "When Mr. Bloss was alive he was promiscuously obligated to go to Ireland on business. I went with him, and raly the manner in which the ladies and gentlemen were accommodated with births, is not creditable."

Tibbs, who had been listening to the dialogue, looked very aghast, and evinced a strong inclination to ask a question, but was checked by a look from his wife. Mr. Wisbottle laughed, and said Tomkins had made a pun; and Tomkins laughed too, and said he had not,

The remainder of the meal passed off as breakfasts usually do. Conversation flagged, and people played with their tea-spoons. The gentlemen looked out at the window; walked about the room, and when they got near the door, dropped off one by one. Tibbs retired to the back parlor, by his wife's orders, to check the greengrocer's weekly account; and ultimately Mrs. Tibbs and Mrs. Bloss were left alone together.

"Oh dear!" said the latter, "I feel alarmingly faint; it's very singular." (It certainly was, for she had eaten four pounds of solids that morning.) "By-the-by," said Mrs. Bloss, "I have not seen Mr. what's his name yet."

"Mr. Gobler?" suggested Mrs. Tibbs.

"Yes."

"Oh!" said Mrs. Tibbs, "he is a most mysterious person. He has his meals regularly sent up stairs, and sometimes don't leave his room for weeks together."

"I haven't seen or heard nothing of him," repeated Mrs. Bloss.

"I dare say you'll hear him to-night," replied Mrs. Tibbs; "he generally groans a good deal on Sunday evenings."

"I never felt such an interest in any one in my life," ejaculated Mrs. Bloss. A finicking double-knock interrupted the conversation; Dr. Wosky was announced, and duly shown in. He was a little man with a red face,—dressed of course in black, with a stiff white neckerchief. He had a very good practice, and plenty of money, which he had amassed by invariably humoring the worst fancies of all the females of all the families he had ever been introduced into. Mrs. Tibbs offered to retire, but was entreated to stay.

"Well, my dear ma'am, and how are we?" inquired Wosky in a soothing tone.

"Very ill, doctor—very ill," said Mrs. Bloss, in a whisper.

"Ah! we must take care of ourselves;—we must indeed,"

said the obsequious Wosky, as he felt the pulse of his interesting patient.

"How is our appetite?"

Mrs. Bloss shook her head.

"Our friend requires great care," said Wosky, appealing to Mrs. Tibbs, who of course assented. "I hope, however, with the blessing of Providence," continued the Doctor, "that we shall be enabled to make her quite stout again." Mrs. Tibbs wondered in her own mind what the patient would be when she had got quite stout.

"We must take stimulants," said the cunning Wosky—"plenty of nourishment, and, above all, we must keep our nerves quiet; we positively must not give way to our sensibilities. We must take all we can get," concluded the doctor, as he pocketed his fee, "and we must keep quiet."

"Dear man!" exclaimed Mrs. Bloss, as the doctor stepped into his carriage.

"Charming creature indeed—quite a lady's man," said Mrs. Tibbs, and Doctor Wosky rattled away to make fresh gulls of delicate females, and pocket fresh fees.

As we had occasion in a former paper to describe a dinner at Mrs. Tibbs's, and as one meal went off very like another on all ordinary occasions, we will not fatigue our readers by entering into any other detailed account of the domestic economy of the establishment. We will therefore proceed to events, merely premising that the mysterious tenant of the back drawing-room was a lazy, selfish hypochondriac; always complaining and never ill. As his character in many respects closely assimilated to that of Mrs. Bloss, a very warm friendship soon sprung up between them. He was tall, thin, and pale; he always fancied he had a severe pain somewhere or other, and his face invariably wore a pinched, screwed-up expression; he looked, indeed, like a man who had got his feet in a tub of exceedingly hot water against his will.

For two or three months after Mrs. Bloss's first appearance in Coram-street, John Everson was observed to become every day more sarcastic and more ill-natured, and there was a degree of additional importance in his manner, which clearly showed that he fancied he had discovered something, which he only wanted a proper opportunity of divulging. He found it at last.

One evening the different inmates of the house were assembled in the drawing-room engaged in their ordinary occupations. Mr. Gobler and Mrs. Bloss were sitting at a small card-table near the centre window playing cribbage; Mr. Wisbottle was describing semi-circles on the music-stool, turning over the leaves of a book on the piano, and humming most melodiously; Alfred Tomkins was sitting at the round table with his elbows duly squared, making a pencil sketch of a head considerably larger than his own; O'Bleary was reading Horace, and trying to look as if he understood it; and John Evenson had drawn his chair close to Mrs. Tibbs's work-table, and was talking to her very earnestly in a low tone.

"I can assure you, Mrs. Tibbs," said the radical, laying his forefinger on the muslin she was at work on; "I can assure you, Mrs. Tibbs, that nothing but the interest I take in your welfare would induce me to make this communication. I repeat that I fear Wisbottle is endeavoring to gain the affections of that young woman, Agnes, and that he is in the habit of meeting her in the storeroom on the first floor, over the leads. From my bedroom I distinctly heard voices there last night. I opened my door immediately, and crept very softly on to the landing; there I saw Mr. Tibbs, who, it seems, had been disturbed also.—Bless me, Mrs. Tibbs, you change color!"

"No, no—it's nothing," returned Mrs. T., in a hurried manner; "it's only the heat of the room."

"A flush!" ejaculated Mrs. Bloss from the card-table; "that's good for four.'

"If I thought it was Mr. Wisbottle," said Mrs. Tibbs, after a pause, "he should leave this house instantly."

"Go!" said Mrs. Bloss again.

"And if I thought," continued the hostess with a most threatening air, "if I thought he was assisted by Mr. Tibbs"—

"One for his nob!" said Gobler.

"Oh," said Evenson, in a most soothing tone—he liked to make mischief—"I should hope Mr. Tibbs was not in any way implicated. He always appeared to be very harmless."

"I have generally found him so," sobbed poor little Mrs. Tibbs; crying like a watering-pot in full play.

"Hush! hush! pray—Mrs. Tibbs—consider—we shall be observed—pray, don't!" said John Evenson, fearing his whole plan would be interrupted. "We will set the matter at rest with the utmost care, and I shall be most happy to assist you in doing so."

Mrs. Tibbs murmured her thanks.

"When you think every one has retired to rest to-night," said Evenson very pompously, "if you'll meet me without a light, just outside my bedroom-door, by the staircase-window, I think we can ascertain who the parties really are, and you will afterward be enabled to proceed as you think proper."

Mrs. Tibbs was easily persuaded; her curiosity was excited, her jealousy was roused, and the arrangement was forthwith made. She resumed her work, and John Evenson walked up and down the room with his hands in his pockets, looking as if nothing had happened. The game of cribbage was over, and conversation began again.

"Well, Mr. O'Bleary," said the humming top, turning round on his pivot, and facing the company, "what did you think of Vauxhall the other night?"

"Oh, it's very fair," replied Orson, who had been enthusiastically delighted with the whole exhibition.

"Never saw any thing like that Captain Ross's set-out—eh?"

"No," returned the patriot with his usual reservation—"except in Dublin."

"I saw the Count de Canky and Captain Fitzthompson in the Gardens," said Wisbottle; "they appeared much delighted."

"Then it must be beautiful!" snarled Evenson.

"I think the white bears is partickerlerly well done," suggested Mrs. Bloss. "In their shaggy white coats they look just like Polar bears—don't you think they do, Mr. Evenson?"

"I think they look a great deal more like omnibus cads on all fours," replied the discontented one.

"Upon the whole, I should have liked our evening very well," gasped Gobler; "only I caught a desperate cold which increased my pain dreadfully; I was obliged to have several shower-baths before I could leave my room."

"Capital things those shower-baths!" ejaculated Wisbottle.

"Excellent!" said Tomkins.

"Delightful!" chimed in O'Bleary. (He had once seen one outside a tinman's.)

"Disgusting machines!" rejoined Evenson, who extended his dislike to almost every created object, masculine, feminine, or neuter.

"Disgusting, Mr. Evenson!" said Gobler, in a tone of strong indignation.—"Disgusting! look at their utility—consider how many lives they have saved by promoting perspiration."

"Promoting perspiration, indeed," growled John Evenson, stopping short in his walk across the large squares in the pattern of the carpet—"I was ass enough to be persuaded some time ago to have one in my bedroom. 'Gad, I was in it once, and it effectually cured *me* certainly, for the mere sight of it threw me into a profuse perspiration for six months afterward."

A general titter followed this announcement, and before it had subsided James brought up "the tray," containing the remains of a leg of lamb which had made its *débût* at dinner; bread, cheese, an atom of butter in a forest of parsley; one pickled walnut and the third of another, and so forth. The boy disappeared, and returned again with another tray, containing glasses and jugs of hot and cold water. The gentlemen brought in their spirit-bottles; the housemaid placed divers plated bedroom candlesticks under the card-table, and the servants retired for the night.

Chairs were drawn round the table, and the conversation proceeded in the customary manner. John Evenson, who never eat supper, lolled on the sofa, and amused himself by contradicting every body. O'Bleary eat as much as he could conveniently carry, and Mrs. Tibbs felt a due degree of indignation thereat; Mr. Gobler and Mrs. Bloss conversed most affectionately on the subject of pill-taking and other innocent amusements; and Tomkins and Wisbottle "got into an argument;" that is to say, they both talked very loudly and vehemently, each flattering himself that he had got some advantage about something, and neither of them having more than a very indistinct idea of what they were talking about. An hour or two passed away; and the boarders and the brass candlesticks retired in pairs to their respective bedrooms. John Evenson pulled off his boots, locked his door, and determined to sit up until Mr. Gobler had retired. He always sat in the drawing-room about an hour after every body else had left it, taking medicine, and groaning.

Great Coram-street was hushed into a state of the most profound repose; it was nearly two o'clock. A hackney-coach now and then rumbled slowly by; and occasionally some stray lawyer's clerk on his way home to Somers-town struck his iron heel on the top of the coal-cellar with a noise resembling the click of a smoke-jack. A low, monotonous, gushing sound was heard, which added considerably to the romantic dreariness of the scene. It was the water "coming in" at No. 11.

"He must be asleep by this time," said John Evenson to himself after waiting with exemplary patience for nearly an hour after Mr. Gobler had left the drawing-room. He listened for a few moments; the house was perfectly quiet; he extinguished his rush-light, and opened his bedroom-door. The staircase was so dark that it was impossible to see any thing.

"S—s—s!" whispered the mischief-maker, making a noise like the first indication a catherine-wheel gives of the probability of its going off.

"Hush!" whispered somebody else.

"Is that you, Mrs. Tibbs?"

"Yes, sir."

"Where?"

"Here;" and the misty outline of Mrs. Tibbs appeared at the staircase-window like the ghost of Queen Anne in the tent scene in Richard.

"This way, Mrs. Tibbs," whispered the delighted busybody; "give me your hand—there. Whoever these people are, they are in the storeroom now, for I have been looking down from my window, and I could see that they accidentally upset their candlestick, and are now in darkness. You have no shoes on, have you?"

"No," said little Mrs. Tibbs, who could hardly speak for trembling.

"Well; I have taken my boots off, so we can go down close to the storeroom-door and listen over the banisters," continued

Evenson; and down stairs they both crept accordingly, every board creaking like a patent mangle on a Saturday afternoon.

"It's Wisbottle and somebody I'll swear," exclaimed the radical in an energetic whisper, when they had listened for a few moments.

"Hush—pray let's hear what they say!' exclaimed Mrs. Tibbs, the gratification of whose curiosity was now paramount to every other consideration.

"Ah! if I could but believe you," said a female voice coquettisly, "I'd be bound to settle my missis for life."

"What does she say?" inquired Mr. Evenson, who was not quite so well situated as his companion.

"She says she'll settle her missis's life," replied Mrs. Tibbs. "The wretch! they're plotting murder."

"I know you want money," continued the voice, which belonged to Agnes; "and if you'd secure me the five hundred pounds, I warrant she should take fire soon enough."

"What's that?" inquired Evenson again. He could just hear enough to want to hear more.

"I think she says she'll set the house on fire," replied the affrighted Mrs. Tibbs. "Thank God, I'm insured in the Phœnix!"

"The moment I have secured your mistress, my dear," said a man's voice in a strong Irish brogue, "you may depend on having the money."

"Bless my soul, it's Mr. O'Bleary!" exclaimed Mrs. Tibbs in a parenthesis.

"The villain!" said the indignant Mr. Evenson.

"The first thing to be done," continued the Hibernian, "is to poison Mr. Gobler's mind."

"Oh, certainly!" returned Agnes, with the utmost coolness.

"What's that?" inquired Evenson again, in an agony of curiosity and a whisper.

"He says she's to mind and poison Mr. Gobler," replied Mrs. Tibbs, perfectly aghast at this awful sacrifice of human life.

"And in regard to Mrs. Tibbs," continued O'Bleary—Mrs. Tibbs shuddered.

"Hush!" exclaimed Agnes, in a tone of the greatest alarm.

just as Mrs. Tibbs was on the extreme verge of a fainting-fit. "Hush!"

"Hush!" exclaimed Evenson, at the same moment to Mrs. Tibbs.

"There's somebody coming *up* stairs," said Agnes to O'Bleary.

"There's somebody coming *down* stairs," whispered Evenson to Mrs. Tibbs.

"Go into the parlor, sir," said Agnes to her companion. "You will get there before whoever it is gets to the top of the kitchen-stairs."

"The drawing-room, Mrs. Tibbs!" whispered the astonished Evenson to his equally astonished companion; and for the drawing-room they both made, plainly hearing the rustling of two persons, one coming down stairs, and one coming up.

"What can it be?" exclaimed Mrs. Tibbs. "It's like a dream. I wouldn't be found in this situation for the world!"

"Nor I," returned Evenson, who could never bear a joke at his own expense. "Hush, here they are at the door."

"What fun!" whispered one of the new comers.—It was Wisbottle.

"Glorious!" replied his companion, in an equally low tone—This was Alfred Tomkins. "Who would have thought it?"

"I told you so," said Wisbottle, in a most knowing whisper. "Lord bless you, he has paid her most extraordinary attention for the last two months. I saw 'em when I was sitting at the piano to-night."

"Well, do you know I didn't notice it?" interrupted Tomkins.

"Not notice it!" continued Wisbottle. "Bless you; I saw him whispering to her, and she crying; and then I'll swear I heard him say something about to-night when we are all in bed."

"They are talking of *us!*" exclaimed the agonized Mrs. Tibbs, as the painful suspicion, and a sense of their situation, flashed upon her mind.

"I know it—I know it," replied Evenson, with a melancholy consciousness that there was no mode of escape.

"What's to be done? we cannot both stop here!" ejaculated Mrs. Tibbs, in a state of partial derangement.

"I'll get up the chimney," replied Evenson, who really meant what he said.

"You can't," said Mrs. Tibbs, in despair. "You can't—it's a register stove."

"Hush!" repeated John Evenson.

"Hush—hush!" cried somebody down stairs.

"What a d—d hushing!" said Alfred Tomkins, who began to get rather bewildered.

"There they are!" exclaimed the sapient Wisbottle, as a rustling noise was heard in the storeroom.

"Hark!" whispered both the young men.

"Hark!" repeated Mrs. Tibbs and Evenson.

"Let me alone, sir," said a female voice in the storeroom.

"Oh, Hagnes!" cried another voice, which clearly belonged to Tibbs, for nobody else ever owned one like it. "Oh, Hagnes—lovely creature!"

"Be quiet, sir!" (A bounce.)

"Hag—"

"Be quiet, sir—I am ashamed of you. Think of your wife, Mr. Tibbs. Be quiet, sir!"

"My wife!" exclaimed the valorous Tibbs, who was clearly under the influence of gin-and-water, and a misplaced attachment; "I 'ate her! Oh, Hagnes! when I was in the volunteer corps, in eighteen hundred and—"

"I declare I'll scream. Be quiet, sir, will you!" (Another buunce, and a scuffle.)

"What's that?" exclaimed Tibbs, with a start.

"What's what?" said Agnes, stopping short.

"Why, that!"

"Ah! you have done it nicely now, sir," sobbed the frightened Agnes, as a tapping was heard at Mrs. Tibbs' bed-room door, which would have beaten any twelve woodpeckers hollow.

"Mrs. Tibbs! Mrs. Tibbs!" called out Mrs. Bloss. "Mrs. Tibbs, pray get up." (Here the imitation of a woodpecker was resumed with tenfold violence.)

"Oh, dear—dear!" exclaimed the wretched partner of the depraved Tibbs. "She's knocking at my door. We must be discovered! What will they think?"

"Mrs. Tibbs! Mrs. Tibbs!" screamed the woodpecker again

"What's the matter?" shouted Gobler, bursting out of the back drawing-room, like the dragon at Astley's—only without the portable gas in his countenance.

"Oh, Mr. Gobler!" cried Mrs. Bloss, with a proper approximation to hysterics; "I think the house is on fire, or else there's thieves in it. I have heard the most dreadful noises!"

"The devil you have!" shouted Gobler again, bouncing back into his den, in happy imitation of the aforesaid dragon, and returning immediately with a lighted candle. "Why, what's this? Wisbottle! Tomkins! O'Bleary! Agnes! What the deuce! all up and dressed?"

"Astonishing!" said Mrs. Bloss, who had run down stairs, and taken Mr. Gobler's arm.

"Call Mrs. Tibbs directly, somebody," said Gobler, turning into the front drawing-room.—"What! Mrs. Tibbs and Mr. Evenson!!"

"Mrs. Tibbs and Mr. Evenson!" repeated every body, as that unhappy pair were discovered, Mrs. Tibbs seated in an arm-chair by the fireplace, and Mr. Evenson standing by her side.

We must leave the scene that ensued to the reader's imagination. We could tell how Mrs. Tibbs forthwith fainted away, and how it required the united strength of Mr. Wisbottle and Mr. Alfred Tomkins to hold her in her chair; how Mr. Evenson explained, and how his explanation was evidently disbelieved;—how Agnes repelled the accusations of Mrs. Tibbs, by proving that she was negotiating with Mr. O'Bleary to influence her mistress's affections in his behalf; and how Mr. Gobler threw a damp counterpane on the hopes of Mr. O'Bleary by avowing that he (Gobler) had already proposed to, and been accepted by, Mrs. Bloss; how Agnes was discharged from that lady's service; how Mr. O'Bleary discharged himself from Mrs. Tibbs's house, without going through the form of previously discharging his bill; and how that disappointed young gentleman rails against England and the English, and vows there is no virtue or fine feeling extant, "except in Ireland." We repeat that we *could* tell all this, but we love to exercise our self-denial, and we therefore prefer leaving it to be imagined.

The lady whom we have hitherto described as Mrs. Bloss, is no more. Mrs. Gobler exists: Mrs. Bloss has left us forever.

The Boarding House.

In a secluded retreat in Newington Butts, far—far removed from the noisy strife of that great boarding-house, the world, the enviable Gobler and his pleasing wife revel in retirement; happy in their complaints, their table, and their medicine; wafted through life by the grateful prayers of all the purveyors of animal food within three miles round.

We would willingly stop here, but we have a painful duty imposed upon us, which we must discharge. Mr. and Mrs. Tibbs have separated by mutual consent, Mrs. Tibbs receiving one moiety of 43*l.* 15*s.* 10*d.*, which we before stated to be the amount of her husband's annual income, and Mr. Tibbs the other. He is spending the evening of his days in retirement, and he is spending also annually that small but honorable independence. He resides among the original settlers at Walworth, and it has been stated, on unquestionable authority, that the conclusion of the volunteer story has been heard in a small tavern in that respectable neighborhood.

The unfortunate Mrs. Tibbs has determined to dispose of the whole of her furniture by public auction, and to retire from a residence in which she has suffered so much. Mr. Robins has been applied to, to conduct the sale, and the transcendent abilities of the literary gentlemen connected with his establishment are now devoted to the task of drawing up the preliminary advertisement. It is to contain, among a variety of brilliant matter, seventy-eight words in large capitals, and six *original* quotations in inverted commas.

CHAPTER II.

MR. MINNS AND HIS COUSIN.

MR. AUGUSTUS MINNS was a bachelor, of about forty as he said—of about eight and forty as his friends said. He was always exceedingly clean, precise, and tidy; perhaps somewhat priggish, and the most retiring man in the world. He usually wore a brown frock-coat without a wrinkle, light inexplicables without a spot, a neat neckerchief with a remarkable neat tie, and boots without a fault: moreover, he always carried a brown silk umbrella with an ivory handle. He was a clerk in Somerset-house, or, as he said himself, he held "a responsible situation under Government." He had a good and increasing salary, in addition to some 10,000*l.* of his own (invested in the funds), and he occupied a first floor in Tavistock-street, Covent-garden, where he had resided for twenty years, having been in the habit of quarreling with his landlord the whole time, regularly giving notice of his intention to quit on the first day of every quarter, and as regularly countermanding it on the second. There were two classes of created objects which he held in the deepest and most unmingled horror: they were, dogs and children. He was not unamiable, but he could at any time have viewed the execution of a dog, or the assassination of an infant, with the liveliest satisfaction. Their habits were at variance with his love of order; and his love of order, was as powerful as his love of life. Mr. Augustus Minns had no relations, in or near London, with the exception of his cousin Mr. Octavius Budden, to whose son, whom he had never seen (for he disliked the father), he had consented to become godfather by proxy. Mr. Budden having realized a moderate fortune by exercising the trade or calling of a corn-chandler, and having a great predilection for the country, had purchased a cottage in the vicinity of Stamford-hill, whither he retired with the wife of his bosom, and his only son, Master Alexander Augustus Budden. One evening, as Mr. and Mrs. B. were admiring their son, discussing his various merits, talking over his education, and disputing whether the classics should be made an essential part thereof, the lady pressed so strongly upon her husband the propriety of cultivating the friendship of Mr. Minns in behalf of their son, that Mr. Budden at last made up his mind, that it should not be his fault if he and his cousin were not in future more intimate.

"I'll break the ice, my love," said Mr. Budden, stirring up the sugar at the bottom of his glass of brandy-and-water, and casting a sidelong look at his spouse to see the effect of the announcement of his determination, "by asking Minns down to dine with us, on Sunday."

"Then, pray Mr. Budden write to your cousin at once," replied Mrs. Budden. "Who knows, if we could only get him down here, but that he might take a fancy to our Alexander, and leave him his property?—Alick, my dear, take your legs off the rail of the chair!"

"Very true," said Mr. Budden, musing, "very true, indeed, my love!"

On the following morning, as Mr. Minns was sitting at his breakfast table, alternately biting his dry toast and casting a look upon the columns of his morning paper, which he always read from the title to the printer's name, he heard a loud knock at the street-door which was shortly afterward followed by the entrance of his servant, who put into his hand a particularly small card, on which was engraved in immense letters "Mr. Octavius Budden, Amelia Cottage (Mrs. B.'s name was Amelia), Poplar-walk, Stamford-hill."

"Budden," ejaculated Minns, "what the deuce can bring that vulgar fellow here!—say I'm asleep—say I'm out, and shall never be home again—any thing to keep him down stairs."

"But please, sir, the gentleman's coming up," replied the servant: and the fact was made perfectly evident, by an appalling creaking of boots on the staircase, accompanied by a pattering noise, the cause of which Minns could not, for the life of him divine.

"Hem!—show the gentleman in," said the unfortunate

bachelor. Exit servant, and enter Octavius, preceded by a large white dog, dressed in a suit of fleecy hosiery, with pink eyes, large ears, and no perceptible tail.

The cause of the pattering on the stairs was but too plain. Mr. Augustus Minns staggered beneath the shock of the dog's appearance.

"My dear fellow, how are you?" said Budden, as he entered. He always spoke at the top of his voice, and always said the same thing half a dozen times.

"How are you, my hearty?"

"How do you do, Mr. Budden?"—pray take a chair?" politely stammered the discomfited Minns.

"Thank you—thank you—well—how are you, eh?"

"Uncommonly well, thank ye," said Minns, casting a diabolical look at the dog, who, with his hind legs on the floor, and his fore paws resting on the table, was dragging a bit of bread-and-butter out of a plate, preparatory to devouring it, with the buttered side next the carpet.

"Ah, you rogue!" said Budden to his dog; "you see, Minns, he's like me, always at home, eh, my boy?—Egad, I'm precious hot and hungry! I've walked all the way from Stamford-hill this morning."

"Have you breakfasted?" inquired Minns.

"Oh, no!—came to breakfast with you; so ring the bell, my dear fellow, will you? and let's have another cup and saucer, and the cold ham.—Make myself at home, you see?" continued Budden, dusting his boots with a table napkin. "Ha!—ha! ha!—'pon my life, I'm hungry."

Minns rang the bell, and tried to smile.

"I decidedly never was so hot in my life," continued Octavius, wiping his forehead: well, but how are you, Minns. 'Pon my soul, you wear capitally!"

"D'ye think so?" said Minns; and he tried another smile.

"'Pon my life, I do!"

"Mrs. B. and—what's his name—quite well?"

"Alick—my son, you mean, never better—never better. But at such a place as we've got at Poplar-walk, you know, he couldn't be ill if he tried. When I first saw it, by Jove! it looked so knowing, with the front garden and the green railings, and the brass knocker, and all that—I really thought it was a cut above me."

"Don't you think you'd like the ham better," interrupted Minns, "if you cut it the other way?" He saw, with feelings which it is impossible to describe, that his visitor was cutting, or rather maiming, the ham, in utter violation of all established rules.

"No, thank ye," returned Budden, with the most barbarous indifference to crime, "I prefer it this way—it eats short. But I say, Minns, when will you come down and see us? You will be delighted with the place; I know you will. Amelia and I were talking about you the other night, and Amelia said—another lump of sugar, please; thank ye—she said, don't you think you could contrive, my dear, to say to Mr. Minns, in a friendly way—come down, sir—damn the dog! he's spoiling your curtains, Minns—ha!—ha!—ha!" Minns leaped from his seat as though he had received the discharge from a galvanic battery.

"Come out, sir—go out, hoo!" cried poor Augustus, keeping, nevertheless, at a very respectful distance from the dog, having read of a case of hydrophobia in the paper of that morning. By dint of great exertion, much shouting, and a marvelous deal of poking under the tables with a stick and umbrella, the dog was at last dislodged, and placed on the landing, outside the door, where he immediately commenced a most appalling howling; at the same time vehemently scratching the paint off the two nicely-varnished bottom panels of the door, until they resembled the interior of a back-gammon-board.

"A good dog for the country, that," coolly observed Budden to the distracted Minns—"he's not much used to confinement, though. But now, Minns, when will you come down? I'll take no denial, positively. Let's see: to-day's Thursday.—Will you come on Sunday? We dine at five—don't say no—do."

After a great deal of pressing, Mr. Augustus Minns, driven to despair, accepted the invitation, and promised to be at Poplar-walk on the ensuing Sunday, at a quarter before five to the minute.

"Now mind the direction," said Budden; "the coach goos from the Flowerpot, in Bishopsgate-street, every half hour. When the coach stops at the Swan, you'll see, immediately opposite you, a white house."

"Which is your house—I understand," said Minns, wishing to cut short the visit and the story at the same time.

"No, no, that's not mine; that's Grogus's, the great ironmonger's. I was going to say—you turn down by the side of the white house till you can't go another step further—mind that—and then you turn to your right, by some stables—well; close to you, you'll see a wall with 'Beware of the Dog' written upon it in large letters—(Minns shuddered)—go along by the side of that wall for about a quarter of a mile, and any body will show you which is my place."

"Very well—thank ye—good-by."

"Be punctual."

"Certainly; good-morning."

"I say, Minns, you've got a card?"

"Yes, I have: thank ye." And Mr. Octavius Budden departed leaving his cousin looking forward to his visit of the following Sunday, with the feelings of a penniless poet to the weekly visit of his Scotch landlady.

Sunday arrived; the sky was bright and clear; crowds of people were hurrying along the streets, intent on their different schemes of pleasure for the day; and every thing and every body looked cheerful and happy but Mr. Augustus Minns.

The day was fine, bnt the heat was considerable; and by the time Mr. Minns had fagged up the shady side of Fleet-street, Cheapside, and Threadneedle-street, he had become pretty warm, tolerably dusty, and it was getting late into the bargain. By the most extraordinary good fortune, however, a coach was waiting at the Flowerpot, into which Mr. Augustus Minns got, on the solemn assurance of the cad that the vehicle would start in three minutes—that being the very utmost extremity of time it was allowed to wait by Act of Parliament. A quarter of an hour elapsed, and there were no signs of moving. Minns looked at his watch for the sixth time.

"Coachman, are you going or not?" bawled Mr. Minns, with his head and half his body out of the coach-window.

"Di—rectly, sir," said the coachman, with his hands in his pockets, looking as much unlike a man in a hurry as possible.

"Bill, take them cloths off." Five minutes more elapsed; at the end of which time the coachman mounted the box, from whence he looked down the street and up the street, and hailed all the pedestrians for another five minutes.

"Coachman! if you don't go this moment, I shall get out," said Mr. Minns, rendered desperate by the lateness of the hour, and the impossibility of being in Poplar-walk at the appointed time.

"Going this minute, sir," was the reply;—and, accordingly the machine trundled on for a couple of hundred yards, and then stopped again. Minns doubled himself up into a corner of the coach, and abandoned himself to fate, as a child, a mother, a bandbox, and a parasol became his fellow-passengers.

The child was an affectionate and an amiable infant; the little dear mistook Minns for its other parent, and screamed to embrace him.

"Be quiet, dear," said the mamma, restraining the impetuosity of the darling, whose little fat legs were kicking, and stamping, and twining themselves into the most complicated forms, in an ecstasy of impatience. "Be quiet, dear, that's not your papa."

"Thank Heaven I am not"—thought Minns, as the first gleam of pleasure he had experienced that morning shone like a meteor through his wretchedness.

Playfulness was agreeably mingled with affection in the disposition of the boy. When satisfied that Mr. Minns was not his parent, he endeavored to attract his notice by scraping his drab trousers with his dirty shoes, poking his chest with his mamma's parasol, and other nameless endearments peculiar to infancy, with which he beguiled the tediousness of the ride, apparently very much to his own satisfaction.

When the unfortunate gentleman arrived at the Swan, he found to his great dismay, that it was a quarter past five. The white house, the stables, the "Beware of the Dog,"—every landmark was passed, with a rapidity not unusual to a gentleman of a certain age when too late for dinner. After the lapse of a few minutes, Mr. Minns found himself opposite a yellow-brick house with a green door, brass knocker and door-plate, green window-frames and ditto railings, with a "garden" in front, that is to say, a small loose bit of graveled ground, with one round and two scalene triangular beds, containing a fir-tree, twenty or thirty bulbs, and an unlimited number of marigolds. The taste of Mr. and Mrs. Budden was further displayed by the appearance of a Cupid on each side of the door, perched upon a heap of large chalk flints, variegated with pink cone-shells. His knock at the door was answered by a stumpy boy, in drab livery, cotton stockings and high-lows, who, after hanging his hat on one of the dozen brass pegs which ornamented the passage, denominated by courtesy "The Hall," ushered him into a front drawing-room commanding a very extensive view of the back of the neighboring houses. The usual ceremony of introduction, and so forth, over, Mr. Minns took his seat, not a little agitated at finding that he was the last comer, and, somehow or other, the Lion of about a dozen people, sitting together in a small drawing-room, getting rid of that most tedious of all time, the time preceding dinner.

"Well, Brogson," said Budden, addressing an elderly gentleman in a black coat, drab knee-breeches, and long gaiters, who under pretense of inspecting the prints in an Annual, had been engaged in satisfying himself upon the subject of Mr. Minns's general appearance, by looking at him over the tops of the leaves—"Well, Brogson, what do Ministers mean to do? Will they go out, or what?"

"Oh—why—really, you know, I'm the last person in the world to ask for news. Your cousin, from his situation, is the most likely person to answer the question."

Mr. Minns assured the last speaker, that although he was in Somerset-house, he possessed no official communication relative to the projects of his Majesty's Ministers. But his remark was evidently received incredulously; and no further conjectures being hazarded on the subject, a long pause ensued, during which the company occupied themselves in coughing and blowing their noses, until the entrance of Mrs. Budden caused a general rise.

The ceremony of introduction being over, dinner was announced, and down stairs the party proceeded accordingly—Mr. Minns escorting Mrs. Budden as far as the drawing-room door, but being prevented, by the narrowness of the staircase, from extending his gallantry any further. The dinner passed off as such dinners usually do. Ever and anon amidst the clatter of knives and forks, and the hum of conversation, Mr. B.'s voice might be heard, asking a friend to take wine, and assuring him he was glad to see him; and a great deal of by-play took place between Mrs. B. and the servants, respecting the removal of the dishes, during which her countenance assumed all the variations of a weather-glass, from "stormy" to "set fair."

Upon the dessert and wine being placed on the table, the servant, in compliance with a significant look from Mrs. B. brought down "Master Alexander," habited in a sky-blue suit with silver buttons, and with hair of nearly the same color as the metal. After sundry praises from his mother, and various admonitions as to his behavior from his Pa, he was introduced to his godfather.

"Well my little fellow—you are a fine boy, ain't you?" said Mr. Minns, as happy as a tomtit on birdlime.

"Yes."

"How old are you?"

"Eight, next We'nsday. How old are *you*?"

"Alexander," interrupted his mother, "how dare you ask Mr. Minns how old he is!"

"He asked me how old *I* was," said the precocious child, to whom Minns had from that moment internally resolved he never would bequeath one shilling. As soon as the titter occasioned by the observation had subsided, a little smirking man with red whiskers, sitting at the bottom of the table, who during the whole of dinner had been endeavoring to obtain a listener to some stories about Sheridan, called out, with a very patronizing air—"Alick, what part of speech is *be*?"

"A verb."

"That's a good boy," said Mrs. Budden with all a mother's pride. "Now, you know what a verb is?"

"A verb is a word which signifies to be, to do, or to suffer; as, I am—I rule—I am ruled. Give me an apple, Ma."

"I'll give you an apple," replied the man with the red whiskers, who was an established friend of the family, or in other words was always invited by Mrs. Budden, whether Mr. Budden liked it or not, "if you'll tell me what is the meaning of *be?*"

"Be ?" said the prodigy, after a little hesitation--"an insect that gathers honey."

"No, dear," frowned Mrs. Budden—"B double E is the substantive."

"I don't think he knows much yet about *common* substantives," said the smirking gentleman, who thought this an admirable opportunity for letting off a joke. "It's clear he's not very well acquainted with *proper names.* He! he! he!"

"Gentlemen," called out Mr. Budden, from the end of the table, in a stentorian voice, and with a very important air, "will you have the goodness to charge your glasses? I have a toast to propose."

"Hear! hear!" cried the gentlemen, passing the decanters. After they had made the round of the table, Mr. Budden proceeded—"Gentlemen; there is an individual present—"

"Hear! hear!" said the little man with red whiskers.

"*Pray* be quiet, Jones," remonstrated Budden.

"I say, gentlemen, there is an individual present," resumed the host, "in whose society I am sure we must take great delight—and—and—the conversation of that individual must have afforded to every one present the utmost pleasure." ["Thank Heaven, he does not mean me!" thought Minns, conscious that his diffidence and exclusiveness had prevented his saying above a dozen words since he entered the house.] "Gentlemen, I am but a humble individual myself, and I perhaps ought to apologize for allowing my individual feelings of friendship and affection for the person I allude to, to induce me to venture to rise, to propose the health of that person—a person that, I am sure—that is to say, a person whose virtues must endear him to those who know him—and those who have not the pleasure of knowing him, cannot dislike him."

"Hear! hear!" said the company, in a tone of encouragement and approval.

"Gentlemen," continued Budden, "my cousin is a man who

—who is a relation of my own." (Hear! hear!) Minns groaned audibly. "Who I am most happy to see here, and who, if he were not here, would certainly have deprived us of the great pleasure we all feel in seeing him. (Loud cries of hear!) Gentlemen, I feel that I have already trespassed on your attention for too long a space. With every feeling——of ——with every sentiment of——of——"

"Gratification"—suggested the friend of the family.

"——Of gratification, I beg to propose the health of Mr. Minns."

"Standing, gentlemen!" shouted the indefatigable little man with the whiskers—"and with the honors. Take your time from me, if you please. Hip! hip! hip!—Za!—Hip! hip! hip!—Za!—Hip! hip!—Za—a—a!"

All eyes were now fixed on the subject of the toast, who, by gulping down port wine at the imminent hazard of suffocation, endeavored to conceal his confusion. After as long a pause as decency would admit, he rose, but, as the newspapers sometimes say in their reports, "we regret that we are quite unable to give even the substance of the honorable gentleman's observations." The words "present company—honor—present occasion," and "great happiness"—heard occasionally, and repeated at intervals, with a countenance expressive of the utmost confusion and misery, convinced the company that he was making an excellent speech; and accordingly, on his resuming his seat, they cried "Bravo!" and manifested tumultuous applause. Jones, who had been long watching his opportunity, then darted up.

"Budden," said he, "will you allow *me* to propose a toast?"

"Certainly," replied Budden, adding in an undertone to Minns right across the table—"Devilish sharp fellow that: you'll be very much pleased with his speech. He talks equally well on any subject." Minns bowed, and Mr. Jones proceeded:

"It has on several occasions, in various instances, under many circumstances, and in different companies, fallen to my lot to propose a toast to those by whom, at the time, I have had the honor to be surrounded. I have sometimes, I will cheerfully own—for why should I deny it?—felt the overwhelming nature of the task I have undertaken, and my own utter incapability to do justice to the subject. If such have been my feelings, however, on former occasions, what must they be now—now—under the extraordinary circumstances in which I am placed. (Hear! hear!) To describe my feelings accurately would be impossible; but I cannot give you a better idea of them, gentlemen, than by referring to a circumstance which happens, oddly enough, to occur to my mind at the moment. On one occasion, when that truly great and illustrious man, Sheridan, was——"

Now, there is no knowing what new villainy in the form of a joke would have been heaped upon the memory of that very ill-used man, Mr. Sheridan, if the boy in drab had not at that moment entered the room in a breathless state, to report that, as it was a very wet night, the nine o'clock stage had come round to know whether there was any body going to town, as, in that case, he (the nine o'clock) had room for one inside.

Mr. Minns started up; and despite countless exclamations of surprise, and entreaties to stay, persisted in his determination to accept the vacant place. But the brown silk umbrella was nowhere to be found; and as the coachman couldn't wait, he drove back to the Swan, leaving word for Mr. Minns to "run round" and catch him. But as it did not occur to Mr. Minns for some ten minutes or so, that he had left the brown silk umbrella with the ivory handle in the other coach, coming down; and, moreover, as he was by no means remarkable for speed, it is no matter of surprise that when he accomplished the feat of "running round" to the Swan, the coach—the last coach—had gone without him.

It was somewhere about three o'clock in the morning, when Mr. Augustus Minns knocked feebly at the street-door of his lodgings in Tavistock-street, cold, wet, cross, and miserable. He made his will next morning, and his professional man informs us, in that strict confidence in which we inform the public, that neither the name of Mr. Octavius Budden, nor of Mrs. Amelia Budden, nor of Master Alexander Augustus Budden, appears therein.

CHAPTER III.

SENTIMENT.

The Miss Crumptons, or to quote the authority of the inscription on the garden-gate of Minerva House, Hammersmith—"The Misses Crumpton," were two unusually tall, particularly thin, and exceedingly skinny personages: very upright, and very yellow. Miss Amelia Crumpton owned to thirty-eight, and Miss Maria Crumpton admitted she was forty; an admission which was rendered perfectly unnecessary by the self-evident fact of her being fifty at least. They dressed in the most interesting manner—like twins, and looked about as happy and comfortable as a couple of marigolds run to seed. They were very precise, had the strictest possible ideas of propriety, wore false hair, and always smelt very strongly of lavender.

Minerva House, conducted under the auspices of the two sisters, was a "finishing establishment for young ladies," where some twenty girls of the ages of from thirteen to nineteen inclusive, acquired a smattering of every thing, and a knowledge of nothing; instruction in French and Italian, dancing lessons twice a-week, and other necessaries of life. The house was a white one, a little removed from the road-side, with close palings in front. The bed-room windows were always left partly open to afford a bird's-eye view of numerous little bedsteads with very white dimity furniture, and thereby impress the passer-by with a due sense of the luxuries of the establishment; and there was a front parlor hung round with highly varnished maps which nobody ever looked at, and filled with books which no one ever read, appropriated exclusively to the reception of parents, who, whenever they called could not fail to be struck with the very knowledge-imparting appearance of the place.

"Amelia, my dear," said Miss Maria Crumpton, entering the school-room one morning, with her false hair in papers, as she occasionally did, in order to impress the young ladies with a conviction of its reality—"Amelia, my dear, here's a most gratifying note I have just received. You needn't mind reading it aloud"

Miss Amelia, thus advised, proceeded to read the following note with an air of great triumph:—

"Cornelius Brook Dingwall, Esq., M.P., presents his compliments to Miss Crumpton, and will feel much obliged by Miss Crumpton's calling on him, if she conveniently can, to-morrow morning at one o'clock, as Cornelius Brook Dingwall, Esq., M.P., is anxious to see Miss Crumpton on the subject of placing Miss Brook Dingwall under her charge.

"Adelphi.

"Monday morning."

"A Member of Parliament's daughter!" ejaculated Amelia, in an ecstatic tone.

"A Member of Parliament's daughter!" repeated Miss Maria, with a smile of delight, which of course elicited a concurrent titter of pleasure from all the young ladies.

"It's exceedingly delightful!" said Miss Amelia; whereupon all the young ladies murmured their admiration again. Courtiers are but schoolboys, and court-ladies schoolgirls.

So important an announcement at once superseded the business of the day. A holiday was declared in commemoration of the great event: the Miss Crumptons retired to their private apartment to talk it over; the smaller girls discussed the probable manners and customs of the daughter of a Member of Parliament: and the young ladies verging on eighteen wondered whether she was engaged, whether she was pretty, whether she wore much bustle, and many other *whethers* of equal importance.

The two Miss Crumptons proceeded to the Adelphi at the appointed time next day, dressed, of course, in their best style, and looking as amiable as they possibly could—which, by-the-by, is not saying much for them. Having sent in their cards, through the medium of a red-hot looking footman in bright livery, they were ushered into the august presence of the profound Dingwall.

Cornelius Brook Dingwall, Esq., M.P., was very haughty, solemn and portentous. He had naturally a somewhat spasmodic expression of countenance, which was not rendered the less remarkable by his wearing an extremely stiff cravat. He was wonderfully proud of the "M.P." attached to his name, and never lost an opportunity of reminding people of his dignity. He had a great idea of his own abilities, which must have been a great comfort to him, as no one else had; and in diplomacy, on a small scale in his own family arrangements, he considered himself unrivaled. He was a country magistrate, and discharged the duties of his station with all due justice and impartiality, frequently committing poachers, and occasionally committing himself. Miss Brook Dingwall was one of that numerous class of young ladies, who, like adverbs, may be known by their answering to a common-place question, and doing nothing else.

On the present occasion this talented individual was seated in a small library at a table covered with papers, doing nothing, but trying to look busy—playing at shop. Acts of Parliament, and letters directed to "Cornelius Brook Dingwall, Esq., M.P.," were ostentatiously scattered over the table, at a little distance from which Mrs. Brook Dingwall was seated at work. One of those public nuisances, a spoiled child, was playing about the room, dressed after the most approved fashion, in a blue tunic with a black belt a quarter of a yard wide, fastened with an immense buckle, and looking like a robber in a melodrama seen through a diminishing-glass.

After a little pleasantry from the sweet child, who amused himself by running away with Miss Maria Crumpton's chair as fast as it was placed for her, the visitors were seated, and Cornelius Brook Dingwall, Esq., opened the conversation.

He had sent for Miss Crumpton, he said, in consequence of the high character he had received of her establishment from his friend Sir Alfred Muggs.

Miss Crumpton murmured her acknowledgments to him (Muggs), and Cornelius proceeded.

"One of my principal reasons, Miss Crumpton, for parting with my daughter is, that she has lately acquired some sentimental ideas, which it is most desirable to eradicate from her young mind." (Here the little innocent before noticed fell out of an arm-chair with an awful crash.)

"Naughty boy!" said his mamma, who appeared more surprised at his taking the liberty of falling down, than at any thing else; "I'll ring the bell for James to take him away."

"Pray don't check him, my love," said the diplomatist, as soon as he could make himself heard amidst the unearthly howling consequent upon the threat and tumble. "It all arises from his great flow of spirits." This last explanation was addressed to Miss Crumpton.

"Certainly, sir," replied the antique Maria, not exactly seeing, however, the connection between a flow of animal spirits and a fall from an arm-chair.

Silence was restored, and the M. P. resumed: "Now, I know nothing so likely to effect this object, Miss Crumpton, as her mixing constantly in the society of girls of her own age; and as I know that in your establishment she will meet such as are not likely to contaminate her young mind, I propose to send her to you."

The youngest Miss Crumpton expressed the acknowledgments of the establishment generally. Maria was rendered perfectly speechless by bodily pain—the dear little fellow, having recovered his spirits, was standing upon her most tender foot, by way of getting his face (which looked like a capital O in a red lettered play-bill) on a level with the writing-table.

"Of course, Lavinia will be a parlor-boarder," continued the enviable father; "and on one point I wish my directions to be strictly observed. The fact is, that some ridiculous love affair with a person much her inferior in life has been the cause of her present state of mind. Knowing that of course, under your care, she can have no opportunity of meeting this person, I do not object to—indeed, I should rather prefer—her mixing with such society as you see yourself."

The important statement was again interrupted by the high-spirited little creature, in the excess of his joyousness breaking a pane of glass, and nearly precipitating himself into an adjacent area. James was rung for; considerable confusion and screaming succeeded; two little blue legs about the size of hoop-sticks were seen to kick violently in the air as the man left the room, and the child was gone.

"Mr. Brook Dingwall would like Miss Brook Dingwall to

learn every thing," said Mrs. Brook Dingwall, who hardly ever said any thing at all.

"Certainly," said both the Miss Crumptons together.

"And as I trust the plan I have devised will be effectual in weaning my daughter from this absurd idea, Miss Crumpton," continued the legislator, "I hope you will have the goodness to comply in all respects with any request I may forward to you."

The promise was of course made; and after a lengthened discussion, conducted on behalf of the Dingwalls with the most becoming diplomatic gravity, and on that of the Crumptons with profound respect, it was finally arranged that Miss Lavinia should be forwarded to Hammersmith on the next day but one, on which occasion the half-yearly ball given at the establishment was to take place. It might divert the dear girl's mind. This, by the way, was another bit of diplomacy.

Miss Lavinia was introduced to her future governess, and both the Miss Crumptons pronounced her "a most charming girl;" an opinion which, by a singular coincidence, they always entertained of any new pupil.

Courtesies were made, acknowledgments expressed, condescension exhibited, and the interview terminated.

Preparations, to make use of theatrical phraseology, "on a scale of magnitude never before attempted," were incessantly made at Minerva House to give every effect to the forthcoming ball. The largest room in the house was pleasingly ornamented with blue calico roses, plaid tulips, and other equally natural-looking artificial flowers, the work of the young ladies themselves. The carpet was taken up, the folding-doors were taken down, the furniture was taken out, and rout-seats were taken in. The linendrapers of Hammersmith were astounded at the sudden demand for blue sarcenet ribbon, and long white gloves. Dozens of geraniums were purchased for boquets, and a harp and two violins were bespoke from town, in addition to the grand-piano already on the premises. The young ladies who were selected to show off on the occasion, and do credit to the establishment, practiced incessantly, much to their own satifaction, and greatly to the annoyance of the lame old gentleman over the way; and a constant correspondence was kept up between the Misses Crumptons and the Hammersmith pastrycook.

The evening came; and then there was such a lacing of stays, and tying of sandals, and dressing of hair, as never can take place with a proper degree of bustle out of a boarding-school. The smaller girls managed to be in every body's way, and were pushed about accordingly; and the elder ones dressed, and tied, and flattered and envied one another, as earnestly and sincerely as if they had actually *come out.*

"How do I look, dear?" inquired Miss Emily Smithers, the belle of the house, of Miss Caroline Wilson, who was her bosom friend, because she was the ugliest girl in Hammersmith, or out of it.

"Oh! charming, dear. How do I?"

"Delightful! you never looked so handsome," returned the belle, adjusting her own dress, and not bestowing a glance on her poor companion.

"I hope young Hilton will come early," said another young lady to Miss somebody else, in a fever of expectation.

"I'm sure he'd be highly flattered if he knew it," returned the other, who was practicing *l'ete* for effect.

"Oh! he's so handsome," said the first.

"Such a charming person!" added a second.

"Such a *distingue* air!" said a third.

"Oh, what *do* you think?" said another girl, running into the room; "Miss Crumpton says her cousin's coming."

"What! Theodosius Butler?" said every body in raptures.

"Is *he* handsome?" inquired a novice.

"No, not particularly handsome," was the general reply; "but, oh, so clever!"

Mr. Theodosius Butler was one of those immortal geniuses who are to be met with in almost every circle. They have usually very deep, monotonous voices. They always persuade themselves that they are wonderful persons, and that they ought to be very miserable, though they don't precisely know why. They are very conceited, and usually possess exactly half an idea; but with enthusiastic young ladies, and silly young gentlemen, they are very wonderful persons. The individual in question, Mr. Theodosius, had written a pamphlet, containing some very weighty considerations on the expediency of doing something or other; and as every sentence contained at least fifty words of four syllables, his admirers took it for granted that he meant a good deal.

"Perhaps that's he," exclaimed several young ladies, as the first pull of the evening threatened destruction to the bell of the gate.

An awful pause ensued. Some boxes arrived, and a young lady—it was Miss Brook Dingwall, in full ball costume, with an immense gold chain round her neck, and her dress looped up with a single rose; an ivory fan in her hand, and a most interesting expression of despair in her face.

The Miss Crumptons inquired after the family with the most excruciating anxiety, and Miss Brook Dingwall was formally introduced to her future companions. The Miss Crumptons conversed with the young ladies in the most mellifluous tones, in order that Miss Brook Dingwall might be properly impressed with their amiable treatment.

Another pull at the bell. Mr. Dadson, the writing-master, and his wife. The wife in green silk, with shoes and cap-trimmings to correspond; and the writing-master in a white waistcoat, black knee-shorts, and ditto silk stockings, displaying a leg large enough for two writing-masters, at least. The young ladies whispered one another, and the writing-master and his wife flattered the Miss Crumptons, who were dressed in amber, with long sashes, like dolls.

Repeated pulls at the bell, and arrivals too numerous to particularize; papas and mammas, and aunts and uncles, the owners and guardians of the different pupils; the singing-master, Signor Lobskini, in a black wig; the piano-forte player and the violins; the harp, in a state of intoxication; and some twenty young men, who stood near the door, and talked to one another, occasionally bursting into a giggle. A general hum of conversation. Coffee handed round and plentifully partaken of by fat mammas, looking like the stout people who come on in pantomimes for the sole purpose of being knocked down.

The popular Mr. Hilton was the next arrival; and having, at the request of the Miss Crumptons, undertaken the office of Master of the Ceremonies, the quadrilles commenced with considerable spirit. The young men by the door gradually advanced into the middle of the room, and in time became sufficiently at ease to consent to be introduced to partners. The writing-master danced every set, springing about with the most fearful agility, and his wife played a rubber in the back parlor—a little room with five book-shelves, dignified by the name of the study. Setting her down to whist was a half-yearly piece of generalship on the part of the Miss Crumptons, as it was necessary to hide her somewhere on account of her being a fright.

The interesting Lavinia Brook Dingwall was the only girl present who appeared to take no interest in the proceedings of the evening. In vain was she solicited to dance; in vain was the universal homage paid to her as the daughter of a member of parliament. She was equally unmoved by the splendid tenor of the inimitable Lobskini, and the brilliant execution of Miss Lætitia Parsons, whose performance of "The Recollections of Ireland" was universally declared to be almost equal to that of Moschelles himself. Not even the announcement of the arrival of Mr. Theodosius Butler could induce her to leave the corner of the back drawing-room in which she was seated.

"Now, Theodosius," said Miss Maria Crumpton, after that enlightened pamphleteer had nearly run the gauntlet of the whole company, "I must introduce you to our new pupil."

Theodosius looked as if he cared for nothing earthly.

"She's the daughter of a member of parliament," said Maria. —Theodosius started.

"And her name is—— ?" he inquired.

"Miss Brook Dingwall."

"Great Heaven!" poetically exclaimed Theodosius in a low tone.

Miss Crumpton commenced the introduction in due form. Miss Brook Dingwall languidly raised her head.

"Edward!" she exclaimed, with a half-shriek, on seeing the well-known nankeen legs.

Fortunately, as Miss Maria Crumpton possessed no remarkable share of penetration, and as it was one of the diplomatic arrangements that no attention was to be paid to Miss Lavinia's incoherent exclamations, she was perfectly unconscious of the mutual agitation of the parties; and therefore, seeing that the offer of his hand for the next quadrille was accepted, she left him by the side of Miss Brook Dingwall.

"Oh, Edward!" exclaimed that most romantic of all romantic young ladies, as the light of science seated himself beside her, "Oh, Edward! is it you?"

Mr. Theodosius assured the dear creature, in the most impassioned manner, that he was not conscious of being any body but himself.

"Then why—why—this disguise? Oh! Edward M'Neville Walter, what have I not suffered on your account!"

"Lavinia, hear me," replied the hero, in his most poetic strain. "Do not condemn me unheard. If any thing that emanates from the soul of such a wretch as I can occupy a place in your recollection—if any being so vile deserve your notice—you may remember that I once published a pamphlet (and paid for its publication) entitled 'Considerations on the Policy of Removing the Duty on Bees'-wax.'"

"I do—I do!" sobbed Lavinia.

"That," continued the lover, "was a subject to which your father was devoted heart and soul."

"He was—he was!" reiterated the sentimentalist.

"I knew it," continued Theodosius, tragically; "I knew it—I forwarded him a copy. He wished to know me. Could I disclose my real name? Never! No, I assumed that name which you have so often pronounced in tones of endearment. As M'Neville Walter, I devoted myself to the stirring cause; as M'Neville Walter I gained your heart; in the same character I was ejected from your house by your father's domestics, and in no character at all have I since been enabled to see you. We now meet again, and I proudly own that I am—Theodosius Butler."

The young lady appeared perfectly satisfied with this very argumentative address, and bestowed a look of the most ardent affection on the immortal advocate of bees'-wax.

"May I hope," said he, "that the promise your father's violent behavior interrupted, may be renewed?"

"Let us join this set," replied Lavinia, coquettishly—for girls of nineteen can coquette.

"No," ejaculated he of the nankeens; "I stir not from this spot writhing under this torture of suspense. May I—may I—hope?"

"You may."

"The promise is renewed?"

"It is."

"I have your permission?"

"You have."

"To the fullest extent?"

"You know it," returned the blushing Lavinia. The contortions of the interesting Butler's visage expressed his raptures.

We could dilate upon the occurrences that ensued. How Mr. Theodosius and Miss Lavinia danced, and talked, and sighed for the remainder of the evening—how the Miss Cruptons were delighted thereat. How the writing master continued to frisk about with one-horse power, and how his wife, from some unaccountable freak, left the whist-table in the little back parlor, and persisted in displaying her green head-dress in the most conspicuous part of the drawing-room. How the supper consisted of small triangular sandwiches in trays, and a tart here and there by way of variety; and how the visitors consumed warm water disguised with lemon, and dotted with nutmeg, under the denomination of negus. These, and other matters of as much interest, however, we pass over, for the purpose of describing a scene of even more importance.

A fortnight after the date of the ball, Cornelius Brook Dingwall, Esq., M.P., was seated at the same library-table, and in the same room as we have before described. He was alone, and his face bore an expression of deep thought and solemn gravity—he was drawing up "A Bill for the better observance of Easter Monday."

The footman tapped at the door—the legislator started from his revery, and "Miss Crumpton" was announced. Permission was given for Miss Crumpton to enter the *sanctum;* Maria came sliding in, and having taken her seat with a due portion of affectation, the footman retired, and the governess was left alone with the M.P. Oh! how she longed for the presence of a third party ! even the facetious young gentleman would have been a relief.

Miss Crumpton began the duet. She hoped Mrs. Brook Dingwall and the handsome little boy were in good health.

They were. Mrs. Brook Dingwall and little Frederick were at Brighton.

"Much obliged to you, Miss Crumpton," said Cornelius in his most dignified manner, "for your attention in calling this morning. I should have driven down to Hammersmith to see Lavinia, but your account was so very satisfactory, and my duties in the House occupy me so much, that I determined to postpone it for a week. How has she gone on ?"

"Very well indeed, sir," returned Maria, dreading to inform the father that she had gone off.

"Ah, I thought the plan on which I proceeded would be a match for her."

Here was a favorable opportunity to say that somebody else had been a match for her. The unfortunate governess was unequal to the task.

"You have persevered strictly in the line of conduct I prescribed, Miss Crumpton ?"

"Strictly, sir."

"You tell me in your note that her spirits gradually improved."

"Very much indeed, sir."

"To be sure. I was convinced they would."

"But I fear, sir," said Miss Crumpton, with visible emotion. "I fear the plan has not succeeded quite so well as we could have wished."

"No!" exclaimed the prophet. "Bless me! Miss Crumpton, you look alarmed. What has happened ?"

Miss Brook Dingwall sir—"

"Yes, ma'am ?"

"Has gone, sir"—said Maria, exhibiting a strong inclination to faint.

"Gone!"

"Eloped, sir."

"Eloped!"—Who with—when—where—how ?" almost shrieked the agitated diplomatist.

The natural yellow of the unfortunate Maria's face changed to all the hues of the rainbow, as she laid a small packet upon the member's table.

He hurriedly opened it. A letter from his daughter, and another from Theodosius. He glanced over their contents—"Ere this reaches you, far distant—appeal to feelings—love to distraction—bees'-wax—slavery," &c., &c. He dashed his hand to his forehead, and paced the room with fearfully long strides, to the great alarm of the precise Maria.

"Now mind; from this time forward," said Mr. Brook Dingwall, suddenly stopping at the table, and beating time upon it with his hand—"from this time forward, I never will, under any circumstances whatever, permit a man who writes pamphlets to enter any room of this house but the kitchen.—I'll allow my daughter and her husband one hundred and fifty pounds a-year, and never see their faces again;—and, damme! ma'am, I'll bring in a bill for the abolition of finishing-schools!"

Some time has elapsed since this passionate declaration. Mr. and Mrs. Butler are at present rusticating in a small cottage at Ball's-pond, pleasantly situated in the immediate vicinity of a brick-field. They have no family. Mr. Theodosius looks very important, and writes incessantly; but, in consequence of some gross combination on the part of the publishers, none of his productions appear in print. His young wife begins to think that ideal misery is preferable to real unhappiness; and that a marriage contracted in haste, and repented at leisure, is the cause of more substantial wretchedness than she ever anticipated.

On cool reflection, Cornelius Brook Dingwall, Esq., M.P., was reluctantly compelled to admit that the untoward result of his admirable arrangements was attributable, not to the Miss Crumptons, but his own diplomacy. He, however, consoles himself, like some other small diplomatists, by satisfactorily proving that if his plans did not succeed, they ought to have done so. Minerva House is in *statu quo*, and "The Misses Crumpton" remain in the peaceable and undisturbed enjoyment of all the advantages resulting from their Fnishing-School.

CHAPTER IV.

THE TUGGS'S AT RAMSGATE.

ONCE upon a time there dwelt, in a narrow street on the Surrey side of the water within three minutes' walk of the old London Bridge, Mr. Joseph Tuggs—a little dark-faced man, with shiny hair, twinkling eyes, short legs, and a body of very considerable thickness, measuring from the centre button of his waistcoat in front, to the ornamental buttons of his coat behind. The figure of the amiable Mrs. Tuggs, if not perfectly symmetrical, was decidedly comfortable; and the form of her only daughter, the accomplished Miss Charlotte Tuggs, was fast ripening into that state of luxuriant plumpness which had enchanted the eyes, and captivated the heart, of Mr. Joseph Tuggs in his earlier days. Mr. Simon Tuggs, his only son, and Miss Charlotte Tuggs's only brother, was as differently formed in body, as he was differently constituted in mind, from the remainder of his family. There was that elongation in his thoughtful face, and that tendency to weakness in his interesting legs, which tells so forcibly of a great mind and romantic disposition. The slightest traits of character in such a being, possess no mean interest to speculative minds. He usually appeared in public in capacious shoes with black-cotton stockings; and was observed to be particularly attached to a black glazed stock, without tie or ornament of any description.

There is perhaps no profession, however useful; no pursuit. however meritorious, which can escape the petty attacks of vulgar minds. Mr. Joseph Tuggs was a grocer. It might be supposed that a grocer was beyond the breath of calumny; but no—the neighbors stigmatized him as a chandler; and the poisonous voice of envy distinctly asserted that he dispensed tea and coffee by the quartern, retailed sugar by the ounce, cheese by the slice, tobacco by the screw, and butter by the pat. These taunts, however, were lost upon the Tuggs's. Mr. Tuggs attended to the grocery department, Mrs. Tuggs to the cheesemongery, and Miss Tuggs to her education. Mr. Simon Tuggs kept his father's books, and his own counsel.

One fine spring afternoon, the latter gentleman was seated on a tub of weekly Dorset behind the little red desk with a wooden rail which ornamented the corner of the counter, when a stranger dismounted from a cab, and hastily entered the shop. He was habited in black cloth, and bore with him a green umbrella and a blue bag.

"Mr. Tuggs ?" said the stranger inquiringly.

"*My* name is Tuggs," replied Mr. Simon.

"It's the other Mr. Tuggs," said the stranger, looking toward the glass-door which led into the parlor behind the shop, and on the inside of which, the round face of Mr. Tuggs, senior, was distinctly visible, peeping over the curtain.

Mr. Simon gracefully waved his pen, as if in intimation of his wish that his father would advance, and Mr. Joseph Tuggs, with considerable celerity, removed his face from the curtain, and placed it before the stranger.

"I come from the Temple," said the man with the bag.

"From the Temple!" said Mrs. Tuggs, flinging open the door of the litttle parlor, and disclosing Miss Tuggs in perspective.

"From the Temple!" said Miss Tuggs and Mr. Simon Tuggs at the same moment.

"From the Temple!" said Mr. Joseph Tuggs, turning as pale as a Dutch cheese.

"From the the Temple," repeated the man with the bag; "from Mr. Cower's, the solicitor's. Mr. Tuggs, I congratulate you, sir. Ladies, I wish you joy of your prosperity! We have been successful." And the man with the bag leisurely divested himself of his umbrella and glove, as a preliminary to shaking hands with Mr. Joseph Tuggs.

Now the words "we have been successful," had no sooner issued from the mouth of the man with the bag, than Mr. Simon Tuggs rose from the tub of weekly Dorset, opened his eyes very wide, gasped for breath, made figures of eight in the air with his pen, and finally fell into the arms of his anxious mother, and fainted away, without the slightest ostensible cause or pretense.

"Water!" screamed Mrs. Tuggs.

"Look up, my son," exclaimed Mr. Tuggs.

"Simon! dear Simon!" shrieked Miss Tuggs.

"I'm better now," said Mr. Simon Tuggs—"What! successful!" And then, as corroborative evidence of his being better, he fainted away again, and was borne into the little parlor by the united effort of the remainder of the family and the man with the bag.

To a casual spectator, or to any one unacquainted with the position of the family, this fainting would have been unaccountable. To those who understood the mission of the man with the bag, and were moreover acquainted with the excitability of the nerves of Mr. Simon Tuggs, it was quite comprehensible. A long pending lawsuit respecting the validity of a will, had been unexpectedly decided; and Mr. Joseph Tuggs was the possessor of twenty thousand pounds.

A prolonged consultation took place that night in the little parlor—a consultation which was to settle the future destinies of the Tuggs's. The shop was shut up at an unusually early hour; and many were the unavailing kicks bestowed upon the closed door by applicants for quarterns of sugar, or half-quarterns of bread, or penn'orths of pepper, which were to have been "left till Saturday," but which fortune had decreed were to be left alone altogether.

"We must certainly give up business," said Miss Tuggs.

"Oh, decidedly," said Mrs. Tuggs.

"Simon shall go to the bar," said Mr. Joseph Tuggs.

"And I shall always sign myself 'Cymon' in future," said his son.

"And I shall call myself Charlotta," said Miss Tuggs.

"And you must always call *me* 'Ma,' and father 'Pa,'" said Mrs. Tuggs.

"Yes, and Pa must leave off all his vulgar habits," interposed Miss Tuggs.

"I'll take care of all that," responded Mr. Joseph Tuggs, complacently.—He was at that very moment eating pickled salmon with a pocket-knife.

"We must leave town immediately," said Mr. Cymon Tuggs.

Every body concurred that this was an indispensable preliminary to being genteel. The question then arose—Where should they go?

"Gravesend," mildly suggested Mr. Joseph Tuggs. The idea was unanimously scouted. Gravesend was *low.*

"Margate," insinuated Mrs. Tuggs. Worse and worse—nobody there but tradespeople.

"Brighton!" Mr. Cymon Tuggs opposed an insurmountable objection. All the coaches had been upset in their turn within the last three weeks; each coach had averaged two passengers killed and six wounded; and in every case the newspapers had distinctly understood that "no blame whatever was attributable to the coachman."

"Ramsgate!" ejaculated Mr. Cymon, thoughtfully.—To be sure: how stupid they must have been not to have thought of that before! Ramsgate was just the place of all others that they ought to go to.

Two months after this conversation, the City of London Ramsgate steamer was running gayly down the river. Her flag was flying, her band was playing, her passengers were conversing; every thing about her seemed gay and lively. No wonder—the Tuggs's were on board.

"Charming, ain't it?" said Mr. Joseph Tuggs, in a bottle-green great-coat, with a velvet collar of the same, and a blue traveling-cap with a gold band.

"Soul-inspiring," replied Mr. Cymon Tuggs—he was entered at the bar—"Soul-inspiring!"

"Delightful morning, sir," said a stoutish, military-looking gentleman in a blue surtout buttoned up to his chin, and white trousers chained down to the soles of his boots.

Mr. Cymon Tuggs took upon himself the responsibility of answering the observation. "Heavenly!" he replied.

"You are an enthusiastic admirer of the beauties of Nature, sir?" said the military gentleman, deferentially.

"I am, sir," replied Mr. Cymon Tuggs.

"Traveled much, sir?" inquired the military gentleman.

"Not much," replied Mr. Cymon Tuggs.

"You've been on the continent, of course?" inquired the military gentleman.

"Not exactly," replied Mr. Cymon Tuggs, in a qualified tone, as if he wished it to be implied that he had gone halfway and come back again.

"You of course intend your son to make the grand tour, sir?" said the military gentleman, addressing Mr. Joseph Tuggs.

As Mr. Joseph Tuggs did not pecisely understand what the grand tour was, or how such an article was manufactured, he replied, "Of course." Just as he said the word, there came tripping up from her seat at the stern of the vessel, a young lady in a puce-colored silk cloak and boots of the same, with long black ringlets, large black eyes, brief petticoats, and unexceptionable ankles.

"Walter, my dear," said the young lady to the military gentleman.

"Yes, Belinda, my love," responded the military gentleman to the black-eyed young lady.

"What have you left me alone so long for?" said the young lady. "I have been stared out of countenance by those rude young men."

"What! stared at?" exclaimed the military gentleman, with an emphasis which made Mr. Cymon Tuggs withdraw his eyes from the young lady's face with inconceivable rapidity.

"Which young men—where?" and the military gentleman clenched his fist, and glared fearfully on the cigar-smokers around.

"Be calm, Walter, I entreat," said the young lady.

"I won't," said the military gentleman.

"Do, sir," interposed Mr. Cymon Tuggs. "They ain't worth your notice."

"No—no—they are not, indeed," urged the young lady.

"I will be calm," said the military gentleman. "You speak truly, sir. I thank you for a timely remonstrance, which may have spared me the guilt of manslaughter." Calming his wrath, the military gentleman wrung Mr. Cymon Tuggs by the hand.

"My sister, sir," said Mr. Cymon Tuggs; seeing that the military gentleman was casting an admiring look toward Miss Charlotta.

"My wife, ma'am—Mrs. Captain Waters," said the military gentleman, presenting the black-eyed young lady.

"My mother ma'am—Mrs. Tuggs," said Mr. Cymon. The

military gentleman and his wife murmured enchanting courtesies; and the Tuggs's looked as unembarrassed as they could.

"Walter, my dear," said the black-eyed young lady, after they had sat chatting with the Tuggs's some half hour.

"Yes, my love," said the military gentleman.

"Don't you think this gentleman" (with an inclination of the head toward Mr. Cymon Tuggs) "is very much like the Marquis Carriwini?"

"God bless me, very!" said the military gentleman.

"It struck me the moment I saw him," said the young lady; gazing intently, and with a melancholy air, on the scarlet countenance of Mr. Cymon Tuggs. Mr. Cymon Tuggs looked at every body; and finding that every body was looking at him, appeared to feel some temporary difficulty in disposing of his eyesight.

"So exactly the air of the Marquis," said the military gentleman.

"Quite extraordinary!" sighed the military gentleman's lady.

"You don't know the Marquis, sir?" inquired the military gentleman.

Mr. Cymon Tuggs stammered a negative.

"If you did," continued Captain Walter Waters, "you would feel how much reason you have to be proud of the resemblance—a most elegant man, with a most prepossessing appearance."

"He is—he is indeed!" exclaimed Belinda Waters energetically; and as her eye caught that of Mr. Cymon Tuggs, she withdrew it from his features in bashful confusion.

All this was highly gratifying to the feelings of the Tuggs's; and when, in the course of further conversation, it was discovered that Miss Charlotta Tuggs was the *fac simile* of a titled relative of Mrs. Belinda Waters, and that Mrs. Tuggs herself was the very picture of the Dowager Duchess of Dobbleton, their delight in the acquisition of so genteel and friendly an acquaintance knew no bounds. Even the dignity of Captain Walter Waters relaxed to that degree that he suffered himself to be prevailed upon by Mr. Joseph Tuggs to partake of cold pigeon-pie and sherry on deck; and a most delightful conversation, aided by these agreeable stimulants, was prolonged until they ran alongside Ramsgate Pier.

"Good-by'e, dear!" said Mrs. Captain Waters to Miss Charlotta Tuggs, just before the bustle of landing commenced; "we shall see you on the sands in the morning; and as we are sure to have found lodgings before then, I hope we shall be inseparables for many weeks to come."

"Oh! I hope so," said Miss Charlotta Tuggs, emphatically.

"Tickets, ladies and gen'lm'n," said the man on the paddle-box.

"Want a porter, sir?" inquired a dozen men in smock-frocks.

"Now, my dear," said Captain Waters.

"Good-by'e!" said Mrs. Captain Waters—"good-by'e, Mr. Cymon!" and with a pressure of the hand that threw the amiable young man's nerves into a state of considerable derangement, Mrs. Captain Waters disappeared among the crowd. A pair of puce-colored boots were seen ascending the steps, a white handkerchief fluttered, a black eye gleamed. The Waters's were gone, and Mr. Cymon Tuggs was alone in a heartless world.

Silently and abstractedly did that too sensitive youth follow his revered parents and a train of smock-frocks and wheelbarrows, along the pier, until the bustle of the scene around recalled him to himself. The sun was shining brightly; the sea, dancing to its own music, rolled merrily in; crowds of people promenaded to and fro, young ladies tittered, old ladies talked, nursemaids displayed their charms to the greatest possible advantage, and their sweet little charges ran up and down, and to and fro, and in and out, under the feet, and between the legs of the assembled concourse, in the most playful and exhilarating manner possible. There were old gentlemen trying to make out objects through long telescopes, and young ones making objects of themselves in open shirt-collars; ladies carrying about portable chairs, and portable chairs carrying about invalids; parties waiting on the pier for parties who had come by the steamboat; and nothing was to be heard but talking, laughing, welcoming, and merriment.

"Fly, sir?" exclaimed a chorus of fourteen men and six boys, the moment that Mr. Joseph Tuggs, at the head of his little party, had set foot in the street.

"Here's the gen'lm'n at last!" said one, touching his hat

with mock politeness. "Werry glad to see you, sir,—been waitin' for you these six weeks. Jump in, if you please, sir."

"Nice light fly and a fast trotter, sir," said another: "fourteen mile an hour, and surroundin' objects rendered inwisible by hextreme welocity!"

"Large fly for your luggage, sir," cried a third. "Werry large fly here, sir—reg'lar bluebottle!"

"Here's your fly, sir!" shouted another aspiring charioteer, mounting the box, and inducing an old gray horse to indulge in some imperfect reminiscences of a canter. Look at him, sir!—temper of a lamb and haction of a steam-ingein."

Resisting even the temptation of securing the services of so valuable a quadruped as the last named, Mr. Joseph Tuggs beckoned to the proprietor of a dingy conveyance of a greenish hue, lined with faded striped calico; and the luggage and the family having been deposited therein, the animal in the shafts, after describing circles in the road for a quarter of an hour, at last consented to depart in quest of lodgings.

"How many beds have you got?" screamed Mrs. Tuggs out of the fly, to the woman who opened the door of the first house which displayed a bill intimating that apartments were to be let within.

"How many did you want, ma'am?" was of course the reply.

"Three."

"Will you step in, ma'am?" Down got Mrs. Tuggs. The family were delighted. Splendid view of the sea from the front windows—charming! A short pause. Back came Mrs. Tuggs again.—One parlor and a mattress.

"Why the devil didn't they say so at first?" inquired Mr. Joseph Tuggs, rather pettishly.

"Don't know," said Mrs. Tuggs.

"Wretches!" exclaimed the nervous Cymon. Another bill—another stoppage. Same question—same answer similar result.

"What do they mean by this?" inquired Mr. Joseph Tuggs, thoroughly out of temper.

"Don't know," said the placid Mrs. Tuggs.

"Orvis the vay here, sir," said the driver, by way of accounting for the circumstance in a satisfactory manner; and off they went again, to make fresh inquiries, and encounter fresh disappointments.

It had grown dusk when the "fly"—the rate of whose progress greatly belied its name—after climbing up four or five perpendicular hills, stopped before the door of a dusty house, with a bay window, from which you could obtain a beautiful glimpse of the sea—if you thrust half your body out of it, at the imminent peril of falling into the area. Mrs. Tuggs alighted. One ground-floor sitting-room, and three cells with beds in them up stairs—a double house—family on the opposite side—five children milk-and-watering in the parlor, one little boy, expelled for bad behavior, screaming on his back in the passage.

"What's the terms?" said Mrs. Tuggs. The mistress of the house was deliberating on the expediency of putting on an extra guinea; so she coughed slightly, and affected not to hear the question.

"What's the terms?" said Mrs. Tuggs, in a louder key.

"Five guineas a week, ma'am, *with* attendance," replied the lodging-house keeper. (Attendance means the privilege of ringing the bell as often as you like, for your own amusement.)

"Rather dear," said Mrs. Tuggs.

"Oh dear, no, ma'am," replied the mistress of the house, with a benign smile of pity at the ignorance of manners and customs, which the observation betrayed." "Very cheap."

Such an authority was indisputable. Mrs. Tuggs paid a week's rent in advance, and took the lodgings for a month. In an hour's time the family were seated at tea in their new abode.

"Capital srimps!" said Mr. Joseph Tuggs.

Mr. Cymon eyed his father with a rebellious scowl, as he emphatically said "*Shrimps.*"

"Well then, shrimps," said Mr. Joseph Tuggs. "Srimps or shrimps, don't much matter."

There was pity, blended with malignity, in Mr. Cymon's eye, as he replied, "Don't matter, father! What would Captain Waters say, if he heard such vulgarity?"

"Or what would dear Mrs. Captain Waters say," added Charlotta, "if she saw mother—ma, I mean—eating them whole heads and all?"

"It won't bear thinking of!" ejaculated Mr. Cymon, with a shudder. "How different," he thought, "from the Dowager Duchess of Dobbleton!"

"Very pretty woman, Mrs. Captain Waters, is she not, Cymon?" inquired Miss Charlotta.

A glow of nervous excitement passed over the countenance of Mr. Simon Tuggs, as he replied, "An angel of beauty!"

"Hallo!" said Mr. Joseph Tuggs. "Hallo, Cymon, my boy, take care—married lady, you know;" and he winked one of his twinkling eyes knowingly.

"Why," exclaimed Cymon, starting up with an ebullition of fury, as unexpected as alarming. "Why am I to be reminded of that blight of my happiness, and ruin of my hopes? Why am I to be taunted with the miseries that are heaped upon my head? Is it not enough to—to—to" and the orator paused; but whether for want of words, or lack of breath, was never distinctly ascertained.

There was an impressive solemnity in the tone of this address, and in the air with which the romantic Cymon at its conclusion rang the bell, and demanded a flat candlestick, which effectually forbade a reply. He stalked dramatically to bed, and the Tuggs's went to bed too, half an hour afterward, in a state of considerable mystification and perplexity.

If the pier had presented a scene of life and bustle to the Tuggs's on their first landing at Ramsgate, it was far surpassed by the appearance of the sands on the morning after their arrival. It was a fine, bright, clear day, with a light breeze from the sea. There were the same ladies and gentlemen, the same children, the same nursemaids, the same telescopes, the same portable chairs; the ladies were employed in needlework, or watchguard making, or knitting, or reading novels; the gentlemen were reading newspapers and magazines; the children were digging holes in the sand with wooden spades, and collecting water therein; the nursemaids, with their youngest charges in their arms, were running in after the waves, and then running back, with the waves after them; and now and and then a little sailing-boat either departed with a gay and talkative cargo of passengers, or returned with a very silent, and particularly uncomfortable-looking one.

"Well, I never!" exclaimed Mrs. Tuggs, as she and Mr. Joseph Tuggs, and Miss Charlotta Tuggs, and Mr. Cymon Tuggs, with their eight feet in a corresponding number of yellow shoes, seated themselves on four rush-bottomed chairs, which, being placed in a soft part of the sand, forthwith sunk down some two feet and a half—"Well, I never!"

Mr. Cymon, by an exertion of great personal strength, uprooted the chairs, and removed them further back.

"Why, I'm bless'd if there ain't some ladies a-going in!" exclaimed Mr. Joseph Tuggs, with intense astonishment.

"Lor, pa!" exclaimed Miss Charlotta.

"There *is*, my dear," said Mr. Joseph Tuggs. And, sure enough, four young ladies, each furnished with a towel, tripped up the steps of a bathing-machine; in went the horse, floundering about in the water: round turned the machine, down sat the driver, and presently out burst the young ladies aforesaid, with four distinct splashes.

"Well, that's sing'ler, too!" ejaculated Mr. Joseph Tuggs, after an awkward pause. Mr. Cymon coughed slightly.

"Why, here's some gentlemen a-going in on this side," exclaimed Mrs. Tuggs, in a tone of horror.

Three machines—three horses—three flounderings—three turnings round—three splashes—three gentlemen, disporting themselves in the water like so many dolphins.

"Well, *that's* sing'ler!" said Mr. Joseph Tuggs again. Miss Charlotta coughed this time, and another pause ensued. It was agreeably broken.

"How d'ye do, dear? We have been looking for you all the morning," said a voice to Miss Charlotta Tuggs. Mrs. Captain Waters was the owner of it.

"How d'ye do?" said Captain Walter Waters, all suavity; and a most cordial interchange of greetings ensued.

"Belinda, my love," said Captain Walter Waters, applying his glass to his eye, and looking in the direction of the sea.

"Yes, my dear," replied Mrs. Captain Waters.

"There's Harry Thompson."

"Where?" said Belinda, applying her glass to her eye.

"Bathing."

"Lor, so it is! He don't see us, does he?"

"No, I don't think he does," replied the captain.—"Bless my soul, how very singular!"

"What?" inquired Belinda.

"There's Mary Golding, too."

"Lor!—where?" (Up went the glass again.)

"There!" said the captain, pointing to one of the young ladies before noticed, who, in her bathing costume, looked as if she was enveloped in a patent Mackintosh, of scanty dimensions.

"So it is, I declare!" exclaimed Mrs. Captain Waters. "How very curious we should see them both!"

"Very," said the captain, with perfect coolness.

"It's the reg'lar thing here, you see," whispered Mr. Cymon Tuggs to his father.

"I see it is," whispered Mr. Joseph Tuggs in reply. "Queer though—ain't it?" Mr. Cymon Tuggs nodded assent.

"What do you think of doing with yourself this morning?" inquired the captain.—"Shall we lunch at Pegwell?"

"I should like that very much indeed," interposed Mrs. Tuggs. She had never heard of Pegwell before; but the word "lunch" had reached her ears, and it sounded very agreeably.

"How shall we go?" inquired the captain; "it's too warm to walk."

"A chay?" suggested Mr. Joseph Tuggs.

"Chaise," whispered Mr. Cymon.

"I should think one would be enough," said Mr. Joseph Tuggs aloud, quite unconscious of the meaning of the correction. "However, two chays if you like."

"I should like a donkey so much," said Belinda.

"Oh, so should I!" echoed Charlotta Tuggs.

"Well, we can have a fly," suggested the captain, "and you can have a couple of donkeys."

A fresh difficulty arose. Mrs. Captain Waters declared it would be decidedly improper for two ladies to ride alone. The remedy was obvious. Perhaps young Mr. Tuggs would be gallant enough to accompany them.

Mr. Cymon Tuggs blushed, smiled, looked vacant, and faintly protested he was no horseman. The objection was at once overruled. A fly was speedily found; and three donkeys—which the proprietor declared on his solemn asseveration to be "three parts blood, and the other corn"—were engaged in the service.

"Kim up!" shouted one of the two boys who followed behind to propel the donkeys, when Belinda Waters and Charlotta Tuggs had been hoisted and pushed and pulled into their respective saddles.

"Hi—hi—hi!" groaned the other boy behind Mr. Cymon Tuggs. Away went the donkey, with the stirrups jingling against the heels of Cymon's boots, and Cymon's boots nearly scraping the ground.

"Way—way! Wo—o—o—o—!" cried Mr. Cymon Tuggs as well as he could, in the midst of the jolting.

"Don't make it gallop!" screamed Mrs. Captain Waters, behind.

"My donkey *will* go into the public-house!" shrieked Miss Tuggs, in the rear.

"Hi—hi—hi!" groaned both the boys together; and on went the donkeys as if nothing would ever stop them.

Every thing has an end, however; and even the galloping of donkeys will cease in time. The animal which Mr. Cymon Tuggs bestrode, feeling sundry uncomfortable tuggs at the bit, the intent of which he could by no means divine, abruptly sidled against a brick wall, and expressed his uneasiness by grinding Mr. Cymon Tuggs's leg on the rough surface. Mrs. Captain Waters's donkey, apparently under the influence of some playfulness of spirit, rushed suddenly, head first, into a hedge, and declined to come out again; and the quadruped on which Miss Tuggs was mounted expressed his delight at this humorous proceeding by firmly planting his fore-feet against the ground, and kicking up his hind-legs in a very agile, but somewhat alarming manner.

This abrupt termination to the rapidity of the ride naturally occasioned some confusion. Both the ladies indulged in vehement screaming for several minutes; and Mr. Cymon Tuggs, besides sustaining intense bodily pain, had the additional mental anguish of witnessing their distressing situation, without the power to rescue them, by reason of his leg being firmly screwed in between the animal and the wall. The efforts of the boys, however, assisted by the ingenious expedient of twisting the tail of the most rebellious donkey, restored order in a much shorter time than could have reasonably been expected, and the little party jogged slowly on together.

"Now let 'em walk," said Mr. Cymon Tuggs. "It's cruel to over-drive 'em."

"Werry well, sir," replied the boy, with a grin at his companion, as if he understood Mr. Cymon to mean that the cruelty applied less to the animals than to their riders.

"What a lovely day, dear!" said Charlotta.

"Charming; enchanting, dear!" responded Mrs. Captain Waters. "What a beautiful prospect, Mr. Tuggs!"

Cymon looked full in Belinda's face, as he responded—"Beautiful indeed!" The lady cast down her eyes, and suffered the animal she was riding to fall a little back. Cymon Tuggs instinctively did the same.

There was a brief silence, broken only by a sigh from Mr. Cymon Tuggs.

"Mr. Cymon," said the lady suddenly, in a low tone, "Mr. Cymon—I am another's."

Mr. Cymon expressed his perfect concurrence in a statement which it was quite impossible to controvert.

"If I had not been," resumed Belinda; and there she stopped.

"What—what?" said Mr. Cymon earnestly. "Do not torture me. What would you say?"

"If I had not been"—continued Mrs. Captain Waters—"if in earlier life, it had been my fate to have known, and been beloved by a noble youth—a kindred soul—a congenial spirit—one capable of feeling and appreciating the sentiments which—"

"Heavens, what do I hear?" exclaimed Mr. Cymon Tuggs. "Is it possible! can I believe my—Come up!" (This last unsentimental parenthesis was addressed to the donkey, who with his head between his fore-legs, appeared to be examining the state of his shoes with great anxiety.)

"Hi—hi—hi," said the boys behind. "Come up," expostulated Cymon Tuggs again." "Hi—hi—hi," repeated the boys: and whether it was that the animal felt indignant at the tone of Mr. Tuggs's command, or alarmed by the noise of the deputy proprietor's boots running behind him, or whether he burned with a noble emulation to outstrip the other donkeys, certain it is that he no sooner heard the second series of "hi—hi's," than he started away with a celerity of pace which jerked Mr. Cymon's hat off instantaneously, and carried him to the Pegwell Bay hotel in no time, where he deposited his rider without giving him the trouble of dismounting, by sagaciously pitching him over his head, into the very door of the tavern.

Great was the confusion of Mr. Cymon Tuggs, when he was put right end uppermost by two waiters; considerable was the alarm of Mrs. Tuggs in behalf of her son; and agonizing were the apprehensions of Mrs. Captain Waters on his account. It was speedily discovered, however, that he had not sustained much more injury than the donkey—he was grazed, and the animal was grazing—and then it *was* a delightful party to be sure! Mr. and Mrs. Tuggs, and the captain, had ordered lunch in the little garden behind:—small saucers of large shrimps, dabs of butter, crusty loaves, and bottled ale. The sky was without a cloud; there were flower-pots and turf before them; the sea at the foot of the cliff, stretching away as far as the eye could discern any thing at all; and vessels in the distance with sails as white, and as small, as nicely-got-up cambric handkerchiefs. The shrimps were delightful, the ale better, and the captain even more pleasant than either. Mrs. Captain Waters was in *such* spirits after lunch—chasing, first the captain across the turf, and among the flower-pots, and then Mr. Cymon Tuggs, and then Miss Tuggs, and laughing too, quite boisterously. But as the captain said, it didn't matter; who knew what they were, there? For all the people of the house knew, they might be common people. To which Mr. Joseph Tuggs responded, "To be sure;" and then they went down the steep wooden steps a little further on, which lead to the bottom of the cliff, and looked at the crabs, and the seaweed, and the eels, till it was more than fully time to go back to Ramsgate again; and finally Mr. Cymon Tuggs ascended the steps last, and Mrs. Captain Waters last but one; and Mr. Cymon Tuggs discovered that the foot and ankle of Mrs. Captain Waters, were even more unexceptionable than he had at first supposed.

Taking a donkey toward his ordinary place of residence, is a very different thing, and a feat much more easily to be accomplished, than taking him from it. It requires a great deal of foresight and presence of mind in the one case, to anticipate the numerous flights of his discursive imagination; whereas in the other case all you have to do is to hold on, and to place a blind confidence in the animal. Mr. Cymon Tuggs adopted the latter expedient on his return; and his nerves were so little discomposed by the journey, that he distinctly understood they were all to meet again at the library in the evening.

The library was crowded. There were the same ladies and the same gentlemen who had been on the sands in the morning, and on the pier the day before. There were young ladies in maroon-colored gowns and black velvet bracelets, dispensing fancy articles in the shop, and presiding over games of chance in the concert room. There were marriageable daughters, and marriage-making mammas, gaming, and promenading, and turning over music, and flirting. There were some male beaux doing the sentimental in whispers, and others doing the ferocious in mustaches. There were Mrs. Tuggs in amber, Miss Tuggs in sky-blue, and Mrs. Captain Waters in pink. There was Captain Waters in a braided surtout; there was Mr. Cymon Tuggs in pumps and a gilt waistcoat; and, moreover, there was Mr. Joseph Tuggs in a blue coat and a shirt frill.

"Number three, eight, and eleven," cried one of the young ladies in the maroon-colored gowns.

"Number three, eight, and eleven," echoed another young lady in the same uniform.

"Number three's gone," said the first young lady. "Number eight and eleven."

"Number eight and eleven," echoed the second young lady.

"Number eight's gone, Mary Ann," said the first young lady.

"Number eleven," screamed the second.

"The numbers are all taken now, ladies, if you please," said the first. The representatives of numbers three, eight, and eleven, and the rest of the numbers crowded around the table.

"Will you throw, ma'am?" said the presiding goddess, handing the dice-box to the eldest daughter of a stout lady, with four girls.

There was a profound silence among the lookers-on.

"Throw Jane, my dear," said the stout lady. An interesting display of bashfulness—a little blushing in a cambric handkerchief—a whispering to a younger sister.

"Amelia, my dear, throw for your sister," said the stout lady; and then she turned to a walking advertisement of Rowland's Macassar Oil, who stood next her, and said, "Jane is so *very* modest and retiring; but I can't be angry with her for it. An artless and unsophisticated girl is *so* truly amiable, that I often wish Amelia was more like her sister."

The gentleman with the whiskers whispered his admiring approval; and the artless young lady glanced across, to observe the effect of her most unqualified simplicity.

"Now, my dear!" said the stout lady. Miss Amelia threw—eight for her sister, ten for herself.

"Nice figure, Amelia," whispered the stout lady to a thin youth beside her.

"Beautiful!"

"And *such* a spirit. I am like you in that respect. I can *not* help admiring that life and vivacity. Ah! (a sigh) I wish I could make poor Jane a little more like my dear Amelia!"

The young gentleman cordially acquiesced in the sentiment; and both he and the individual first addressed, were perfectly contented.

"Who's this?" inquired Mr. Cymon Tuggs of Mrs. Captain Waters, as a short female, in a blue velvet hat and feathers, was led into the orchestra, by a fat man in black tights, and cloudy Berlins.

"Mrs. Tippin, of the London theatres," replied Belinda, referring to the programme of the concert.

The talented Tippin having condescendingly acknowledged the clapping of hands, and shouts of "bravo!" which greeted her appearance, proceeded to sing the popular cavitina of "Bid me discourse," accompanied on the piano by Mr. Tippin; after which Mr. Tippin sang a comic song, accompanied on the piano by Mrs. Tippin, the applause consequent upon which was only to be exceeded by the enthusastic approbation bestowed upon an air with variations on the guitar, by Miss Tippin, accompanied on the chin by Master Tippin.

Thus passed the evening; and thus passed the days and evenings of the Tuggs's, and the Waters's, for six weeks afterward

Sands in the morning—donkeys at noon—pier in the afternoon—library at night; and the same people everywhere.

On that very night six weeks, the moon was shining brightly over the calm sea, which dashed against the feet of the tall gaunt cliffs with just enough noise to lull the old fish to sleep, without disturbing the young ones, when two figures were discernible—or would have been, if any body had looked for them—seated on one of the wooden benches which are stationed near the verge of the western cliff. The moon had climbed higher into the heavens, by two hours' journeying, since those figures first sat down, and yet they had moved not. The crowd of loungers had thinned and dispersed, the noise of itinerant musicians had died away; light after light had appeared in the windows of the different houses in the distance, blockade-man after blockade-man had passed the spot, wending his way toward his solitary post, and yet those figures had remained stationary. Some portions of the two forms were in deep shadow, but the light of the moon fell strongly on a puce-colored boot and a glazed stock. Mr. Cymon Tuggs, and Mrs. Captain Waters were seated on that bench. They spoke not, but were silently gazing on the sea.

"Walter will return to-morrow," said Mrs. Captain Waters, mournfully breaking silence.

Mr. Cymon Tuggs sighed like a gust of wind through a forest of gooseberry-bushes, as he replied—"Alas! he will."

"Oh, Cymon! resumed Belinda, "the chaste delight, the calm happiness of this one week of Platonic love, is too much for me."

Cymon was about to suggest that it was too little for him, but he stopped himself, and murmured unintelligibly.

"And to think that even this glimpse of happiness, innocent as it is," exclaimed Belinda, "is now to be lost forever!"

"Oh, do not say forever, Belinda," exclaimed the excitable Cymon, as two strongly-defined tears chased each other down his pale face—it was so long that there was plenty of room for a chase—"Do not say for ever!"

"I must," replied Belinda.

"Why?" urged Cymon, "oh why? Such Platonic acquaintance as ours is so harmless, that even your husband can never object to it."

"My husband!" exclaimed Belinda. "You little know him. Jealous and revengeful; ferocious in his revenge—a maniac in his jealousy! Would you be assassinated before my eyes?" Mr. Cymon Tuggs, in a voice broken by emotion, expressed his disinclination to undergo the process of assassination before the eyes of any body.

"Then leave me," said Mrs. Captain Waters. "Leave me, this night, for ever. It is late; let us return."

Mr. Cymon Tuggs sadly offered the lady his arm, and escorted her to her lodgings. He paused at the door—he felt a Platonic pressure of his hand. "Good-night," he said, hesitating.

"Good night," sobbed the lady. Mr. Cymon Tuggs paused again.

"Won't you walk in, sir?" said the servant. Mr. Tuggs hesitated. Oh, that hesitation! He *did* walk in.

"Good-night," said Mr. Cymon Tuggs again, when he reached the drawing-room.

"Good-night!" replied Belinda; "and if at any period in my life, I—hush!" The lady paused, and stared with a steady gaze of horror on the ashy countenance of Mr. Cymon Tuggs. There was a double knock at the street-door.

"It is my husband!" said Belinda, as the captain's voice was heard below.

"And my family!" added Cymon Tuggs, as the voices of his relatives floated up the staircase.

"The curtain! the curtain!" gasped Mrs. Captain Waters, pointing to the window, before which some chintz hangings were closely drawn.

"But I have done nothing wrong," said the hesitating Cymon.

"The curtain!" reiterated the frantic lady; "you will be murdered." This last appeal to his feeling was irresistible. The dismayed Cymon concealed himself behind the curtain, with pantomimic suddenness.

Enter the Captain, Joseph Tuggs, Mrs. Tuggs, and Charlotta.

"My dear," said the captain, "Lieutenant Slaughter." Two iron-shod boots and one gruff voice were heard by Mr. Cymon to advance, and acknowledge the honor of the introduction. The sabre of the lieutenant rattled heavily upon the floor, as he seated himself at the table. Mr. Cymon's fears almost overcame his reason.

"The brandy, my dear," said the captain. Here was a situation! They were going to make a night of it: and Mr. Cymon Tuggs was pent up behind the curtain, and afraid to breathe.

"Slaughter," said the captain, "a cigar?"

Now, Mr. Cymon Tuggs never could smoke without feeling it indispensably necessary to retire immediately, and never could smell smoke without a strong disposition to cough. The cigars were introduced; the captain was a professed smoker, so was the lieutenant, so was Joseph Tuggs. The apartment was small, the door was closed, the smoke powerful: it hung in heavy wreaths over the room, and at length found its way behind the curtain. Cymon Tuggs held his nose, then his mouth, then his breath. It was all of no use—out came the cough.

"Bless my soul!" said the captain, "I beg your pardon, Miss Tuggs. You dislike smoking?"

"Oh no; I don't indeed," said Charlotta.

"It makes you cough."

"Oh dear no."

"You coughed just now."

"Me, Captain Waters! Lor! how can you say so?"

"Somebody coughed," said the captain.

"I certainly thought so," said Slaughter. "No; everybody denied it."

"Fancy," said the captain.

"Must be," echoed Slaughter.

"Cigars resumed—more smoke, another cough—smothered, but violent.

"Damned odd!" said the captain, staring about him.

"Sing'ler!" ejaculated the unconscious Mr. Joseph Tuggs.

Lieutenant Slaughter looked first at one person mysteriously, then at another; then laid down his cigar; then approached the window on tiptoe, and pointed with his right thumb over his shoulder, in the direction of the curtain.

The Tuggs at Ramsgate.

"Slaughter!" ejaculated the captain, rising from table, "what do you mean?"

The lieutenant, in reply, drew back the curtain, and discovered Mr. Cymon Tuggs behind it, pallid with apprehension, and blue with wanting to cough.

"Ah!" exclaimed the captain, furiously, "What do I see? Slaughter, your sabre!"

"Cymon!" screamed the Tuggs's.

"Mercy," said Belinda.

"Platonic," gasped Cymon.

"Your sabre!" roared the captain: "Slaughter—unhand me—the villain's life!"

"Murder!" screamed the Tuggs's.

"Hold him fast, sir!" faintly articulated Cymon.

"Water!" exclaimed Joseph Tuggs—and Mr. Cymon Tuggs and all the ladies forthwith fainted away, and formed a tableau.

Most willingly would we conceal the disastrous termination of the six weeks' acquaintance. A troublesome form, and an arbitrary custom, however, prescribe that a story should have a conclusion in addition to a commencement; and we have therefore no alternative. Lieutenant Slaughter brought a message—the captain brought an action, Mr. Joseph Tuggs interposed—the lieutenant negotiated. When Mr. Cymon Tuggs recovered from the nervous disorder into which misplaced affection and exciting circumstances had plunged him, he found that his family had lost their pleasant acquaintance; that his father was minus fifteen hundred pounds; and the captain plus the precise sum. The money was paid to hush the matter up, but it got abroad notwithstanding; and there are not wanting those who affirm that three designing impostors never found more easy dupes than did Captain Waters, Mrs. Waters, and Lieutenant Slaughter, in the Tuggs's at Ramsgate.

CHAPTER V.

HORATIO SPARKINS.

"INDEED, my love, he paid Teresa very great attention on the last assembly night," said Mrs. Malderton, addressing her spouse, who, after the fatigues of the day in the City, was sitting with a silk handkerchief over his head, and his feet on the fender, drinking his port;—"very great attention, and I say again, every possible encouragement ought to be given him. He positively must be asked down here to dine."

"Who must?" inquired Mr. Malderton.

"Why, you know whom I mean, my dear—the young man with the black whiskers and the white cravat who has just come out at our assembly, and whom all the girls are talking about. Young —— dear me! what's his name?—Marianne, what *is* his name?" continued Mrs. Malderton, addressing her youngest daughter, who was engaged in netting a purse, and endeavoring to look sentimental.

"Mr. Horatio Sparkins, ma," replied Miss Marianne, with a Juliet-like sigh.

"Oh! yes to be sure—Horatio Sparkins," said Mrs. Malderton. "Decidedly the most gentleman-like young man I ever saw. I am sure, in the beautifully-made coat he wore the other night, he looked like—like ——"

"Like Prince Leopold, ma,—so noble, so full of sentiment!" suggested Miss Marianne, in a tone of enthusiastic admiration.

"You should recollect, my dear," resumed Mrs. Malderton, "that Teresa is now eight-and-twenty; and that it really is very important that something should be done."

Miss Teresa Malderton was a very little girl, rather fat, with vermillion cheeks, but good-humored, and still disengaged, although to do her justice, the misfortune arose from no lack of perseverance on her part. In vain had she flirted for ten years; in vain had Mr. and Mrs. Malderton assiduously kept up an extensive acquaintance among the young eligible bachelors of Camberwell, and even of Wandsworth and Brixton; to say nothing of those who "dropped in" from town. Miss Malderton was as well known as the lion on the top of Northumberland House, and had an equal chance of "going off."

"I am quite sure you'd like him," continued Mrs. Malderton; "he is so gentlemanly!"

"So clever!" said Miss Marianne.

"And has such a flow of language!" added Miss Teresa.

"He has a great respect for you, my dear," said Mrs. Malderton to her husband, in a confident tone. Mr. Malderton coughed, and looked at the fire.

"Yes, I'm sure he's very much attached to pa's society," said Miss Marianne.

"No doubt of it," echoed Miss Teresa.

"Indeed, he said as much to me in confidence," observed Mrs. Malderton.

"Well, well," returned Mr. Malderton, somewhat flattered; "if I see him at the assembly to-morrow, perhaps I'll ask him down here. I hope he knows we live at Oak Lodge, Camberwell, my dear?"

"Of course—and that you keep a one-horse carriage."

"I'll see about it," said Mr. Malderton, composing himself for a nap; "I'll see about it."

Mr. Malderton was a man whose whole scope of ideas was limited to Lloyd's, the Exchange, the India House, and the Bank. A few successful speculations had raised him from a situation of obscurity and comparative poverty, to a state of affluence. As it frequently happens in such cases, the ideas of himself and his family became elevated to an extraordinary pitch as their means increased; they affected fashion, taste, and many other fooleries, in imitation of their betters, and had a very decided and becoming horror of any thing which could by possibility be considered *low.* He was hospitable from ostentation, illiberal from ignorance, and prejudiced from conceit. Egotism and the love of display induced him to keep an excellent table: convenience, and a love of the good things of this life, ensured him plenty of guests. He liked to have clever men, or what he considered such, at his table, because it was a great thing to talk about; but he never could endure what he called "sharp fellows." Probably he cherished this feeling out of compliment to his two sons, who gave their respected parent no uneasiness in that particular. The family were ambitious of forming acquaintances and connections in some sphere of society superior to that in which they themselves moved; and one of the necessary consequences of this desire, added to their utter ignorance of the world beyond their own small circle, was, that any one who could plausibly lay claim to an acquaintance with people of rank and title, had a sure passport to the table at Oak Lodge, Camberwell.

The appearance of Mr. Horatio Sparkins at the assembly had excited no small degree of surprise and curiosity among its regular frequenters. Who could he be? He was evidently reserved, and apparently melancholy. Was he a clergyman?—He danced too well. A barrister?—he was not called. He used very fine words, and said a great deal. Could he be a distinguished foreigner come to England for the purpose of describing the country, its manners and customs; and frequenting public balls and public dinners, with the view of becoming acquainted with high life, polished etiquette, and English refinement?—No, he had not a foreign accent. Was he a surgeon, a contributor to the magazines, a writer of fashionable novels, or an artist?—No; to each and all of these surmises there existed some valid objection.—"Then," said every body, "he must be *somebody*."—"I should think he must be," reasoned Mr. Malderton, with himself, "because he perceives our superiority, and pays us so much attention."

The night succeeding the conversation we have just recorded was "Assembly night." The double-fly was ordered to be at the door of Oak Lodge at nine o'cclock precisely. The Miss Maldertons were dressed in sky-blue satin trimmed with artificial flowers; and Mrs. M. (who was a little fat woman), in ditto ditto, looked like her eldest daughter multiplied by two. Mr. Frederick Malderton, the eldest son, in full-dress costume, was the very *beau idèal* of a smart waiter; and Mr. Thomas Malderton, the youngest, with his white dress-stock, blue coat, bright buttons, and red watch-ribbon, strongly resembled the portrait of that interesting, though somewhat rash young gentleman, George

Barnwell. Every member of the party had made up his or her mind to cultivate the acquaintance of Mr. Horatio Sparkins. Miss Teresa, of course, was to be as amiable and interesting as ladies of eight-and-twenty on the look-out for a husband usually are; Mrs. Malderton would be all smiles and graces; Miss Marianne would request the favor of some verses for her album; Mr. Malderton would patronize the great unknown by asking him to dinner; and Tom intended to ascertain the extent of his information on the interesting topic of snuff and cigars. Even Mr. Frederick Malderton himself, the family authority on all points of taste, dress, and fashionable arrangement—who had lodgings of his own in town, who had a free admission to Covent-garden theatre, who always dressed according to the fashions of the months, who went up the water twice a week in the season, and who actually had an intimate friend who once knew a gentleman who formerly lived in the Albany,—even he had determined that Mr. Horatio Sparkins must be a devilish good fellow, and that he would do him the honor of challenging him to a game at billiards.

The first object that met the anxious eyes of the expectant family on their entrance into the ball-room, was the interesting Horatio, with his hair brushed off his forehead, and his eyes fixed on the ceiling, reclining in a contemplative attitude on one of the seats.

"There he is, my dear," anxiously whispered Mrs. Malderton to Mr. Malderton.

"How like Lord Byron!" murmured Miss Teresa.

"Or Montgomery!" whispered Miss Marianne.

"Or the portraits of Captain Ross!" suggested Tom.

"Tom—don't be an ass!" said his father, who checked him upon all occasions, probably with a view to prevent his becoming "sharp"—which was very unnecessary.

The elegant Sparkins attitudinized with admirable effect until the family had crossed the room. He then started up with the most natural appearance of surprise and delight; accosted Mrs. Malderton with the utmost cordiality, saluted the young ladies in the most enchanting manner; bowed to, and shook hands with Mr. Malderton, with a degree of respect amounting almost to veneration, and returned the greetings of the two young men in a half-gratified, half-patronizing manner, which fully convinced them that he must be an important, and, at the same time, condescending personage.

"Miss Malderton," said Horatio, after the ordinary salutations, and bowing very low, "may I be permitted to presume to hope that you will allow me to have the pleasure——"

"I don't think I am engaged," said Miss Teresa, with a dreadful affectation of indifference—"but, really—so many——"

Horatio looked as handsomely miserable as a Hamlet sliding upon a bit of orange-peel.

"I shall be most happy," simpered the interesting Teresa, at last; and Horatio's countenance brightened up like an old hat in a shower of rain.

"A very genteel young man, certainly!" said the gratified Mr. Malderton, as the obsequious Sparkins and his partner joined the quadrille which was just forming.

"He has a remarkably good address," said Mr. Frederick.

"Yes, he is a prime fellow," interposed Tom, who always managed to put his foot in it—"he talks just like an auctioneer."

"Tom!" said his father solemnly, "I think I desired you before not to be a fool."—Tom looked as happy as a cock on a drizzly morning.

"How delightful!" said the interesting Horatio to his partner, as they promenaded the room at the conclusion of the set—"how delightful, how refreshing it is, to retire from the cloudy storms, the vicissitudes, and the troubles of life, even if it be but for a few short, fleeting moments; and to spend those moments, fading and evanescent though they be, in the delightful, the blessed society of one individual—of her whose frowns would be death, whose coldness would be madness, whose falsehood would be ruin, whose constancy would be bliss; the possession of whose affection would be the brightest and best reward that Heaven could bestow on man."

"What feeling! what sentiment!" thought Miss Teresa, as she leaned more heavily upon her companion's arm.

"But enough—enough!" resumed the elegant Sparkins, with a theatrical air. "What have I said? what have I—I—to do with sentiments like these? Miss Mallerton—" here he stopped short—"may I hope to be permitted to offer the humble tribute of—"

"Really, Mr. Sparkins," returned the enraptured Teresa, blushing in the sweetest confusion, "I must refer you to papa. I never can, without his consent, venture to—to—"

"Surely he cannot object—"

"Oh, yes. Indeed, indeed, you know him not," interrupted Miss Teresa, well knowing there was nothing to fear, but wishing to make the interview resemble a scene in some romantic novel.

"He cannot object to my offering you a glass of negus," returned the adorable Sparkins, with some surprise.

"Is that all?' said the disappointed Teresa to herself. "What a fuss about nothing!"

"It will give me the greatest pleasure, sir, to see you to dinner at Oak Lodge, Camberwell, on Sunday next at five o'clock, if you have no better engagement," said Mr. Malderton, at the conclusion of the evening, as he and his sons were standing in conversation with Mr. Horatio Sparkins.

Horatio bowed his acknowledgments, and accepted the flattering invitation.

"I must confess," continued the maneuvering father, offering his snuff-box to his new acquaintance, "that I don't enjoy these assemblies half so much as the comfort—I had almost said the luxury—of Oak Lodge: they have no great charms for an elderly man."

"And after all, sir, what is man!" said the metaphysical Sparkins—"I say, what is man?"

"Ah! very true," said Mr. Malderton—"very true."

"We know that we live and breathe," continued Horatio; "that we have wants and wishes, desires and appetites—"

"Certainly," said Mr. Frederick Malderton, looking very profound.

"I say, we know that we exist," repeated Horatio, raising his voice, "but there we stop; there is an end to our knowledge; there is the summit of our attainments; there is the termination of our ends. What more do we know?"

"Nothing," replied Mr. Frederick—than whom no one was more capable of answering for himself in that particular.

Tom was about to hazard something, but, fortunately for his reputation, he caught his father's angry eye, and slunk off like a puppy convicted of petty larceny.

"Upon my word," said Mr. Malderton the elder, as they were returning home in the 'Fly,' "that Mr. Sparkins is a wonderful young man. Such surprising knowledge! such extraordinary information! and such a splendid mode of expressing himself!"

"I think he must be somebody in disguise," said Miss Marianne. "How charmingly romantic!"

"He talks very loud and nicely," timidly observed Tom, "but I don't exactly understand what he means."

"I almost begin to despair of *your* understanding any thing, sir," said his father, who, of course, had been much enlightened by Mr. Horatio Sparkins' conversation.

"It strikes me, Tom," said Miss Teresa, "that you have have made yourself very ridiculous this evening."

"No doubt of it," cried every body—and the unfortunate Tom reduced himself into the least possible space. That night Mr. and Mrs. Malderton had a long conversation respecting their daughter's prospects and future arrangements. Miss Teresa went to bed, considering whether, in the event of her marrying a title, she could conscientiously encourage the visits of her present associates; and dreampt all night of disguised noblemen, large routs, ostrich plumes, bridal favors, and Horatio Sparkins.

Various surmises were hazarded, on the Sunday morning, as to the mode of conveyance which the anxiously-expected Horatio would adopt. Did he keep a gig?—was it possible he could come on horseback?—or would he patronize the stage? These, and various other conjectures of equal importance, engrossed the attention of Mrs. Malderton and her daughters during the whole morning.

"Upon my word, my dear, it's a most annoying thing that that vulgar brother of yours should have invited himself to dine here to-day," said Mr. Malderton to his wife. "On account of Mr. Sparkins's coming down, I purposely abstained from asking any one but Flamwell. And then to think of your brother—a tradesman—it's insufferable. I declare I wouldn't have him mention his shop before our new guests—no, not for a thousand pounds! I wouldn't care, if he had the good sense to conceal the disgrace he is to the family; but he's so cursedly fond of his horrid business that he *will* let people know what he is."

Mr. Jacob Barton, the individual alluded to, was a large grocer; so vulgar, and so lost to all sense of feeling, that he actually never scrupled to avow that he wasn't above his business; "he'd made his money by it, and he didn't care who know'd it."

"Ah, Flamwell, my dear fellow, how d'ye do?" said Mr. Malderton, as a little spoffish man, with green spectacles, entered the room. "You got my note?"

"Yes, I did; and here I am in consequence."

"You don't happen to know this Mr. Sparkins by name?—You know every body."

Mr. Flamwell was one of those gentlemen of remarkably extensive information whom one occasionally meets in society, who pretend to know every body, but in reality know nobody. At Malderton's, where any stories about great people were received with a greedy ear, he was an especial favorite; and knowing the kind of people he had to deal with, he carried his passion of claiming acquaintance with every body to the most immoderate length. He had rather a singular way of telling his greatest lies in a parenthesis, and with an air of self-denial, as if he feared being thought egotistical.

"Why, no, I don't know him by that name," returned Flamwell, in a low tone, and with an air of immense importance.—"I have no doubt I know him, though. Is he tall?"

"Middle-sized," said Miss Teresa.

"With black hair?" inquired Flamwell, hazarding a bold guess.

"Yes," returned Miss Teresa, eagerly.

"Rather a snub nose?"

"No," said the disappointed Teresa, "he has a Roman nose."

"I said a Roman nose, didn't I?" inquired Flamwell. "He's an elegant young man?"

"Oh, certainly."

"With remarkably prepossessing manners?"

"Oh, yes!" said all the family together. "You must know him."

"Yes, I thought you knew him, if he was any body," triumphantly exclaimed Mr. Malderton. "Who d'ye think he is?"

"Why, from your description," said Flamwell, ruminating, and sinking his voice almost to a whisper, "he bears a strong resemblance to the Honorable Augustus Fitz-Edward Fitz-John Fitz-Osborne. He's a very talented young man, and rather eccentric. It's extremely probable he may have changed his name for some temporary purpose."

Teresa's heart beat high. Could he be the Honorable Augustus Fitz-Edward Fitz-John Fitz-Osborne! What a name to be elegantly engraved upon two glazed cards, tied together with a piece of white satin ribbon! "The Honorable Mrs. Augustus Fitz-Edward Fitz-John Fitz-Osborne." The thought was transport.

"It's five minutes to five," said Mr. Malderton, looking at his watch: "I hope he's not going to disappoint us."

"There he is!" exclaimed Miss Teresa, as a loud double-knock was heard at the door. Every body endeavored to look—as people when they particularly expect a visitor always do—as if they were perfectly unsuspicious of the approach of any body.

The room-door opened—"Mr. Barton!" said the servant.

"Confound the man!" murmured Malderton. "Ah! my dear sir, how d'ye do! Any news?"

"Why, no," returned the grocer, in his usual honest, bluff manner, "No, none partickler. None that I am much aware of.—How d'ye do, gals and boys?—Mr. Flamwell, sir—glad to see you."

"Here's Mr. Sparkins," said Tom, who had been looking out at the window, "on *such* a black horse!"—There was Horatio, sure enough, on a large black horse!" curvetting and prancing along like an Astley's supernumerary. After a great deal of reining in and pulling up, with the usual accompaniments of snorting, rearing, and kicking, the animal consented to stop at about a hundred yards from the gate, where Mr. Sparkins dismounted, and confided him to the care of Mr. Malderton's groom. The ceremony of introduction was gone through in all due form. Mr. Flamwell looked from behind his green spectacles at Horatio with an air of mysterious importance; and the gallant Horatio looked unutterable things at Teresa, who tried in her turn to appear uncommonly lackadaisical.

"Is he the Honorable Mr. Augustus—what's his name?" whispered Mrs. Malderton to Flamwell, as he was escorting her to the dining-room.

"Why, no—at least not exactly," returned that great authority—"not exactly."

"Who *is* he then?"

"Hush!" said Flamwell, nodding his head with a grave air, importing that he knew very well; but was prevented by some grave reasons of state from disclosing the important secret. It might be one of the ministers making himself acquainted with the views of the people.

"Mr. Sparkins," said the delighted Mrs. Malderton, "pray divide the ladies. John, put a chair for the gentleman between Miss Teresa and Miss Marianne." This was addressed to a man who on ordinary occasions acted as half-groom, half-gardener; but who, as it was most important to make an impression on Mr. Sparkins, had been forced into a white neckerchief and shoes, and touched up and brushed to look like a second footman.

The dinner was excellent; Horatio was most attentive to Miss Teresa, and every one felt in high spirits, except Mr. Malderton, who knowing the propensity of his brother-in-law, Mr. Barton, endured that sort of agony which the newspapers inform us is experienced by the surrounding neighborhood when a pot-boy hangs himself in a hay-loft, and which is "much easier to be imagined than described."

"Have you seen your friend, Sir Thomas Noland, lately, Flamwell?" inquired Mr. Malderton, casting a side-long look at Horatio, to see what effect the mention of so great a man had upon him.

"Why, no—not very lately: I saw Lord Gubbleton the day before yesterday."

"Ah! I hope his lordship is very well," said Malderton in a tone of the greatest interest. It is scarcely necessary to say that until that moment he had been quite innocent of the existence of such a person.

"Why, yes; he was very well—very well indeed. He's a devilish good fellow; I met him in the city, and had a long chat with him. Indeed, I'm rather intimate with him. I couldn't stop to talk to him as long as I could wish though, because I was on my way to a banker's, a very rich man, and a Member of Parliament, with whom I am also rather, indeed I may say very, intimate.

"I know whom you mean," returned the host, consequentially, in reality knowing as much about the matter as Flamwell himself.

"He has a capital business."

This was touching on a dangerous topic.

"Talking of business," interposed Mr. Barton, from the centre of the table. "A gentleman that you knew very well, Malderton, before you made that first lucky spec of yours, called at our shop the other day, and——"

"Barton, may I trouble you for a potato," interrupted the wretched master of the house, hoping to nip the story in the bud.

"Certainly," returned the grocer, quite insensible of his brother-in-law's object—"and he said in a very plain manner——"

"*Floury*, if you please," interrupted Malderton again; dreading the termination of the anecdote, and fearing a repetition of the word "shop."

"He said, says he," continued the culprit, after dispatching the potato—"says he, how goes on your business? So I said, jokingly—you know my way—says I, I'm never above my business, and I hope my business will never be above me. Ha, ha!"

"Mr. Sparkins," said the host, vainly endeavoring to conceal his dismay, "a glass of wine?"

"With the utmost pleasure, sir."

"Happy to see you."

"Thank you."

"We were talking the other evening," resumed the host, addressing Horatio, partly with the view of displaying the con versational powers of his new acquaintance, and partly in the hope of drowning the grocer's stories—we were talking the other day about the nature of man. Your argument struck me very forcibly "

"And me," said Mr. Frederick. Horatio made a graceful inclination of the head.

"Pray, what is your opinion of woman, Mr. Sparkins?" inquired Mrs. Malderton. The young ladies simpered.

"Man," replied Horatio, "man, whether he ranged the bright, gay, flowery plains of a second Eden, or the more sterile, barren, and, I may say, commonplace regions, to which we are compelled to accustom ourselves in times such as these; man, I say, under any circumstances, or in any place—whether he were bending beneath the withering blasts of the frigid zone, or scorching under the rays of a vertical sun—man, without woman, would be—alone."

"I'm very happy to find you entertain such honorable opinions, Mr. Sparkins," said Mrs. Malderton.

"And I," added Miss Teresa. Horatio looked his delight, and the young lady blushed like a full-blown peony.

"Now it's my opinion," said Mr. Barton——

"I know what you're going to say," interposed Malderton, determined not to give his relation another opportunity, "and I don't agree with you."

"What?" inquired the astonished grocer.

"I am sorry to differ from you, Barton," said the host, in as positive a manner as if her were really contradicting a position which the other had laid down, "but I cannot give my assent to what I consider a very monstrous proposition."

"But I meant to say—"

"You never can convince me," said Malderton, with an air of obstinate determination. "Never."

"And I," said Mr. Frederick, following up his father's attack, "cannot entirely agree in Mr. Sparkins' argument."

"What!" said Horatio, who became more metaphysical, and more argumentative, as he saw the female part of the family listening in wondering delight—"what! is effect the consequence of cause? Is cause the precursor of effect?"

"That's the point" said Flamwell.

"To be sure," said Mr. Malderton.

"Because, if effect is the consequence of cause, and if cause does precede effect, I apprehend you are decidedly wrong," added Horatio.

"Decidedly," said the toad-eating Flamwell.

"At least I apprehend that to be the just and logical deduction," said Sparkins, in a tone of interrogation.

"No doubt of it," chimed in Flamwell again. "It settles the point."

"Well, perhaps it does," said Mr. Frederick; "I didn't see it before."

"I don't exactly see it now," thought the grocer; "but I suppose it's all right."

"How wonderfully clever he is!" whispered Mrs. Malderton to her daughters, as they retired to the drawing-room.

"Oh, he's quite a love!" said both the young ladies together; "He talks like an oracle. He must have seen a great deal of life."

The gentlemen being left to themselves, a pause ensued, during which every body looked very grave, as if they were quite overcome by the profound nature of the previous discussion. Flamwell, who had made up his mind to find out who and what Mr. Horatio Sparkins really was, first broke silence.

"Excuse me, sir," said that distinguished personage—"I presume you have studied for the bar? I thought of entering once myself—indeed I'm rather intimate with some of the highest ornaments of that distinguished profession."

"No—no!" said Horatio, with a little hesitation; "not exactly."

"But you have been much among the silk gowns, or I mistake?" inquired Flamwell, deferentially.

"Nearly all my life," returned Sparkins.

The question was thus pretty well settled in the mind of Mr. Flamwell.—He was a young gentleman "about to be called."

"I shouldn't like to be a barrister," said Tom, speaking for the first time, and looking round the table to find somebody who would notice the remark.

No one made any reply.

I shouldn't like to wear a wig," added Tom, hazarding another observation.

"Tom, I beg you'll not make yourself ridiculous," said his father. "Pray listen, and improve yourself by the conversation you hear, and don't be constantly making these absurd remarks."

"Very well, father," replied the unfortunate Tom, who had not spoken a word since he had asked for another slice of beef at a quarter past five o'clock, P. M., and it was then eight.

"Well, Tom," observed his good-natured uncle, "never mind; I think with you. *I* shouldn't like to wear a wig. I'd rather wear an apron."

Mr. Malderton coughed violently. Mr. Barton resumed—"For if a man's above his business——"

The cough returned with tenfold violence, and did not cease until the unfortunate cause of it, in his alarm, had quite forgotten what he intended to say.

"Mr. Sparkins," said Flamwell, returning to the charge, "do you happen to know Mr. Delafontaine, of Bedford-square?"

"I have exchanged cards with him; since which, indeed, I have had an opportunity of serving him considerably," replied Horatio, slightly coloring, no doubt, at having been betrayed into making the acknowledgment.

"You are very lucky, if you have had an opportunity of obliging that great man," observed Flamwell with an air of great respect.

"I don't know who he is," he whispered to Mr. Malderton confidentially, as they followed Horatio up to the drawing-room. "It's quite clear, however that he belongs to the law, and that he is somebody of great importance, and very highly connected."

"No doubt, no doubt," returned his companion.

The remainder of the evening passed away most delightfully. Mr. Malderton, relieved from his apprehensions by the circumstance of Mr. Barton's falling into a profound sleep, was as affable and gracious as possible. Miss Teresa played the "Fall of Paris," as Mr. Sparkins declared in a most masterly manner, and both of them, assisted by Mr. Frederick, tried over glees and trios without number; they having made the pleasing discovery that their voices harmonized beautifully. To be sure, they all sang the first part; and Horatio, in addition to the slight drawback of having no ear, was perfectly innocent of knowing a note of music; still they passed the time away very agreeably, and it was past twelve o'clock before Mr. Sparkins ordered the mourning-coach-looking steed to be brought out—an order which was only complied with, upon the distinct understanding that he was to repeat his visit on the following Sunday.

"But, perhaps, Mr. Sparkins will form one of our party to-morrow evening?" suggested Mrs. M. "Mr. Malderton intends taking the girls to see the pantomime."—Mr. Sparkins bowed, and promised to join the party in box 48, in the course of the evening.

"We will not tax you for the morning," said Miss Teresa, bewitchingly; "for ma is going to take us to all sorts of places, shopping. But I know that the gentleman have a great horror of that employment." Mr. Sparkins bowed again, and declared that he should be delighted, but business of importance occupied him in the morning. Flamwell looked at Malderton significantly.—"It's term time!" he whispered.

At twelve o'clock on the following morning, the "fly" was at the door of Oak Lodge, to convey Mrs. Malderton and her daughters on their expedition for the day. They were to dine and dress for the play at a friend's house; first driving thither with their bandboxes, they departed on their first errand to make some purchases at Messrs. Jones, Spruggins, and Smith's, of Tottenham-court-road; after which they were to go to Redmayne's, in Bond-street; and thence to innumerable places that no one ever heard of. The young ladies beguiled the tediousness of the ride by eulogizing Mr. Horatio Sparkins, scolding their mamma for taking them so far to save a shilling, and wondering whether they should ever reach their destination. At length the vehicle stopped before a dirty-looking ticketed linen-draper's shop, with goods of all kinds, and labels of all sorts and sizes in the window. There were dropsical figures of a seven with a little three-farthings in the corner, something like the aquatic animalculæ disclosed by the gas microscope, "perfectly invisible to the naked eye;" three hundred and fifty thousand ladies' boas, *from* one shilling and a penny halfpenny; real French kid shoes, at two and ninepence per pair; green parasols, with handles like carving-forks, at an equally cheap rate; and "every description of goods," as the proprietors said —and they must know best—"fifty per cent. under cost price."

"La! ma, what a place you have brought us to!" said Miss Teresa; "what would Mr. Sparkins say if he could see us!"

"Ah! what, indeed!" said Miss Marianne, horrified at the idea

"Pray be seated, ladies. What is the first article?" inquired the obsequious master of the ceremonies of the establishment, who, in his large white neckcloth and formal tie, looked like a bad "portrait of a gentleman" in the Somerset-house Exhibition.

"I want to see some silks," answered Mrs. Malderton.

"Directly, ma'am.—Mr. Smith! Where *is* Mr. Smith?"

"Here, sir," cried a voice at the back of the shop.

"Pray make haste, Mr. Smith," said the M. C. "You never are to be found when you're wanted, sir."

Mr. Smith thus enjoined to use all possible dispatch, leaped over the counter with great agility, and placed himself before the newly-arrived customers. Mrs. Malderton uttered a faint scream; Miss Teresa, who had been stooping down to talk to her sister, raised her head, and beheld—Horatio Sparkins!

"We will draw a vail," as novel writers say, over the scene that ensued. The mysterious, philosophical, romantic, metaphysical Sparkins—he who, to the interesting Teresa, seemed like the embodied idea of the young dukes and poetical exquisites in blue silk dressing-gowns, and ditto ditto slippers, of whom she had read and dreamt, but had never expected to behold—was suddenly converted into Mr. Samuel Smith, the assistant at a "cheap shop;" the junior partner in a slippery firm of some three weeks' existence. The dignified evanishment of the hero of Oak Lodge on this unexpected announcement, could only be equaled by that of a furtive dog with a considerable kettle at his tail. All the hopes of the Maldertons were destined at once to melt away, like the lemon-ices at a Company's dinner; Almacks was still to them as distant as the

North Pole; and Miss Teresa had about as much chance of a husband as Captain Ross had of a north-west passage.

Years have elapsed since the occurrence of this dreadful morning. The daisies have thrice bloomed on Camberwell-green—the sparrows have thrice repeated their vernal chirps in Camberwell-grove; but the Miss Maldertons are still unmated. Miss Teresa's case is more desperate than ever; but Flamwell is yet in the zenith of his reputation; and the family have the same predilection for aristocratic personages, with an increased aversion to any thing *low*.

CHAPTER VI.

THE BLACK VAIL.

One winter's evening, toward the close of the year 1800, or within a year or two of that time, a young medical practitioner, recently established in business, was seated by a cheerful fire in his little parlor, listening to the wind which was beating the rain in pattering drops against the window, and rumbling dismally in the chimney. The night was wet and cold: he had been walking through mud and water the whole day, and was now comfortably reposing in his dressing-gown and slippers, more than half asleep and less than half awake, revolving a thousand matters in his wandering imagination. First he thought how hard the wind was blowing, and how the cold, sharp rain would be at that moment beating in his face if he were not comfortably housed at home. Then his mind reverted to his annual Christmas visit to his native place and dearest friends; he thought how glad they would all be to see him, and how happy it would make Rose if he could only tell her that he had got a patient at last, and hoped to have more, and to come down again in a few months' time and marry her, and take her home to gladden his lonely fireside, and stimulate him to fresh exertions. Then he began to wonder when his first patient would appear, or whether he was destined by a special dispensation of Providence never to have any patients at all; and then he thought about Rose again, and dropped to sleep and dreamed about her, till the very tones of her sweet, merry voice sounded in his ears, and her soft, tiny hand rested on his shoulder.

There *was* a hand upon his shoulder, but it was neither soft nor tiny; its owner being a corpulent, round-headed boy, who, in consideration of the sum of one shilling per week and his food, was let out by the parish to carry medicine and messages. As there was no demand for the one, however, and no necessity for the other, he usually occupied his unemployed hours—averaging fourteen a day—in abstracting peppermint drops, taking animal nourishment, and going to sleep.

"A lady, sir—a lady!" whispered the boy, rousing his master with a shake.

"What lady?" cried our friend, starting up, and not quite certain that his dream was an illusion, and half expecting that it might be Rose herself. "What lady? Where?"

"*There*, sir," replied the boy, pointing to the glass-door leading into the surgery, with an expression of alarm which the very unusual apparition of a customer might have tended to excite.

The surgeon looked toward the door, and started himself, for an instant, on beholding the appearance of his unlooked-for visitor.

It was a singularly tall female, dressed in deep mourning, and standing so close to the door that her face almost touched the glass. The upper part of her person was carefully muffled in a black shawl, as if for the purpose of concealment, and her face was shrouded by a thick black vail. She stood perfectly erect; her figure was drawn up to its full height, and though the surgeon *felt* that the eyes beneath the vail were fixed on him, she stood perfectly motionless, and evinced, by no gesture whatever, the slightest consciousness of his having turned toward her.

"Do you wish to consult me?" he inquired, with some hesitation, holding open the door. It opened inward, and therefore the action did not alter the position of the figure, which still remained motionless on the same spot.

The female slightly inclined her head, in token of acquiescence.

"Pray walk in," said the surgeon.

The figure moved a step forward: and then turning its head in the direction of the boy—to his infinite horror—appeared to hesitate.

"Leave the room, Tom," said the young man, addressing the boy, whose large round eyes had been extended to their utmost width during this brief interview.—"Draw the curtain, and shut the door."

The boy drew a green curtain across the glass part of the door, retired into the surgery, closed the door after him, and immediately applied one of his large eyes to the key-hole on the other side.

The surgeon drew a chair to the fire, and motioned the visitor to a seat. The mysterious figure slowly moved toward it, and as the blaze shone upon the black dress, the surgeon observed that the bottom of it was saturated with mud and rain.

"You are very wet," he said.

"I am," said the stranger, in a low, deep voice.

"And you are ill?" added the surgeon, compassionately, for the tone was that of a person in severe pain.

"I am," was the reply—"very ill: not bodily, but mentally. It is not for myself, or on my own behalf," continued the stranger, "that I come to you. If I labored under bodily disease, I should not be out alone at such an hour, or on such a night as this; and if I were afflicted with it twenty-four hours hence, God knows how gladly I would lie down and pray to die. It is for another that I beseech your aid, sir. I may be mad to ask it for him—I think I am: but, night after night, through the long, dreary hours of watching and weeping, the thought has been ever present to my mind; and though even *I* see the hopelessness of human assistance availing him, the bare thought of laying him in his grave without it, makes my blood run cold!" And a shudder, such as the surgeon well knew art could not produce, trembled through the speaker's frame.

There was a desperate earnestness in this woman's manner that went to the young man's heart. He was young in his profession, and had not yet witnessed enough of the miseries which are daily presented before the eyes of its members, to have grown comparatively callous to human suffering.

"If," he said, rising hastily, "the person of whom you speak be in so hopeless a condition as you describe, not a moment is to be lost. I will go with you instantly. Why did you not obtain medical advice before?"

"Because it would have been useless before—because it is useless even now," replied the woman, clasping her hands passionately.

The surgeon gazed for a moment on the black vail, as if to

ascertain the expression of the features beneath it; its thickness, however, rendered such a result impossible.

"You *are* ill," he said gently, "although you do not know it. The fever which has enabled you to bear without feeling the fatigue you have evidently undergone, is burning within you now. Put that to your lips," he continued, pouring out a glass of water—"to compose yourself for a few moments, and then tell me, as calmly as you can, what the disease of the patient is, and how long he has been ill. The moment I know what it is necessary I should know, to render my visit serviceable to him, I am ready to accompany you."

The stranger lifted the glass of water to her mouth without raising the vail, put it down again untasted, and burst into tears.

"I know," she said, sobbing aloud, "that what I say to you now, seems like the ravings of fever. I have been told so before, less kindly than by you. I am not a young woman, sir; and they do say, that as life steals on toward its final close, the last short remnant, worthless as it may seem to all beside, is dearer to its possessor than all the years that have gone before, connected though they be with the recollection of old friends long since dead, and young ones—children, perhaps—who have fallen off from, and forgotten one as completely as if they had died too. My natural term of life cannot be many years longer, and should be dear on that account; but I would lay it down without a sigh—with cheerfulness—with joy—if what I tell you now were only false, or imaginary. To-morrow morning he of whom I speak will be, I *know*, though I would fain think otherwise, beyond the reach of human aid; and yet, to-night, though he is in deadly peril, you must not see, and could not serve him."

"I am unwilling to increase your distress," said the surgeon, after a short pause, "by making any comment on what you have just said, or appearing desirous to investigate a subject you seem so anxious to conceal; but there is an inconsistency in your statement which I cannot reconcile with probability. This person is dying to-night, and I cannot see him when my assistance might possibly avail; you apprehend it will be useless to-morrow, and yet you would have me see him then. If he be indeed as dear to you, as your words and manner would imply, why not try to save his life before delay and the progress of his disease render it impracticable ?"

"God help me!" exclaimed the woman, weeping bitterly, "how can I hope strangers will believe what appears incredible, even to myself? You will *not* see him then, sir?" she added, rising suddenly.

"I did not say that I declined to see him," replied the surgeon; "but I warn you, that if you persist in this extraordinary procrastination, and the individual dies, a fearful responsibility rests with you."

"The responsibility will rest heavily somewhere," replied the stranger bitterly. "Whatever responsibility rests with me, I am content to bear and ready to answer."

"As I incur none," continued the surgeon, "by acceding to your request, I will see him in the morning, if you leave me the address. At what hour can he be seen?"

"*Nine,*" replied the stranger.

"You must excuse my pressing these inquiries," said the surgeon. "But is he in your charge now?"

"He is not," was the rejoinder.

"Then if I gave you instructions for his treatment through the night, you could not assist him?"

The woman wept bitterly, as she replied, "I could not."

Finding that there was but little prospect of obtaining further information by prolonging the interview, and anxious to spare the woman's feelings, which, subdued at first by a violent effort, were now irrepressible and most painful to witness, the surgeon repeated his promise of calling in the morning at the appointed hour; and his visitor, after giving him a direction to an obscure part of Walworth, left the house in the same mysterious manner as she had entered it.

It will be readily believed that so extraordinary a visit produced a considerable impression on the mind of the young surgeon, and that he speculated a great deal and to very little purpose on the possible circumstances of the case. In common with the generality of people, he had often heard and read of singular instances, in which a presentiment of death at a particular day or even minute had been entertained and realized.

At one moment he was inclined to think that the present might be such a case, but then it occurred to him that all the anecdotes of the kind he had ever heard, were of persons who had been troubled with a foreboding of their own death. This woman, however, spoke of another person—a man ; and it was impossible to suppose that a mere dream or delusion of fancy would induce her to speak of his approaching dissolution with such terrible certainty as she had done. It could not be that the man was to be murdered in the morning, and that the woman, originally a consenting party and bound to secrecy by an oath, had relented, and, though unable to prevent the commission of some outrage on the victim had determined to prevent his death if possible by the timely interposition of medical aid. The idea of such things happening within two miles of the metropolis appeared too wild and preposterous to be entertained beyond the instant. Then his original impression that the woman's intellects were disordered, recurred ; and as it was the only mode of solving the difficulty with any degree of satisfaction, he obstinately made up his mind to believe she was mad. Certain misgivings upon this point, however, stole upon his thoughts at the time, and presented themselves again and again through the long dull course of a sleepless night, during which, despite of all his efforts to the contrary, he was unable to banish the black vail from his disturbed imagination.

The back part of Walworth, at its greatest distance from town, is a straggling, miserable place enough, even in these days; but five-and-thirty years ago the greater portion of it was little better than a dreary waste, inhabited by a few scattered people of most questionable character, whose poverty prevented their living in any better neighborhood, or whose pursuits and mode of life rendered its solitude peculiarly desirable. Very many of the houses which have since sprung up on all sides, were not built until some years afterward; and the great majority even of those which were sprinkled about at irregular intervals, were of the rudest and most miserable description.

The appearance of the place through which he walked was not calculated to raise the spirits of the young surgeon, or to dispel any feeling of anxiety or depression which the singular kind of visit he was about to make might have awakened.— Striking off from the high road, his way lay across a marshy common, through irregular lanes, with here and there a ruinous and dismantled cottage fast falling to pieces with decay and neglect. A stunted tree, or pool of stagnant water, roused into a creeping sluggish action by the heavy rain of the preceding night, skirted the path occasionally; and now and then a miserable patch of garden-ground, with a few old boards knocked together for a summer-house, and old palings imperfectly mended with stakes pilfered from the neighboring hedges, bore testimony at once to the poverty of the inhabitants, and the little scruple they entertained in appropriating the property of other people to their own use. Occasionally, a filthy-looking woman would make her appearance from the door of a dirty house, to empty the contents of some cooking utensil into the gutter in front, or to scream after a little slip-shod girl, who had contrived to stagger a few yards from the door under the weight of a sallow infant almost as big as herself; but scarcely any thing was stirring around, and so much of the prospect as could be faintly traced through the cold damp mist which hung heavily over it, presented a lonely and dreary appearance perfectly in keeping with the objects we have described.

After plodding wearily through the mud and mire; making many inquiries for the place to which he had been directed; and receiving as many contradictory and unsatisfactory replies in return, the young man at length arrived before the house which had been pointed out to him as the object of his destination. It was a small low building, one story above the ground, with a more desolate and unpromising exterior than any he had yet passed. An old yellow curtain was closely drawn across the window up stairs, and the parlor shutters were closed, but not fastened. The house was detached from any other, and, as it stood at an angle of a narrow lane, there was no other habitation in sight.

When we say that the surgeon hesitated, and walked a few paces beyond the house before he could prevail upon himself to lift the knocker, we say nothing that need raise a smile upon the face of the boldest reader. The police of London were a very different body in that day to what they are now: the isolated position of the suburbs, when the rage for building and the progress of improvement had not yet begun to connect them with the main body of the city and its environs, rendered many of them (and this in particular) a place of resort for the worst and most depraved characters. Even the streets in the gayest parts of London were imperfectly lighted at that time, and such places as these were left entirely to the mercy of the moon and stars. The chances of detecting desperate characters, or of tracing them to their haunts, were thus rendered very few, and their offenses naturally increased in boldness, as the consciousness of comparative security became the more impressed upon them by daily experience. Added to these considerations, it must be remembered that the young man had spent some time in the public hospitals of the metropolis; and although neither Burke nor Bishop had then gained a horrible notoriety, still his own observation might have suggested to him how easily the atrocities to which the former has since given his name, might be committed. Be this as it may, whatever reflection made him hesitate, he *did* hesitate; but, being a young man of strong mind and great personal daring, it was only for an instant; he stepped briskly back, and knocked gently at the door.

A low whispering was audible immediately afterward, as if some person at the end of the passage were conversing stealthily with another on the landing above. It was succeeded by the noise of a pair of heavy boots upon the bare floor. The door-chain was softly unfastened; the door opened, and a tall, ill-favored man, with black hair, and a face, as the surgeon often afterward declared, as pale and haggard as the countenance of any dead man he ever saw, presented himself.

"Walk in, sir," he said in a low tone.

The surgeon did so, and the man having secured the door again by the chain, led the way to a small back parlor at the extremity of the passage.

"Am I in time?"

"Too soon," replied the man. The surgeon turned hastily round, with a gesture of astonishment not unmixed with alarm, which he found it impossible to repress, though he would gladly have recalled it.

"If you'll step in here, sir," said the man, who had evidently noticed the action—" if you will step in here, sir, you won't be detained five minutes, I assure you."

The surgeon at once walked into the room. The man closed the door, and left him alone.

It was a little cold room, with no other furniture than two deal chairs, and a table of the same material. A handful of fire, unguarded by any fender, was burning in the grate, which brought out the damp if it served no more comfortable purpose; for the unwholsome moisture was stealing down the walls in long, slug-like tracks. The window, which was broken and patched in many places, looked into a small enclosed piece of ground almost covered with water. Not a sound was to be heard, either within the house or without. The young surgeon sat down by the fire-place, to await the result of his first professional visit.

He had not remained in this position many minutes when the noise of some approaching vehicle struck his ear. It stopped; the street-door was opened; a low talking succeeded, accompanied with a shuffling noise of footsteps along the passage and on the stairs, as if two or three men were engaged in carrying some heavy body to the room above. The creaking of the stairs a few seconds afterward, announced that the new-comers having completed their task, whatever it was, were leaving the house. The door was again closed, and the former silence was restored.

Another five minutes elapsed, and the surgeon had just resolved to explore the house in search of some one to whom he might make his errand known, when the room-door opened, and his last night's visitor, dressed in exactly the same manner, with the vail lowered as before, motioned him to advance. The singular height of her form, coupled with the circumstance of her not speaking, caused the idea to pass across his brain for an instant that it might be a man disguised in woman's attire. The hysteric sobs which issued from beneath the vail, and the convulsive attitude of grief of the whole figure, however, at once exposed the absurdity of the suspicion, and he hastily followed.

The woman led the way up stairs to the front room, and paused at the door to let him enter first. It was scantily furnished with an old deal box, a few chairs, and a tent bedstead without hangings or cross-rails, which was covered with a patch-work counterpane. The dim light, admitted through the curtain which he had noticed from the outside, rendered the objects in the room so indistinct, and communicated to all of them so uniform a hue, that he did not at first perceive the object on which his eye at once rested when the woman rushed frantically past him, and flung herself on her knees by the bedside.

Stretched upon the bed, closely enveloped in a linen wrapper, and covered with blankets, lay a human form stiff and motionless. The head and face, which were those of a man, were uncovered, save by a bandage which passed over the head and under the chin. The eyes were closed. The left arm lay heavily across the bed, and the woman held the passive hand.

The surgeon gently pushed the woman aside, and took the hand in his.

"My God!" he exclaimed, letting it fall involuntarily—"the man is dead!"

The woman started to her feet and beat her hands together.—"Oh! don't say so, sir," she exclaimed with a burst of passion, amounting almost to frenzy—"Oh! don't say so, sir! I can't bear it—indeed I can't! Men have been brought to life before when unskillful people have given them up for lost; and men have died who might have been restored, if proper means had been resorted to. Don't let him lie here, sir, without one effort to save him. This very moment life may be passing away. Do try, sir,—do, for God's sake!"—And while speaking, she hurriedly chafed, first the forehead and then the breast of the senseless form before her, and then wildly beat the cold hands, which, when she ceased to hold them, fell listlessly and heavily back on the coverlet.

"It is of no use, my good woman," said the surgeon soothingly, as he withdrew his hand from the man's breast. "Stay—undo that curtain."

"Why?" said the woman, starting up.

"Undo that curtain," repeated the surgeon in an agitated tone.

"I darkened the room on purpose," said the woman, throwing herself before him as he rose to undraw it.—"Oh! sir, have pity on me? If it can be of no use, and he is really dead, do not—do not expose that corpse to other eyes than mine!"

"This man died no natural or easy death," said the surgeon. "I *must* see the body!" and with a motion so sudden, that the woman hardly knew that he had slipped from beside her, he tore open the curtain, admitted the full light of day, and returned to the bedside.

"There has been violence here," he said, pointing toward the body, and gazing intently on her face, from which the black vail was now for the first time removed. In the excitement of a minute before, the female had dashed off the bonnet and vail, and now stood with her eyes fixed upon him. Her features were those of a woman of about fifty, who had once been handsome. Sorrow and weeping had left traces upon them which not time itself would ever have produced without their aid: her face was deadly pale, and there was a nervous contortion of the lip, and an unnatural fire in her eye, which showed too plainly that her bodily and mental powers had nearly sunk beneath an accumulation of misery.

"There has been violence here," said the surgeon, preserving his searching glance.

"There has!" replied the woman.

"This man has been murdered."

"That I call God to witness he has," said the woman, passionately; "pitilessly, inhumanly murdered!"

"By whom?" said the surgeon, seizing the woman by the arm.

"Look at the butchers' marks, and then ask me," she replied.

The surgeon turned his face toward the bed, and bent over the body, which lay full in the light of the window. The throat was swollen, and a blue livid mark encircled it. The truth flashed suddenly upon him.

"This is one of the men who were hung this morning!" he exclaimed, turning away with a shudder.

"It is," replied the woman, with a cold, unmeaning stare.

"Who was he?" inquired the surgeon.

"*My son*," rejoined the woman; and fell senseless at his feet.

It was true. A companion, equally guilty with himself, had been acquitted for want of evidence; and this man had been left for death, and executed. To recount the circumstances of the case at this distant period, must be unnecessary, and might give pain to some persons still alive. The history was an every-day one. The mother was a widow without friends or money, and had denied herself necessaries to bestow them on her orphan boy. That boy, unmindful of her prayers, and forgetful of the sufferings she had endured for him—incessant anxiety of mind, and voluntary starvation of body—had plunged into a career of dissipation and crime. And this was the result: his own death by the hangman's hands, and his mother's shame, and incurable insanity.

For many years after this occurrence, and when profitable and arduous avocations would have led many men to forget that such a miserable being existed, the young surgeon was a daily visitor at the side of the harmless mad woman; not only soothing her by his presence and kindness, but alleviating the rigor of her condition by pecuniary donations for her comfort and support, bestowed with no sparing hand. In the transient gleam of recollection and consciousness which preceded her death, a prayer for his welfare and protection as fervent as mortal ever breathed, rose from the lips of this poor friendless creature. That prayer flew to Heaven, and was heard. The blessings he was instrumental in conferring have been repaid to him a thousand fold; but, amid all the honors of rank and station which have since been heaped upon him, and which he has so well earned, he can have no one reminiscence more gratifying to his feelings than that connected with—The Black Vail.

CHAPTER VII.

THE STEAM EXCURSION.

Mr. Percy Noakes was a law-student, inhabiting a set of chambers on the fourth floor, in one of those houses in Gray's-inn-square which command an extensive view of the gardens, and their usual adjuncts—flaunting nursery-maids and town-made children with parenthetical legs. Mr. Percy Noakes was what is generally termed—"a devilish good fellow." He had a large circle of acquaintance, and seldom dined at his own expense. He used to talk politics to papas, flatter the vanity of mammas, do the amiable to their daughters, make pleasure engagements with their sons, and romp with the younger branches. Like those paragons of perfection, advertising footmen out of place, he was always "willing to make himself generally useful." If any old lady, whose son was in India, gave a ball, Mr. Percy Noakes was master of the ceremonies; if any young lady made a stolen match, Mr. Percy Noakes gave her away; if a juvenile wife presented her husband with a blooming cherub, Mr. Percy Noakes was either godfather, or deputy-godfather; and if any member of a friend's family died, Mr. Percy Noakes was invariably to be seen in the second mourning coach, with a white handkerchief to his eyes, sobbing—to use his own appropriate and expressive description—"like winkin!"

It may readily be imagined that these numerous avocations were rather calculated to interfere with Mr. Percy Noakes's professional studies. Mr. Percy Noakes was perfectly aware of the fact, and he had, therefore, after mature reflection, made up his mind not to study at all—a laudable determination, to which he adhered in the most praiseworthy manner. His sitting-room presented a strange chaos of dress-gloves, boxing-gloves, caricatures, albums, invitation-cards, foils, cricket-bats, card-board drawings, paste, gum, and fifty other extraordinary articles heaped together in the strangest confusion. He was always making something for somebody, or planning some party of pleasure, which was his great forte. He invariably spoke with astonishing rapidity; was smart, spoffish, and eight-and-twenty.

"Splendid idea, 'pon my life!" soliloquized Mr. Percy Noakes, over his morning's coffee, as his mind reverted to a suggestion which had been thrown out the previous night, by a lady at whose house he had spent the evening. "Glorious idea!—Mrs. Stubbs," cried the student, raising his voice.

"Yes, sir," replied a dirty old woman with an inflamed countenance, emerging from the bed-room, with a barrel of dirt and cinders.—This was the laundress. "Did you call, sir?"

"Oh! Mrs. Stubbs, I'm going out: if that tailor should call again, you'd better say—you'd better say, I'm out of town, and shan't be back for a fortnight; and if that bootmaker should come, tell him I've lost his address, or I'd have sent him that little amount. Mind he writes it down; and if Mr. Hardy should call—you know Mr. Hardy?"

"The funny gentleman, sir?"

"Ah! the funny gentleman. If Mr. Hardy should call, say I've gone to Mrs. Taunton's about that water-party."

"Yes, sir."

"And if any fellow calls, and says he's come about a steamer, tell him to be here at five o'clock this afternoon, Mrs. Stubbs."

"Very well, sir."

Mr. Percy Noakes brushed his hat, whisked the crumbs off his inexplicables with a silk handkerchief, gave the ends of his hair a persuasive roll round his forefinger, and sallied forth for Mrs. Taunton's domicile in Great Marlborough-street, where she and her daughters occupied the upper part of a house. She was a good-looking widow of fifty, with the form of a giantess and the mind of a child. The pursuit of pleasure, and some means of killing time, appeared the sole end of her existence. She doted on her daughters, who were as frivolous as herself.

A general exclamation of satisfaction hailed the arrival of Mr. Percy Noakes, who went through the ordinary salutations and threw himself into an easy chair near the ladies' work-table, with all the ease of a regularly established friend of the family. Mrs. Taunton was busily engaged in planting immense bright bows on every part of a smart cap, on which it was possible to stick one; Miss Emily Taunton was making a watch-guard; and Miss Sophia was at the piano, practicing a new song—poetry by the young officer, or the police-officer, or the custom-house officer, or some equally interesting amateur.

"You good creature!" said Mrs. Taunton, addressing the gallant Percy. "You really are a good soul! You've come about the water-party, I know."

"I should rather suspect I had," replied Mr. Noakes, triumphantly. "Now, come here, girls, and I'll tell you all about it." Miss Emily and Miss Sophia advanced to the table, with that ballet sort of step which some young ladies seem to think so fascinating—something between a skip and a canter.

"Now," continued Mr. Percy Noakes, "it seems to me that the best way will be to have a committee of ten, to make all the arrangements, and manage the whole set-out. Then I propose that the expenses shall be paid by these ten fellows jointly."

"Excellent, indeed!" said Mrs. Taunton, who highly approved of this part of the arrangements.

"Then my plan is, that each of these ten fellows shall have the power of asking five people. There must be a meeting of the committee at my chambers, to make all the arrangements, and these people shall be then named; every member of the committee shall have the power of black-balling any one who is proposed, and one black-ball shall exclude that person. This will ensure our having a pleasant party, you know."

"What a manager you are!" interrupted Mrs. Taunton again.

"Charming!" said the lovely Emily.

"I never did!" ejaculated Sophia.

"Yes, I think it'll do," replied Mr. Percy Noakes, who was now quite in his element. "I think it'll do. Then you know we shall go down to the Nore and back, and have a regular capital cold dinner laid out in the cabin before we start, so that every thing may be ready without any confusion; and we shall have the lunch laid out on deck in those little tea-garden-looking concerns by the paddle-boxes—I don't know what you call 'em. Then we shall hire a steamer expressly for our party, and a band, and have the deck chalked, and we shall be able to dance quadrilles all day: and then whoever we know that's musical, you know, why they'll make themselves useful and agreeable; and—and—upon the whole, I really hope we shall have a glorious day, you know."

The announcement of these arrangements was received with the utmost enthusiasm. Mrs. Taunton, Emily, and Sophia, were loud in their praises.

"Well, but tell me, Percy," said Mrs. Taunton, "who are the ten gentlemen to be?"

"Oh! I know plenty of fellows who'll be delighted with the scheme," replied Mr. Percy Noakes; "of course, we shall have—"

"Mr. Hardy," interrupted the servant, announcing a visitor. Miss Sophia and Miss Emily hastily assumed the most interesting attitudes that could be adopted on so short a notice.

"How are you?" said a stout gentleman of about forty, pausing at the door in the attitude of an awkward harlequin. This was Mr. Hardy, whom we have before described, on the authority of Mr. Stubbs, as "the funny gentleman." He was an Astley-Cooperish Joe Miller—a practical joker, immensely popular with married ladies, and a general favorite with young men. He was always engaged in some pleasure excursion or other, and delighted in getting somebody into a scrape on such occasions. He could sing comic songs, imitate hackney-coachmen and fowls, play airs on his chin, and execute concertos on the Jews'-harp. He always eat and drank most immoderately, and was the bosom friend of Mr. Percy Noakes. He had a red face, a somewhat husky voice, and a tremendously loud laugh.

"How are you?" said this worthy, laughing, as if it were the finest joke in the world to make a morning call, and shaking hands with the ladies with as much vehemence as if their arms were so many pump-handles.

"You're just the very man I wanted," said Mr. Percy Noakes, who proceeded to explain the cause of his being in requisition.

"Ha! ha! ha!" shouted Hardy, after hearing the statement, and receiving a detailed account of the proposed excursion.

'Oh, capital! glorious! What a day it will be! what fun!—But, I say, when are you going to begin making the arrangements?"

"No time like the present—at once, if you please."

"Oh, charming!" cried the ladies. "Pray do."

Writing materials were laid before Mr. Percy Noakes, and the names of the different members of the committee were agreed on, after as much discussion between him and Mr. Hardy as if at least the fate of nations had depended on their appointment. It was then agreed that a meeting should take place at Mr. Percy Noakes's chambers on the ensuing Wednesday evening at eight o'clock, and the visitors departed.

Wednesday evening arrived; eight o'clock came, and eight members of the committee were punctual in their attendance. Mr. Loggins, the solicitor, of Boswell-court, sent an excuse, and Mr. Samuel Briggs, the ditto of Furnival's Inn, sent his brother, much to his (the brother's) satisfaction, and greatly to the discomfiture of Mr. Percy Noakes. Between the Briggses and the Tauntons there existed a degree of implacable hatred, quite unprecedented. The animosity between the Montagues and Capulets was nothing to that which prevailed between these two illustrious houses. Mrs. Briggs was a widow, with three daughters and two sons; Mr. Samuel, the eldest, was an attorney, and Mr. Alexander, the youngest, was under articles to his brother. They resided in Portland-street, Oxford-street, and moved in the same orbit as the Tauntons—hence their mutual dislike. If the Miss Briggses appeared in smart bonnets, the Miss Tauntons eclipsed them with smarter. If Mrs. Taunton appeared in a cap of all the hues of the rainbow, Mrs. Briggs forthwith mounted a toque, with all the patterns of a kaleidoscope. If Miss Sophia Taunton learnt a new song, two of the Miss Briggses came out with a new duet. The Tauntons had once gained a temporary triumph, with the assistance of a harp, but the Briggses brought three guitars into the field, and effectually routed the enemy. There was no end to the rivalry between them.

Now, as Mr. Samuel Briggs was a mere machine, a sort of self-acting legal walking-stick; and as the party was known to have originated, however remotely, with Mrs. Taunton, the female branches of the Briggs family had arranged that Mr. Alexander should attend instead of his brother; and as the said Mr. Alexander was deservedly celebrated for possessing all the pertinacity of a bankruptcy-court attorney, combined with the obstinacy of that pleasing animal which browses upon the thistle, he required but little tuition. He was especially enjoined to make himself as disagreeable as possible; and, above all, to black-ball the Tauntons at every hazard.

The proceedings of the evening were opened by Mr. Percy Noakes. After successfully urging upon the gentlemen present the propriety of their mixing some brandy-and-water, he briefly stated the object of the meeting, and concluded by observing that the first step must be a selection of a chairman, necessarily possessing some arbitrary—he trusted not unconstitutional—powers, to whom the personal direction of the whole of the arrangements (subject to the approval of the committee) should be confided. A pale young gentleman in a green stock and spectacles of the same, a member of the honorable society of the Inner Temple, immediately rose for the purpose of proposing Mr. Percy Noakes. He had known him long, and this he would say, that a more honorable, a more excellent, or a better-hearted fellow, never existed—(hear, hear!) The young gentleman, who was a member of a debating society, took this opportunity of entering into an examination of the state of the English law, from the days of William the Conqueror down to the present period: he briefly adverted to the code established by the ancient Druids: slightly glanced at the principles laid down by the Athenian lawgivers; and concluded with a most glowing eulogium on pic-nics and constitutional rights.

Mr. Alexander Briggs opposed the motion. He had the highest esteem for Mr. Percy Noakes as an individual, but he did consider that he ought not to be intrusted with these immense powers—(oh, oh!)—He believed that in the proposed capacity Mr. Percy Noakes would not act fairly, impartially, or honorably; but he begged it to be distinctly understood, that he said this without the slightest personal disrespect. Mr. Hardy defended his honorable friend, in a voice rendered partially unintelligible by emotion and brandy-and-water. The proposition was put to the vote, and there appearing to be only one dissentient voice, Mr. Percy Noakes was declared duly elected, and took the chair accordingly.

The business of the meeting now proceeded with great rapidity. The chairman delivered in his estimate of the probable expense of the excursion, and every one present subscribed his proportion thereof. The question was put that "The Endeavor" be hired for the occasion; Mr. Alexander Briggs moved as an amendment, that the word "Fly" be substituted for the word "Endeavor;" but after some debate consented to withdraw his opposition. The important ceremony of balloting then commenced. A tea-caddy was placed on a table in a dark corner of the apartment, and every one was provided with two backgammon men, one black and one white.

The chairman with great solemnity then read the following list of the guests whom he proposed to introduce:—Mrs. Taunton and two daughters, Mr. Wizzle, Mr. Simson. The names were respectively balloted for, and Mrs. Taunton and her daughters were declared to be black-balled. Mr. Percy Noakes and Mr. Hardy exchanged glances.

"Is your list prepared, Mr. Briggs?" inquired the chairman.

"It is," replied Alexander, delivering in the following:—"Mrs. Briggs and three daughters, Mr. Samuel Briggs." The previous ceremony was repeated, and Mrs. Briggs and three daughters were declared to be black-balled. Mr. Alexander Briggs looked rather foolish, and the remainder of the company appeared somewhat overawed by the mysterious nature of the proceedings.

The balloting proceeded; but one little circumstance which Mr. Percy Noakes had not originally foreseen, prevented the system working quite as well as he had anticipated—every body was blackballed. Mr. Alexander Briggs, by way of retaliation, exercised his power of exclusion in every instance, and the result was, that after three hours had been consumed in incessant balloting, the names of only three gentlemen were found to have been agreed to. In this dilemma what was to be done? either the whole plan must fall to the ground, or a compromise must be effected. The latter alternative was preferable; and Mr. Percy Noakes therefore proposed that the form of balloting should be dispensed with, and that every gentleman should merely be required to state whom he intended to bring. The proposal was readily acceded to; the Tauntons and the Briggses were reinstated, and the party was formed.

The next Wednesday was fixed for the eventful day, and it was unanimously resolved that every member of the committee should wear a piece of blue sarsenet ribbon round his left arm. It appeared from the statement of Mr. Percy Noakes, that the boat belonged to the General Steam Navigation Company, and was then lying off the Custom-House; and as he proposed that the dinner and wines should be provided by an eminent city purveyor, it was arranged that Mr. Percy Noakes should be on board by seven o'clock to superintend the arrangements, and that the remaining members of the committee, together with the company generally, should be expected to join her by nine o'clock. More brandy-and-water was dispatched; several speeches were made by the different law students present; thanks were voted to the chairman, and the meeting separated.

The weather had been beautiful up to this period, and beautiful it continued to be. Sunday passed over, and Mr. Percy Noakes became unusually fidgety—rushing constantly to and from the Steam Packet Wharf, to the astonishment of the clerks, and the great emolument of the Holborn cabmen. Tuesday arrived, and the anxiety of Mr. Percy Noakes knew no bounds; he was every instant running to the window to look out for clouds; and Mr. Hardy astonished the whole square by practicing a new comic song for the occasion, in the chairman's chambers.

Uneasy were the slumbers of Mr. Percy Noakes that night: he tossed and tumbled about, and had confused dreams of steamers starting off, and gigantic clocks with the hands pointing to a quarter past nine, and the ugly face of Mr. Alexander Briggs looking over the boat's side, and grinning as if in derision of his fruitless attempts to move. He made a violent effort to get on board, and awoke. The bright sun was shining cheerfully into the bed-room, and Mr. Percy Noakes started up for his watch, in the dreadful expectation of finding his worst dreams realized.

It was just five o'clock. He calculated the time—he should be a good half-hour dressing himself; and as it was a lovely morning, and the tide would be then running down, he would walk leisurely to Strand-lane, and have a boat to the Custom-house.

He dressed himself, took a hasty apology for a breakfast, and sallied forth. The streets looked as lonely and deserted as if they had been crowded overnight for the last time. Here and there an early apprentice, with quenched-looking sleepy eyes, was taking down the shutters of a shop; and a policeman or milk-woman might occasionally be seen pacing slowly along; the servants had not yet begun to clean the doors, or light the fires, and London looked the picture of desolation. At the corner of a bye-street, near Temple-bar, was stationed a "street-breakfast." The coffee was boiling over a charcoal fire, and large slices of bread and butter were piled one upon the other like deals in a timber-yard. The company were seated on a form, which, with a view both to security and comfort, was placed against a neighboring wall. Two young men, whose uproarious mirth and disordered dress bespoke the conviviality of the preceding evening, were treating three "ladies" and an Irish laborer. A little sweep was standing at a short distance, casting a longing eye at the tempting delicacies; and a policeman was watching the group from the opposite side of the street. The wan looks, and gaudy finery of the wretched thinly-clad females, contrasted as strangely with the gay sun-light, as did their forced merriment with the boisterous hilarity of the two young men, who now and then varied their amusements by "bonneting" the proprietor of this itinerant coffee-house.

Mr. Percy Noakes walked briskly by, and when he turned down Strand-lane, and caught a glimpse of the the glistening water, he thought he had never felt so important or so happy in his life.

"Boat, sir!" cried one of the three watermen who were mopping out their boats, and all whistling different tunes. "Boat, sir!"

"No," replied Mr. Percy Noakes, rather sharply; for the inquiry was not made in a manner at all suitable to his dignity.

"Would you prefer a wessel, sir?" inquired another, to the infinite delight of the "Jack-in-the-water."

Mr. Percy Noakes replied with a look of the most supreme contempt.

"Did you want to be put on board a steamer, sir?" inquired an old fireman-waterman, very confidentially. He was dressed in a faded red suit, just the color of the cover of a very old Court-guide.

"Yes, make haste—the Endeavor—off the Custom-house."

"Endeavor!" cried the man who had convulsed the "Jack" before. "Vy, I see the Endeavor go up half an hour ago."

"So did I," said another; "and I should think she'd gone down by this time, for she's a precious sight too full of ladies and gen'l'men."

Mr. Percy Noakes affected to disregard these representations, and stepped into the boat, which the old man, by dint of scrambling, and shoving, and grating, had brought up to the causeway. "Shove her off," cried Mr. Percy Noakes, and away the boat glided down the river, Mr. Percy Noakes seated on the recently mopped seat, and the watermen at the stairs offering to bet him any reasonable sum that he'd never reach the "Custum-us."

"Here she is, by Jove!" said the delighted Percy, as they ran alongside the Endeavor.

"Hold hard!" cried the steward over the side, and Mr. Percy Noakes jumped on board.

"Hope you'll find every thing as you wished, sir. She looks uncommon well this morning."

"She does, indeed," replied the manager, in a state of ecstasy which it is impossible to describe. The deck was scrubbed, and the seats were scrubbed, and there was a bench for the band, and a place for dancing, and a pile of camp-stools, and an awning: and then Mr. Percy Noakes bustled down below, and there were the pastrycook's men and the steward's wife laying out the dinner on two tables, the whole length of the cabin; and then Mr. Percy Noakes took off his coat, and rushed backward and forward, doing nothing, but quite convinced he was assisting everybody; and the steward's wife laughed till she cried, and Mr. Percy Noakes panted with the violence of his exertions. And then the bell at London-bridge wharf rang, and a Margate boat was just starting, and a Gravesend boat was just starting, and people shouted, and porters ran down the steps with luggage that would crush any men but porters; and sloping boards, with bits of wood nailed on them, were placed between the outside boat and the inside boat, and the passengers ran along them, and looked like so many fowls coming out of an area; and then the bell ceased, and the boards were taken away, and the boats started: and the whole scene was one of the most delightful bustle and confusion that can be imagined.

The time wore on; half-past eight o'clock arrived; the pastrycook's men went ashore; the dinner was completely laid out, and Mr. Percy Noakes locked the principal cabin, and put the key into his pocket, in order that it might be suddenly disclosed in all its magnificence to the eyes of the astonished company. The band came on board, and so did the wine.

Ten minutes to nine, and the committee embarked in a body. There was Mr. Hardy in a blue jacket and waistcoat, white trousers, silk stockings, and pumps; habited in full aquatic costume, with a straw hat on his head, and an immense telescope under his arm; and there was the young gentleman with the green spectacles, in nankeen inexplicables, with a ditto waistcoat and bright buttons, like the pictures of Paul—not the saint, but he of Virginia notoriety. The remainder of the committee dressed in white hats, light jackets, waistcoats and trousers, looked something between waiters and West India planters.

Nine o'clock struck, and the company arrived in shoals. Mr. Samuel Briggs, Mrs. Briggs and the Misses Briggs made their appearance in a smart private wherry. The three guitars, in their respective dark-green cases, were carefully stowed away in the bottom of the boat, accompanied by two immense portfolios of music, which it would take at least a week's incessant playing to get through. The Tauntons arrived at the same moment with more music, and a lion—a gentleman with a bass voice and an incipient red mustache. The colors of the Taunton party were pink; those of the Briggses a light blue. The Tauntons had artificial flowers in their bonnets; here the Briggses gained a decided advantage—they wore feathers.

"How d'ye do, dear?" said the Misses Briggs to the Misses

Taunton. (The word "dear," among girls is frequently synonimous with "wretch.")

"Quite well, thank you, dear," replied the Misses Taunton to the Misses Briggs; and then there was such a kissing, and congratulating, and shaking of hands, as would induce one to suppose that the two families were the best friends in the world, instead of each wishing the other overboard, as they most sincerely did.

Mr. Percy Noakes received the visitors, and bowed to the strange gentleman, as if he should like to know who he was. This was just what Mrs. Taunton wanted. Here was an opportunity to astonish the Briggses.

"Oh! I beg your pardon," said the general of the Taunton party, with a careless air — "Captain Helves—Mr. Percy Noakes—Mrs. Briggs—Captain Helves."

Mr. Percy Noakes bowed very low; the gallant captain did the same with all due ferocity, and the Briggses were clearly overcome.

"Our friend, Mr. Wizzle, being unfortunately prevented from coming," resumed Mrs. Taunton, "I did myself the pleasure of bringing the captain, whose musical talents I knew would be a great acquisition."

"In the name of the committee I have to thank you for doing so, and to offer you a most sincere welcome, sir," replied Percy. (Here the scraping was renewed.) "But pray be seated—won't you walk aft? Captain, will you conduct Miss Taunton?—Miss Briggs, will you allow me?"

"Where could they have picked up that military man?" inquired Mrs. Briggs of Miss Kate Briggs, as they followed the little party.

"I can't imagine," replied Miss Kate, bursting with vexation; for the very fierce air with which the gallant captain regarded the company, had impressed her with a high sense of his importance.

Boat after boat came alongside, and guest after guest arrived. The invites had been excellently arranged, Mr. Percy Noakes having considered it as important that the number of young men should exactly tally with that of the young ladies, as that the quantity of knives on board should be in precise proportion to the forks.

"Now, is every one on board?" inquired Mr. Percy Noakes.

The committee (who, with their bits of blue ribbon, looked as if they were all going to be bled) bustled about to ascertain the fact, and reported that they might safely start.

"Go on," cried the master of the boat from the top of one of the paddle-boxes.

"Go on," echoed the boy, who was stationed over the hatchway to pass the directions down to the engineer; and away went the vessel with that agreeable noise which is peculiar to steamers, and which is composed of a pleasant mixture of creaking, gushing, clanging, and snorting.

"Hoi—oi— oi — oi — oi — oi—o—i—i—i!" shouted half-a-dozen voices from a boat about a quarter of a mile astern.

"Ease her!" cried the captain: "do these people belong to us, sir?"

"Noakes," exclaimed Hardy, who had been looking at every object, far and near, through the large telescope, "it's the Fleetwoods and the Wakefields—and two children with them, by Jove!"

"What a shame to bring children!" said everybody; "how very inconsiderate!"

"I say, it would be a good joke to pretend not to see 'em, wouldn't it?" suggested Hardy, to the immense delight of the company generally. A council of war was hastily held, and it was resolved that the new comers should be taken on board, on Mr. Hardy's solemnly pledging himself to tease the children during the whole of the day.

"Stop her!" cried the captain.

"Stop her!" repeated the boy; whizz went the steam, and all the young ladies, as in duty bound, screamed in concert. They were only appeased by the assurance of the martial Helves, that the escape of steam consequent on stopping a vessel was seldom attended with any great loss of human life.

Two men ran to the side, and after a good deal of shouting, and swearing, and angling for the wherry with a boat-hook, Mr. Fleetwood, and Mrs. Fleetwood, and Master Fleetwood, and Mr. Wakefield, and Mrs. Wakefield, and Miss Wakefield, were safely deposited on the deck. The girl was about six years old, the boy about four; the former was dressed in a white frock with a pink sash and a dog's-eared looking little spencer, a straw bonnet and green vail, six inches by three and a half: the latter was attired for the occasion in a nankeen frock, between the bottom of which and the top of his plaid socks a considerable portion of two small mottled legs was discernible. He had a light blue cap with a gold band and tassel on his head, and a damp piece of gingerbread in his hand, with which he had slightly embossed his dear little countenance.

The boat once more started off; the band played "Off she goes;" the major part of the company conversed cheerfully in groups, and the old gentlemen walked up and down the deck in pairs, as perseveringly and gravely as if they were doing a match against time for an immense stake. They ran briskly down the Pool; the gentlemen pointed out the Docks, the Thames Police-office, and other elegant public edifices; and the young ladies exhibited a proper display of horror and bashfulness at the appearance of the coal-whippers and ballast-heavers. Mr. Hardy told stories to the married ladies at which they laughed very much in their pocket-handkerchiefs, and hit him on the knuckles with their fans, declaring him to be "a naughty man—a shocking creature"—and so forth; and Captain Helves gave slight descriptions of battles and duels, with a most bloodthirsty air, which made him the admiration of the women, and the envy of the men. Quadrilling commenced; Captain Helves danced one set with Miss Emily Taunton, and another set with Miss Sophia Taunton. Mrs. Taunton was in ecstasies. The victory appeared to be complete; but, alas! the inconstancy of man! Having performed this necessary duty, he attached himself solely to Miss Julia Briggs, with whom he danced no less than three sets consecutively, and from whose side he evinced no intention of stirring for the remainder of the day.

Mr. Hardy having played one or two very brilliant fantasias on the Jews'-harp, and having frequently repeated the exquisitely amusing joke of slily chalking a large cross on the back of some member of the committee, Mr. Percy Noakes expressed his hope that some of their musical friends would oblige the company by a display of their abilities.

"Perhaps," he said in a very insinuating manner, "Captain Helves will oblige us." Mrs. Taunton's countenance lighted up, for the captain only sang duets, and couldn't sing them with any body but one of her daughters.

"Really," said that warlike individual, "I should be very happy, but—"

"Oh! pray do," cried all the young ladies.

"Miss Sophia, have you any objection to join in a duet?"

"Oh! not the slightest," returned the young lady, in a tone which clearly showed she had the greatest possible objection.

"Shall I accompany you, dear?" inquired one of the Miss Briggses, with the bland intention of spoiling the effect.

"Very much obliged to you, Miss Briggs," sharply retorted Mrs. Taunton, who saw through the maneuvre; "my daughters always sing without accompaniments."

"And without voices," tittered Mrs. Briggs, in a low tone.

"Perhaps," said Mrs. Taunton, reddening, for she guessed the tenor of the observation, though she had not heard it clearly —"Perhaps it would be as well for some people, if their voices were not quite so audible as they are to other people."

"And perhaps, if gentlemen, who are kidnapped to pay attention to some persons' daughters, had not sufficient discernment to pay attention to other persons' daughters," returned Mrs. Briggs, "some persons would not be so ready to display that ill-temper, which, thank God, distinguishes them from other persons."

"Persons!" ejaculated Mrs. Taunton.

"Yes; persons, ma'am," replied Mrs. Briggs.

"Insolence!"

"Creature!"

"Hush! hush!" interrupted Mr. Percy Noakes, who was one of the very few by whom this dialogue had been overheard. "Hush!—pray silence for the duet."

After a great deal of preparatory crowing and humming, the captain began the following duet from the opera of Paul and Virginia, in that grunting tone in which a man gets down, Heaven knows where, without the remotest chance of ever getting up again. This in private circles, is frequently designated "a bass voice."

"See (sung the captain) from o—ce—an ri—sing
Bright flames the or—b of d—ay.
From yon gro—ve, the varied so—ngs——"

Here the singer was interrupted by varied cries of the most dreadful description, proceeding from some grove in the immediate vicinity of the starboard paddle-box.

"My child!" screamed Mrs. Fleetwood. "My child! it is his voice—I know it."

Mr. Fleetwood, accompanied by several gentlemen, here rushed to the quarter from whence the noise proceeded, and an exclamation of horror burst from the company; the general impression being that the little innocent had either got his head in the water or or his legs in the machinery.

"What is the matter?" shouted the agonized father, as he returned with the child in his arms.

"Oh! oh! oh!" screamed the small sufferer again.

"What is the matter, dear?" inquired the father once more, hastily stripping off the nankeen frock, for the purpose of ascertaining whether the child had one bone which was not smashed to pieces.

"Oh! oh!—I'm so frightened."

"What at, dear?—what at?" said the mother, soothing the sweet infant.

"Oh! he's been making such dreadful faces at me," cried the boy, relapsing into convulsions at the bare recollection.

"He!—who?" cried every body, crowding round him.

"Oh!—him!" replied the child, pointing at Hardy, who affected to be the most concerned of the whole group.

The real state of the case at once flashed upon the minds of all present, with the exception of the Fleetwoods and the Wakefields. The facetious Hardy, in fulfillment of his promise, had watched the child to a remote part of the vessel, and, suddenly appearing before him with the most awful contortions of visage, had produced his paroxysm of terror. Of course, he now observed that it was hardly necessary for him to deny the accusation; and the unfortunate little victim was accordingly led below, after receiving sundry thumps on the head from both his parents, for having the wickedness to tell a story.

This little interruption having been adjusted, the captain resumed, and Miss Emily chimed in, in due course. The duet was loudly applauded, and, certainly, the perfect independence of the parties deserved great commendation. Miss Emily

Steam Excursion.

sung her part without the slightest reference to the captain, and the captain sang so loud that he had not the slightest idea of what was being done by his partner. After having gone through the last eighteen or nineteen bars by himself, therefore, he acknowledged the plaudits of the circle with that air of self-denial which men always assume when they think they have done something to astonish the company, though they don't exactly know what.

"Now," said Mr. Percy Noakes, who had just ascended from the fore-cabin, where he had been busily engaged in decanting the wine; "if the Misses Briggs will oblige us with something before dinner, I am sure we shall be very much delighted."

One of those hums of admiration followed the suggestion which one frequently hears in society, when nobody has the most distant notion of what he is expressing his approval of. The three Misses Briggs looked modestly at their mamma, and the mamma looked approvingly at her daughters, and Mrs. Taunton looked scornfully at all of them. The Misses Briggs asked for their guitars, and several gentlemen seriously damaged the cases in their anxiety to present them. Then there was a very interesting production of three little keys for the aforesaid cases, and a melodramatic expression of horror at finding a string broken; and a vast deal of screwing and tightening, and winding and tuning, during which Mrs. Briggs expatiated to those near her on the immense difficulty of playing a guitar, and hinted at the wondrous proficiency of her daughters in that mystic art. Mrs. Taunton whispered to a neighbor that it was "quite sickening!" and the Misses Taunton tried to look as if they knew how to play, but disdained to do so.

At length the Misses Briggs began in real earnest. It was a new Spanish composition, for three voices and three guitars. The effect was electrical. All eyes were turned upon the captain, who was reported to have once passed through Spain with his regiment, and who, of course, must be well acquainted with the national music. He was in raptures. This was sufficient; the trio was encored—the applause was universal, and never had the Tauntons suffered such a complete defeat.

"Bravo! bravo!" ejaculated the captain;—"Bravo!"

"Pretty, isn't it, sir?" inquired Mr. Samuel Briggs, with

the air of a self-satisfied showman. By-the-by, these were the first words he had been heard to utter since he left Boswell-court the evening before.

"De—lightful!" returned the captain, with a flourish, and a military cough;—"de—lightful!"

"Sweet instrument!" said an old gentleman with a bald head, who had been trying all the morning to look through a telescope, inside the glass of which Mr. Hardy had fixed a large black wafer.

"Did you ever hear a Portuguese tambarine?" inquired that jocular individual.

"Did *you* ever hear a tom-tom, sir?" sternly inquired the captain, who lost no opportunity of showing off his travels real or pretended.

"A what?" asked Hardy, rather taken aback.

"A tom-tom."

"Never!"

"Nor a gum-gum?'

"Never!"

"What *is* a gum-gum?" eageriy inquired several young ladies.

"When I was in the East Indies," replied the captain, (here was a discovery—he had been in the East Indies!)—"when I was in the East Indies, I was once stopping a few thousand miles up the country, on a visit at the house of a very particular friend of mine, Ram Chowdar Doss Azuph Al Bowlar—a devilish pleasant fellow. As we were enjoying our hookahs one evening in the cool verandah in the front of his villa, we were rather surprised by the sudden appearance of thirty-four of his Kit-ma-gars (for he had rather a large establishment there), accompanied by an equal number of Consumars, approaching the house with a threatening aspect, and beating a tom-tom. The Ram started up——"

"The who?" inquired the bald gentleman, intensely interested.

"The Ram—Ram Chowdar—"

"Oh!" said the old gentleman, "I beg your pardon; it really didn't occur to me; pray go on."

"—Started up and drew a pistol. 'Helves,' said he, 'my boy,'—he always called me, my boy—'Helves,' said he, 'do you hear that tom-tom?'—'I do,' said I. His countenance, which before was pale, assumed a most frightful appearance; his whole visage was distorted, and his frame shaken by violent emotions. 'Do you see that gum-gum?' said he. 'No,' said I, staring about me. 'You don't?' said he. 'No, I'll be damned if I do,' said I, 'and what's more, I don't know what a gum-gum is,' said I. I really thought the man would have dropped. He drew me aside, and, with an expression of agony I shall never forget, said in a low whisper——"

"Dinner's on the table, ladies," interrupted the steward's wife.

"Will you allow me?" said the captain, immediately suiting the action to the word, and escorting Miss Julia Briggs to the cabin, with as much ease as if he had finished his story.

"What an extraordinary circumstance!" ejaculated the same old gentleman, preserving his listening attitude.

"What a traveler!" said the young ladies.

"What a singular name!" exclaimed the gentlemen, rather confused by the coolness of the whole affair.

"I wish he had finished the story," said an old lady. "I wonder what a gum-gum really is?"

"By Jove!" exclaimed Hardy, who until now had been lost in utter amazement, "I don't know what it may be in India, but in England I think a gum-gum has very much the same meaning as a humbug."

"How illiberal! how envious!" said every body, as they made for the cabin, fully impressed with a belief in the captain's amazing adventures. Helves was the sole lion for the remainder of the day—impudence and the marvelous are sure passports to any society.

The party had by this time reached their destination, and put about on their return home. The wind, which had been with them the whole day, was now directly in their teeth; the weather had become gradually more and more overcast; and the sky, water, and shore, were all of that dull, heavy, uniform lead-color, which house-painters daub in the first instance over a street-door which is gradually approaching a state of convalescence. It had been "spitting" with rain for the last half-hour, and now began to pour in good earnest. The wind was freshening very fast, and the waterman at the wheel had unequivocally expressed his opinion that there would shortly be a squall. A slight emotion on the part of the vessel now and then, seemed to suggest the possibility of its pitching to a very uncomfortable extent in the event of its blowing harder; and every timber began to creak as if the boat were an overladen clothes-basket. Sea-sickness, however, is like a belief in ghosts—every one entertains some misgivings on the subject, but few will acknowledge them. The majority of the company, therefore, endeavored to look peculiarly happy, feeling all the while especially miserable.

"Don't it rain?" inquired the old gentleman before noticed, when, by dint of squeezing and jamming, they were all seated at table.

"I think it does—a little," replied Mr. Percy Noakes, who could hardly hear himself speak, in consequence of the pattering on the deck.

"Don't it blow?" inquired some one else.

"No—I don't think it does," responded Hardy, sincerely wishing that he could persuade himself it did not, for he sat near the door, and was almost blown off his seat.

"It'll soon clear up," said Mr. Percy Noakes, in a cheerful tone.

"Oh, certainly!" ejaculated the committee generally.

"No doubt of it," said the remainder of the company, whose attention was now pretty well engrossed by the serious business of eating, carving, taking wine, and so forth.

The throbbing motion of the engine was but too perceptible. There was a large, substantial cold boiled leg of mutton at the bottom of the table, shaking like blanc-mange; a hearty sirloin of beef looked as if it had been suddenly seized with the palsy; and some tongues, which were placed on dishes rather too large for them, were going through the most surprising evolutions, darting from side to side, and from end to end, like a fly in an inverted wine-glass. Then the sweets shook and trembled till it was quite impossible to help them, and people gave up the attempt in despair; and the pigeon-pies looked as if the birds, whose legs were stuck outside, were trying to get them in. The table vibrated and started like a feverish pulse, and the very legs were slightly convulsed—every thing was shaking and jarring. The beams in the roof of the cabin seemed as if they were put there for the sole purpose of giving people headaches, and several elderly gentleman became ill-tempered in consequence. As fast as the steward put the fire-irons up, they would fall down again; and the more the ladies and gentlemen tried to sit comfortably on their seats, the more the seats seemed to slide away from the ladies and gentlemen. Several ominous demands were made for small glasses of brandy; the countenances of the company gradually underwent the most extraordinary changes; and one gentleman was observed suddenly to rush from the table without the slightest ostensible reason, and dart up the steps with incredible swiftness, thereby greatly damaging both himself and the steward, who happened to be coming down at the same moment.

The cloth was removed; the dessert was laid on the table, and the glasses were filled. The motion of the boat increased; several members of the party began to feel rather vague and misty, and looked as if they had only just got up. The young gentleman with the spectacles, who had been in a fluctuating state for some time—one moment bright, and another dismal, like a revolving light on the sea-coast—rashly announced his wish to propose a toast. After several ineffectual attempts to preserve his perpendicular, the young gentleman, having managed to hook himself to the centre leg of the table with his left hand, proceeded as follows:

"Ladies and gentlemen.—A gentleman is among us—I may say a stranger—(here some painful thought seemed to strike the orator; he paused, and looked extremely odd) whose talents, whose travels, whose cheerfulness—"

"I beg your pardon, Edkins," hastily interrupted Mr. Percy Noakes—"Hardy, what's the matter?"

"Nothing," replied the 'funny gentleman,' who had just life enough left to utter two consecutive syllables.

"Will you have some brandy?"

"No," replied Hardy, in a tone of great indignation, and looking about as comfortable as Temple-bar in a Scotch mist; "what should I want brandy for?"

"Will you go on deck?"

"No, I will not." This was said with a most determined

air, and in a voice which might have been taken for an imitation of any thing; it was quite as much like a guinea-pig as a bassoon.

"I beg your pardon, Edkins," said the courteous Percy; "I thought our friend was ill. Pray go on."

A pause.

"Pray go on."

"Mr. Edkins *is* gone," cried somebody.

"I beg your pardon, sir," said the steward, running up to Mr. Percy Noakes, "I beg your pardon, sir, but the gentleman as just went on deck—him with the green spectacles—is uncommon bad, to be sure; and the young man as played the wiolin says, that unless he has some brandy he can't answer for the consequences. He says he has a wife and two children, whose werry subsistence depends on his breaking a wessel, and that he expects to do so every moment. The flageolet's been very ill, but he's better, only he's in such a dreadful prusperation."

All disguise was now useless; the company staggered on deck, the gentlemen tried to see nothing but the clouds, and the ladies, muffled up in such shawls and cloaks as they had brought with them, laid about on the seats and under the seats, in the most wretched condition. Never was such a blowing, and raining, and pitching, and tossing, endured by any pleasure party before. Several remonstrances were sent down below on the subject of Master Fleetwood, but they were totally unheeded in consequence of the indisposition of his natural protectors. That interesting child screamed at the very top of his voice, until he had no voice left to scream with, and then Miss Wakefield began, and screamed for the remainder of the passage.

Mr. Hardy was observed some hours afterward in an attitude which induced his friends to suppose that he was busily engaged in contemplating the beauties of the deep; they only regretted that his taste for the picturesque should lead him to remain so long in a position, very injurious at all times, but especially so to an individual laboring under the tendency of blood to the head.

The party arrived off the Custom-house at about two o'clock on the Thursday morning—dispirited and worn out. The Tauntons were too ill to quarrel with the Briggses, and the

Steam Excursion.

Briggses were too wretched to annoy the Tauntons. One of the guitar-cases was lost on its passage to a hackney-coach, and Mrs. Briggs has not scrupled to state that the Tauntons bribed a porter to throw it down an area. Mr. Alexander Briggs opposes vote by ballot—he says from personal experience of its inefficacy; and Mr. Samnel Briggs, whenever he is asked to express his sentiments on the point, says that he has no opinion on that or any other subject.

Mr. Edkins—the young gentleman in the green spectacles—makes a speech on every occasion on which a speech can possibly be made, the eloquence of which can only be equaled by its length. In the event of his not being previously appointed to a judgeship, it is most probable that he will practice as a barrister in the New Central Criminal Court.

Captain Helves continued his attention to Miss Julia Briggs, whom he might possibly have espoused, if it had not unfortunately happened that Mr. Samuel arrested him in the way of business, pursuant to instructions received from Messrs. Scroggins and Payne, whose town debts the gallant captain had condescended to collect, but whose accounts, with the indiscretion so peculiar to military minds, he had omitted to keep with that dull accuracy which custom has rendered necessary. Mrs. Taunton complains that she has been much deceived in him. He introduced himself to the family on board a Gravesend steam-packet, and certainly, therefore, ought to have proved respectable.

Mr. Percy Noakes is as light-hearted and careless as ever. We have described him as a general favorite in his private circle, and trust he may find a kindly-disposed friend or two in public.

CHAPTER VIII.

THE GREAT WINGLEBURY DUEL.

THE little town of Great Winglebury is exactly forty-two miles and three quarters from Hyde Park corner. It has a long, straggling, quiet High-street, with a great black and white clock at a small red Town-hall, half-way up—a market-place—a cage—an assembly-room—a church—a bridge—a chapel—a theatre—a library—an inn—a pump—and a Post-office. Tradition tells of a "Little Winglebury" down some cross-road about two miles off; and as a square mass of dirty paper, supposed to have been originally intended for a letter, with certain tremulous characters inscribed thereon, in which a lively imagination might trace a remote resemblance to the word "Little," was once stuck up to be owned in the sunny window of the Great Winglebury Post-office, from which it only disappeared when it fell to pieces with dust and extreme old age, there would appear to be some foundation for the legend. Common belief is inclined to bestow the name upon a little hole at the end of a muddy lane about a couple of miles long, colonized by one wheelwright, four paupers, and a beer-shop; but even this authority, slight as it is, must be regadred with extreme suspicion, inasmuch as the inhabitants of the hole aforesaid concur in opining that it never had any name at all, from the earliest ages down to the present day.

The Winglebury Arms in the centre of the High-street, opposite the small building with the big clock, is the principal inn of Great Winglebury—the commercial inn, posting-house, and excise office; the "Blue" house at every election, and the Judges' house at every assizes. It is the head-quarters of the Gentlemen's Whist Club of Winglebury Blues (so called in opposition to the Gentlemen's Whist Club of Winglebury Buffs, held at the other house, a little further down); and whenever a juggler, or wax-work man, or concert-giver, takes Great

Winglebury in his circuit, it is immediately placarded all over the town that Mr. So-and-so, "trusting to that liberal support which the inhabitants of Great Winglebury have long been so liberal in bestowing, has at a great expense engaged the elegant and commodious assembly-rooms, attached to the Winglebury Arms." The house is a large one, with a red brick and stone front; a pretty spacious hall ornamented with evergreen plants, terminates in a perspective view of the bar, and a glass-case, in which are displayed a choice variety of delicacies ready for dressing, to catch the eye of a new-comer the moment he enters, and excite his appetite to the highest possible pitch. Opposite doors lead to the "coffee" and "commercial" rooms; and a great wide, rambling staircase,—three stairs and a landing—four stairs and another landing—one step and another landing—half a dozen stairs and another landing—and so on—conducts to galleries of bed-rooms, and labyrinths of sitting-rooms, denominated "private," where you may enjoy yourself as privately as you can in any place where some bewildered being or other walks into your room every five minutes by mistake, and then walks out again, to open all the doors along the gallery till he finds his own.

Such is the Winglebury Arms at this day, and such was the Winglebury Arms sometime since—no matter when—two or three minutes before the arrival of the London stage. Four horses with cloths on—change for a coach—were standing quietly at the corner of the yard, surrounded by a listless group of post-boys in shiny hats and smock-frocks, engaged in discussing the merits of the cattle; half a dozen ragged boys were standing a little apart, listening with evident interest to the conversation of these worthies; and a few loungers were collected round the horse-trough, awaiting the arrival of the coach.

The day was hot and sunny, the town in the zenith of its dullness, and with the exception of these few idlers, not a living creature was to be seen. Suddenly the loud notes of a key-bugle broke the monotonous stillness of the street; in came the coach, rattling over the uneven paving with a noise startling enough to stop even the large-faced clock itself. Down got the outsides, up went the windows in all directions; out came the waiters, up started the ostlers, and the loungers, and the post-boys, and the ragged boys, as if they were electrified—unstrapping, and unchaining, and unbuckling, and dragging willing horses out, and forcing reluctant horses in, and making a most exhilarating bustle. "Lady inside, here," said the guard. "Please to alight, ma'am," said the waiter. "Private sitting-room?" interrogated the lady.—"Certainly, ma'am," responded the chambermaid. "Nothing but these 'ere trunks, ma'am?" inquired the guard. "Nothing more," replied the lady. Up got the outsides again, and the guard, and the coachman; off came the cloths, with a jerk—"All right," was the cry; and away they went. The loungers lingered a minute or two in the road, watching the coach till it turned the corner, and then loitered away one by one. The street was clear again, and the town, by contrast, quieter than ever.

"Lady in number twenty-five," screamed the landlady.—"Thomas!"

"Yes, ma'am."

"Letter just been left for the gentleman in number nineteen.—Boots at the Lion left it.—No answer."

"Letter for you sir," said Thomas, depositing the letter on number nineteen's table.

"For me?" said number nineteen, turning from the window, out of which he had been surveying the scene we have just described.

"Yes, sir,—(waiters always speak in hints, and never utter complete sentences)—yes, sir,—Boots at the Lion, sir—Bar, sir—Misses said number nineteen, sir—Alexander Trott, Esq., sir?—Your card at the bar, sir, I think, sir?"

"My name *is* Trott," replied number nineteen, breaking the seal. "You may go, waiter." The waiter pulled down the window-blind, and then pulled it up again—for a regular waiter must do something before he leaves the room—adjusted the glasses on the sideboard, brushed a place that was *not* dusty, rubbed his hands very hard, walked stealthily to the door, and evaporated.

There was evidently something in the contents of the letter of a nature, if not wholly unexpected, certainly extremely disagreeable. Mr. Alexander Trott laid it down and took it up again, and walked about the room on particular squares of the carpet, and even attempted, though very unsuccessfully, to whistle an air. It wouldn't do. He threw himself into a chair and read the following epistle aloud:

"*Blue Lion and Stomach-warmer,*
"*Great Winglebury.*

Wednesday Morning.

"Sir,

"Immediately on discovering your intentions, I left our counting-house and followed you. I know the purport of your journey;—that journey shall never be completed.

"I have no friend here just now, on whose secrecy I can rely. This shall be no obstacle to my revenge. Neither shall Emily Brown be exposed to the mercenary solicitations of a scoundrel, odious in her eyes, and contemptible in every body else's: nor will I tamely submit to the clandestine attacks of a base umbrella-maker.

"Sir,—from Great Winglebury Church, a footpath leads through four meadows to a retired spot known to the townspeople as Stiffun's Acre (Mr. Trott shuddered). I shall be waiting there alone at twenty minutes before six o'clock to-morrow morning. Should I be disappointed of seeing you there, I will do myself the pleasure of calling with a horse whip.

"HORACE HUNTER.

"PS. There is a gunsmith's in the High-street; and they won't sell gunpowder after dark—you understand me.

"PPS. You had better not order your breakfast in the morning till you have seen me. It may be an unnecessary expense."

"Desperate-minded villain! I knew how it would be!" ejaculated the terrified Trott. "I always told father, that once start me on this expedition, and Hunter would pursue me like the wandering Jew. It's bad enough as it is, to marry with the old people's commands, and without the girl's consent; but what will Emily think of me, if I go down there, breathless with running away from this infernal salamander? What *shall* I do. What *can* I do? If I go back to the city I'm disgraced for ever—lose the girl, and what's more, lose the money too. Even if I did go on to the Browns' by the coach, Hunter would be after me in a post-chaise; and if I go to this place, this Stiffun's Acre, (another shudder,) I'm as good as dead. I've seen him hit the man at the Pall-mall shooting gallery, in the second button-hole of the waistcoat five times out of every six, and when he didn't hit him there, he hit him in the head." And with this consolatory reminiscence, Mr. Alexander Trott again ejaculated, "What shall I do?"

Long and weary were his reflections as, burying his face in his hands, he sat ruminating on the best course to be pursued. His mental direction-post pointed to London. He thought of "the governor's" anger, and the lost of the fortune which the paternal Brown had promised the paternal Trott his daughter should contribute to the coffers of his son. Then the words "To Brown's" were legibly inscribed on the said direction-post, but Horace Hunter's denunciation rung in his ears;—last of all it bore, in red letters, the words, "To Stiffun's Acre;" and then Mr. Alexander Trott decided on adopting a plan which he presently matured.

First and foremost he dispatched the under-boots to the Blue Lion and Stomach-warmer, with a gentlemanly note to Mr. Horace Hunter, intimating that he thirsted foi his destruction and would do himself the pleasure of slaughtering him next morning without fail. He then wrote another letter, and requested the attendance of the other boots—for they kept a pair. A modest knock at the room-door was heard—"Come in," said Mr. Trott. A man thrust in a red head with one eye in it, and being again desired to "come in," brought in the body and legs to which the head belonged, and a fur cap which belonged to the head.

"You are the upper-boots, I think?" inquired Mr. Trott.

"Yes, I am the upper-boots," replied a voice from inside a velveteen case with mother-of-pearl buttons—"that is, I'm the boots as b'longs to the house; the other man's my man, as goes errands and does odd jobs—top-boots and half-boots I calls us."

"You're from London?" inquired Mr. Trott.

"Driv a cab once," was the laconic reply.

"Why don't you drive it now?" asked Mr. Trott.

"Cos I over-driv the cab, and driv over a 'ooman," replied the top-boots, with brevity.

"Do you know the mayor's house?" inquired Trott.

"Rather," replied the boots, significantly, as if he had some good reason to remember it.

"Do you think you could manage to leave a letter there?" interrogated Trott.

"Shouldn't wonder," responded boots.

"But this letter," said Trott, holding a deformed note with a paralytic direction in one hand, and five shillings in the other—"this letter is anonymous."

"A—what?" interrupted the boots.

"Anonymous—he's not to know who it comes from."

"Oh! I see," responded the rig'lar, with a knowing wink, but without evincing the slightest disinclination to undertake the charge—"I see—bit o' sving, eh?" and his one eye wandered round the room as if in quest of a dark lantern and phosphorous-box. "But I say," he continued, recalling the eye from its search, and bringing it to bear on Mr. Trott—"I say, he's a lawyer, our mayor, and insured in the County. If you've a spite agen him, you'd better not burn his house down—blessed if I don't think it would be the greatest favor you could do him." And he chuckled inwardly.

If Mr. Alexander Trott had been in any other situation, his first act would have been to kick the man down stairs by deputy; or, in other words, to ring the bell, and desire the landlord to take his boots off. He contented himself, however, with doubling the fee and explaining that the letter merely related to a breach of the peace. The top-boots retired, solemnly pledged to secrecy; and Mr. Alexander Trott sat down to a fried sole, maintenon cutlet, Madeira, and sundries, with much greater composure than he had experienced since the receipt of Horace Hunter's letter of defiance.

The lady who alighted from the London coach had no sooner been installed in number twenty-five, and made some alteration in her traveling-dress, than she indited a note to Joseph Overton, Esquire, solicitor, and mayor of Great Winglebury, requesting his immediate attendance on private business of paramount importance—a summons which that worthy functionary lost no time in obeying; for after sundry openings of his eyes, divers ejaculations of "Bless me!" and other manifestations of surprise, he took his broad-brimmed hat from its accustomed peg in his little front office, and walked briskly down the High-street to the Winglebury Arms; through the hall and up the staircase of which establishment he was ushered by the landlady, and a crowd of officious waiters, to the door of number-twenty-five.

"Show the gentleman in," said the stranger lady, in reply to the foremost waiter's announcement. The gentleman was shown in accordingly.

The lady rose from the sofa; the mayor advanced a step from the door, and there they both paused for a minute or two, looking at one another as if by mutual consent. The mayor saw before him a buxom, richly-dressed female of about forty; and the lady looked upon a sleek man about ten years older, in drab shorts and continuations, black coat, neckcloth, and gloves.

"Miss Julia Manners!" exclaimed the mayor at length, "you astonish me."

"That's very unfair of you, Overton," replied Miss Julia, "for I have known you long enough not to be surprised at any thing you do, and you might extend equal courtesy to me."

"But to run away—actually run away—with a young man!" remonstrated the mayor.

"You would not have me actually run away with an old one, I presume," was the cool rejoinder.

"And then to ask me—me—of all people in the world, a man of my age and appearance—mayor of the town—to promote such a scheme!" pettishly ejaculated Joseph Overton; throwing himself into an arm chair, and producing Miss Julia's letter from his pocket, as if to corroborate the assertion that he had been asked.

"Now, Overton," replied the lady, impatiently, "I want your assistance in this matter, and I must have it. In the life-time of that poor old dear, Mr. Cornberry, who—who—"

"Who was to have married you, and didn't, because he died first; and who left you his property unincumbered with the addition of himself," suggested the mayor, in a sarcastic tone.

"Well," replied Miss Julia, reddening slightly, "in the lifetime of the poor old dear, the property had the incumbrance of your management; and all I will say of that is, that I only wonder *it* didn't die of consumption instead of its master. You helped yourself then;—help me now."

Mr. Joseph Overton was a man of the world, and an attorney; and as certain indistinct recollections of an odd thousand pounds or two, appropriated by mistake, passed across his mind, he hemmed deprecatingly, smiled blandly, remained silent for a few seconds; and finally inquired, "What do you wish me to do?"

"I'll tell you," replied Miss Julia—"I'll tell you in three words. Dear Lord Peter—"

"That's the young man, I suppose," interrupted the mayor.

"That's the young nobleman," replied the lady, with a great stress on the last word. "Dear Lord Peter is considerably afraid of the resentment of his family; and we have therefore thought it better to make the match a stolen one. He left town to avoid suspicion, on a visit to his friend, the Honorable Augustus Flair, whose seat, as you know, is about thirty miles from this, accompanied only by his favorite "tiger." We arranged that I should come here alone in the London coach; and that he, leaving his "tiger" and cab behind him, should come on, and arrive here as soon as possible this afternoon."

"Very well," observed Joseph Overton, "and then he can order the chaise, and you can go on to Gretna Green together, without requiring the presence or interference of a third party, can't you?"

"No," replied Miss Julia. "We have every reason to believe—dear Lord Peter not being considered very prudent or sagacious by his friends, and they having discovered his attachment to me—that immediately on his absence being observed, pursuit will be made in this direction: to elude which, and to prevent our being traced, I wish it to be understood in this house that dear Lord Peter is slightly deranged, though perfectly harmless; and that I am, unknown to him, awaiting his arrival to convey him in a post-chaise to a private asylum—at Berwick, say. If I don't show myself much, I dare say I can manage to pass for his mother."

The thought occurred to the mayor's mind that the lady might show herself a good deal without fear of detection; seeing that she was about double the age of her intended husband. He said nothing, however, and the lady proceeded—

"With the whole of this arrangement, dear Lord Peter is acquainted: and all I want you to do is, to make the delusion more complete by giving it the sanction of your influence in this place, and assigning this as a reason to the people of the house for my taking the young gentleman away. As it would not be consistent with the story that I should see him until after he has entered the chaise, I also wish you to communicate with him, and inform him that it is all going on well."

"Has he arrived?" inquired Overton.

"I don't know," replied the lady.

"Then how am I to know?" inquired the mayor. "Of course he will not give his own name at the bar."

"I begged him, immediately on his arrival, to write you a note," replied Miss Manners; "and to prevent the possibility of our project being discovered through its means, I desired him to write anonymously, and in mysterious terms to acquaint you with the number of his room."

"God bless me!" exclaimed the mayor, rising from his seat, and searching his pockets—"most extraordinary circumstance—he *has* arrived—mysterious note left at my house in a most mysterious manner, just before yours—didn't know what to make of it before, and certainly shouldn't have attended to it. Oh! here it is." And Joseph Overton pulled out of an inner coat-pocket the identical letter penned by Alexander Trott. "Is this his lordship's hand?"

"Oh yes," replied Julia; "good, punctual creature! I have not seen it more than once or twice, but I know he writes very badly and very large. These dear, wild young noblemen, you know, Overton—"

"Ay, ay, I see," replied the mayor.—"Horses and dogs. play and wine—grooms, actresses, and cigars,—the stable, the green-room, the brothel, and the tavern; and the legislative assembly at last."

"Here's what he says," pursued the mayor; "'Sir,—A young gentleman in number nineteen at the Winglebury Arms, is bent on committing a rash act to-morrow morning at an early hour. (That's good—he means marrying.) If you have any regard for the peace of this town, or the preservation of one—it may be two—human lives'—What the deuce does he mean by that?"

"That he's so anxious for the ceremony, he will expire if it's put off, and that I may possibly do the same," replied the lady with great complacency.

"Oh! I see—not much fear of that;—well—'two human lives, you will cause him to be removed to-night.—(He wants to start at once.) Fear not to do this on your responsibility; for to-morrow, the absolute necessity of the proceeding will be but too apparent. Remember: number nineteen. The name is Trott. No delay; for life and death depend upon your promptitude.'—Passionate language, certainly. Shall I see him?"

"Do," replied Miss Julia; "and entreat him to act his part well. I am half afraid of him. Tell him to be cautious."

"I will," said the mayor.

"Settle all the arrangements."

"I will," said the mayor again.

"And say I think the chaise had better be ordered for one o'clock."

"Very well," cried the mayor once more; and ruminating on the absurdity of the situation in which fate and old acquaintance had placed him, he desired a waiter to herald his approach to the temporary representative of number nineteen.

The announcement—"Gentleman to speak with you, sir," induced Mr. Trott to pause half-way in the glass of port, the contents of which he was in the act of imbibing at the moment; to rise from his chair, and retreat a few paces toward the window, as if to secure a retreat in the event of the visitor assuming the form and appearance of Horace Hunter. One glance at Joseph Overton, however, quieted his apprehensions. He courteously motioned the stranger to a seat. The waiter, after a little jingling with the decanter and glasses, consented to leave the room; and Joseph Overton placing the broad-brimmed hat on the chair next to him, and bending his body gently forward, opened the business by saying in a very low and cautious tone,

"My lord—"

"Eh?" said Mr. Alexander Trott in a very loud key, with the vacant and mystified stare of a chilly somnambulist.

"Hush—hush!" said the cautious attorney: "to be sure—quite right—no titles here—my name is Overton, sir."

"Overton!"

"Yes: the mayor of this place—you sent me a letter with anonymous information, this afternoon."

"I, sir?" exclaimed Trott with ill-dissembled surprise; for, coward as he was, he would willingly have repudiated the authorship of the letter in question. "I, sir?"

"Yes, you, sir; did you not?" responded Overton, annoyed with what he supposed to be an extreme degree of unnecessary suspicion. "Either this letter is yours, or it is not. If it be, we can converse securely upon the subject at once. If it be not, of course I have no more to say."

"Stay, stay," said Trott, "it *is* mine; I *did* write it. What could I do, sir? I had no friend here."

"To be sure—to be sure," said the mayor, encouragingly, "you could not have managed it better. Well, sir; it will be necessary for you to leave here to-night in a post-chaise and four. And the harder the boys drive the better. You are not safe from pursuit here."

"Bless me!" exclaimed Trott, in an agony of apprehension, "can such things happen in a country like this? Such unrelenting and cold-blooded hostility!" He wiped off the concentrated essence of cowardice that was oozing fast down his forehead, and looked aghast at Joseph Overton.

"It certainly is a very hard case," replied the mayor with a smile, "that, in a free country, people can't marry whom they like without being hunted down as if they were criminals. However, in the present instance, the lady is willing, you know, and that's the main point, after all."

"Lady willing!" repeated Trott, mechanically—"How do you know the lady's willing?"

"Come, that's a good one," said the mayor, benevolently tapping Mr. Trott on the arm with his broad-brimmed hat, "I have known her well for a long time, and if any body could entertain the remotest doubt on the subject, I assure you I have none, nor need you."

"Dear me!" said Mr. Trott, ruminating—"Dear me!—this is very extraordinary!"

"Well, Lord Peter," said the mayor, rising.

"Lord Peter!" repeated Mr. Trott.

"Oh—ah, I forgot; well, Mr. Trott, then—Trott—very good, ha! ha!—Well, sir, the chaise shall be ready at half-past twelve."

"And what is to become of me till then?" inquired Mr. Trott, anxiously. "Wouldn't it save appearances if I were placed under some restraint?"

"Ah!" replied Overton, "very good thought—capital idea indeed. I'll send somebody up directly. And if you make a little resistance when we put you in the chaise it wouldn't be amiss—look as if you didn't want to be taken away, you know."

"To be sure," said Trott—"to be sure."

"Well, my lord," said Overton, in a low tone, "till then I wish your lordship a good-evening."

"Lord—lordship!" ejaculated Trott again, falling back a step or two, and gazing in unutterable wonder on the countenance of the mayor.

"Ha-ha! I see, my lord—practicing the madman?—very good indeed—very vacant look—capital, my lord, capital—good-evening, Mr.—Trott—ha! ha! ha!"

"That mayor's decidedly drunk," soliloquized Mr. Trott, throwing himself back in his chair, in an attitude of reflection.

"He is a much cleverer fellow than I thought him, that young nobleman—he carries it off uncommonly well," thought Overton, as he wended his way to the bar, there to complete his arrangements. This was soon done: every word of the story was implicitly believed, and the one-eyed boots was immediately instructed to repair to number nineteen, to act as custodian of the person of the supposed lunatic until half-past twelve o'clock. In pursuance of this direction, that somewhat eccentric gentleman armed himself with a walking-stick of gigantic dimensions, and repaired with his usual equanimity of manner to Mr. Trott's apartment, which he entered without any ceremony, and mounted guard in, by quietly depositing himself upon a chair near the door, where he proceeded to beguile the time by whistling a popular air with great apparent satisfaction.

"What do you want here, you scoundrel?" exclaimed Mr. Alexander Trott, with a proper appearance of indignation at his detention.

The boots beat time with his head, as he looked gently round at Mr. Trott with a smile of pity, and whistled an *adagio* movement.

"Do you attend in this room by Mr. Overton's desire?" inquired Trott, rather astonished at the man's demeanor.

"Keep yourself to yourself, young feller," calmly responded the boots, "and don't say nothin' to nobody." And he whistled again.

"Now mind," ejaculated Mr. Trott, anxious to keep up the farce of wishing with great earnestness to fight a duel if they'd let him,—"I protest against being kept here. I deny that I have any intention of fighting with any body. But as it's useless contending with superior numbers, I shall sit quietly down."

"You'd better," observed the placid boots, shaking the large stick expressively.

"Under protest, however," added Alexander Trott, seating himself with indignation in his face but great content in his heart. "Under protest."

"Oh, certainly!" responded the boots;" any thing you please. If you're happy, I'm transported; only don't talk too much—it'll make you worse."

"Make me worse!" exclaimed Trott, in unfeigned astonishment: "the man's drunk!"

"You'd better be quiet, young feller," remarked the boots, going through a most threatening piece of pantomime with the stick.

"Or mad!" said Mr. Trott, rather alarmed. "Leave the room, sir, and tell them to send somebody else."

"Won't do!" replied the boots.

"Leave the room!" shouted Trott, ringing the bell violently; for he began to be alarmed on a new score.

"Leave that 'ere bell alone, you wretched loo-natic!" said the boots, suddenly forcing the unfortunate Trott back into his chair, and brandishing the stick aloft. "Be quiet, you mis-'rable object, and don't let every body know there's a madman in the house."

"He *is* a madman! He *is* a madman!" exclaimed the terrified Mr. Trott, gazing on the one eye of the red-headed boots with a look of abject horror.

"Madman!" replied the boots—"dam'me, I think he *is* a madman with a vengeance! Listen to me, you unfort'nate. Ah! would you?—[a slight tap on the head with the large stick, as Mr. Trott made another move toward the bell-handle] I caught you there! did I?"

"Spare my life!" exclaimed Trott, raising his hands imploringly.

"I don't want your life," replied the boots, disdainfully, "though I think it 'ud be a charity if somebody took it."

"No, no, it wouldn't," interrupted poor Mr. Trott, hurriedly; "no no, it wouldn't! I—I—'d rather keep it!"

"O werry well," said the boots; "that's a mere matter of taste—ev'ry one to his liking. Hows'ever, all I've got to say is this here: You sit quietly down in that chair, and I'll sit hoppersite you here, and if you keep quiet and don't stir, I won't damage you; but if you move hand or foot till half-past twelve o'clock, I shall alter the expression of your countenance so completely, that the next time you look in the glass you'll ask vether you're gone out of town, and ven you're likely to come back again. So sit down."

"I will—I will," responded the victim of mistakes; and down sat Mr. Trott and down sat the boots too, exactly opposite him, with the stick ready for immediate action in case of emergency.

Long and dreary were the hours that followed. The bell of Great Winglebury church had just struck ten, and two hours and a half would probably elapse before succor arrived. For half an hour the noise occasioned by shutting up the shops in the street beneath betokened something like life in the town, and rendered Mr. Trott's situation a little less insupportable; but when even these ceased, and nothing was heard beyond the occasional rattling of a post-chaise as it drove up the yard to change horses, and then drove away again, or the clattering of horses' hoofs in the stables behind, it became almost unbearable. The boots occasionally moved an inch or two, to knock superfluous bits of wax off the candles, which were burning low, but instantaneously resumed his former position; and as he remembered to have heard somewhere or other that the human eye had an unfailing effect in controlling mad people, he kept his solitary organ of vision constantly fixed on Mr. Alexander Trott. That unfortunate individual stared at his companion in his turn, until his features grew more and more indistinct—his hair gradually less red—and the room more misty and obscure. Mr. Alexander Trott fell into a sound sleep, from which he was awakened by a rumbling in the street, and a cry of—"Chaise-and-four for number twenty-five!" A bustle on the stairs succeeded; the room-door was hastily thrown open; and Mr. Joseph Overton entered, followed by four stout waiters, and Mrs. Williamson, the stout landlady of the Winglebury Arms.

"Mr. Overton!" exclaimed Mr. Alexander Trott, jumping up in a frenzy of passionate excitement—"Look at this man, sir; consider the situation in which I have been placed for three hours past—the person you sent to guard me, sir, was a madman—a madman—a raging, ravaging, furious madman."

"Bravo!" whispered Overton.

"Poor dear!" said the compassionate Mrs. Williamson, "mad people always think other people's mad."

"Poor dear!" ejaculated Mr. Alexander Trott. "What the devil do you mean by poor dear! are you the landlady of this house?"

"Yes, yes," replied the stout old lady, "don't exert yourself, there's a dear—consider your health, now; do."

"Exert myself!" shouted Mr. Alexander Trott, it's a mercy, ma'am, that I have any breath to exert myself with, I might have been assassinated three hours ago by that one-eyed monster with the oakum head. How dare you have a madman, ma'am—how dare you have a madman, to assault and terrify the visitors to your house?"

"I'll never have another," said Mrs. Williamson, casting a look of reproach at the mayor.

"Capital—capital," whispered Overton again, as he enveloped Mr. Alexander Trott in a thick traveling-cloak.

"Capital, sir!" exclaimed Trott, aloud, "it's horrible. The very recollection makes me shudder. I'd rather fight four duels in three hours, if I survived the first three, than I'd sit for that time face to face with a madman."

"Keep it up as you go down stairs," whispered Overton; "your bill is paid, and your portmanteau in the chaise." And then he added aloud, "Now, waiters, the gentleman's ready."

At this signal, the waiters crowded round Mr. Alexander Trott. One took one arm, another the other, a third walked before with a candle, the fourth behind with another candle; the boots and Mrs. Williamson brought up the rear, and down stairs they went, Mr. Alexander Trott expressing alternately at the very top of his voice, either his feigned reluctance to go, or his unfeigned indignation at being shut up with a madman.

Mr. Overton was waiting at the chaise-door, the boys were ready mounted, and a few ostlers and stable nondescripts were standing round to witness the departure of "the mad gentleman." Mr. Alexander Trott's foot was on the step, when he observed (which the dim light had prevented his doing before) a human figure seated in the chaise, closely muffled up in a cloak like his own.

"Who's that?" he inquired of Overton, in a whisper.

"Hush, hush," replied the mayor; "the other party, of course."

"The other party!" exclaimed Trott, with an effort to retreat.

"Yes, yes; you'll soon find out, before you go far, I should think—but make a noise, you'll excite suspicion if you whisper to me so much."

"I won't go in this chaise," shouted Mr. Alexander Trott, all his original fears recurring with tenfold violence. "I shall be assassinated—I shall be—"

"Bravo, bravo," whispered Overton. "I'll push you in.

"But I won't go," exclaimed Mr. Trott. "Help here, help! they're carrying me away against my will. This is a plot to murder me.'

"Poor dear!" said Mrs. Williamson again.

"Now, boys, put 'em along," cried the mayor, pushing Trott in and slamming the door. "Off with you as quick as you can, and stop for nothing till you come to the next stage—all right."

"Horses are paid, Tom," screamed Mrs. Williamson, and away went the chaise at the rate of fourteen miles per hour, with Mr. Alexander Trott and Miss Julia Manners carefully shut up in the inside.

Mr. Alexander Trott remained coiled up in one corner of the chaise, and his mysterious companion in the other, for the first two or three miles; Mr. Trott edging more and more into his corner as he felt his companion gradually edging more and more from hers; and vainly endeavoring in the darkness to catch a glimpse of the furious face of the supposed Horace Hunter.

"We may speak now," said his fellow-traveler, at length; "the post-boys can neither see nor hear us."

"That's not Hunter's voice!"—thought Alexander, astonished.

"Dear Lord Peter!" said Miss Julia, most winningly; putting her arm on Mr. Trott's shoulder—"Dear Lord Peter. Not a word?"

"Why, it's a woman!" exclaimed Mr. Trott, in a low tone of excessive wonder.

"Ah—whose voice is that?" said Julia—"'tis not Lord Peter's."

"No,—it's mine," replied Mr. Trott.

"Yours!" ejaculated Miss Julia Manners. "A strange man! Gracious Heaven—how came you here?"

"Whoever you are, you might have known that I came against my will, ma'am," replied Alexander, "for I made noise enough when I got in."

"Do you come from Lord Peter?" inquired Miss Manners.

"Damn Lord Peter," replied Trott, pettishly—"I don't know any Lord Peter—I never heard of him before to-night, when I've been Lord Peter'd by one and Lord Peter'd by another, till I verily believe I'm mad, or dreaming—"

"Whither are we going?" inquired the lady, tragically.

"How should *I* know, ma'am?" replied Trott, with singular

coolness; for the events of the evening had completely hardened him.

"Stop! stop!" cried the lady, letting down the front glasses of the chaise.

"Stay, my dear ma'am!" said Mr. Trott, pulling the glasses up again with one hand, and gently squeezing Miss Julia's waist with the other. "There is some mistake here; give me till the end of this stage to explain my share of it. We must go so far; you can not be set down here alone, at this hour of the night."

The lady consented; the mistake was mutually explained. Mr. Trott was a young man, had highly promising whiskers, an undeniable tailor, and an insinuating address—he wanted nothing but valor, and who wants that with three thousand a-year? The lady had this, and more; she wanted a young husband, and the only course open to Mr. Trott to retrieve his disgrace was a rich wife. So they came to the conclusion that it would be a pity to have all this trouble and expense for nothing, and that, as they were so far on the road already, they had better go to Gretna Green, and marry each other; and they did so. And the very next preceding entry in the Blacksmith's book, was an entry of the marriage of Emily Brown with Horace Hunter. Mr. Hunter took his wife home, and begged pardon, and *was* pardoned; and Mr. Trott took *his* wife home, begged pardon too, and was pardoned also. And Lord Peter, who had been detained beyond his time by drinking champagne and riding a steeple-chase, went back to the Honorable Augustus Flair's, and drank more champagne, and rode another steeple-chase, and was thrown and killed. And Horace Hunter took great credit to himself for practicing on the cowardice of Alexander Trott; and all these circumstances were discovered in time, and carefully noted down; and if ever you stop a week at the Winglebury arms, they'll give you just this account of The Great Winglebury Duel.

CHAPTER IX.

MRS. JOSEPH PORTER.

Most extensive were the preparations at Rose Villa, Clapham Rise, in the occupation of Mr. Gattleton (a stockbroker in especially comfortable circumstances), and great was the anxiety of Mr. Gattleton's interesting family, as the day fixed for the representation of the Private Play, which had been "many months in preparation," approached. The whole family was infected with the mania for Private Theatricals; the house, usually so clean and tidy, was, to use Mr. Gattleton's expressive description, "regularly turned out o' windows;" the large dining-room, dismantled of its furniture and ornaments, presented a strange jumble of flats, fly-wings, lamps, bridges, clouds, thunder and lightning, festoons and flowers, daggers and foil, and all the other messes which in theatrical slang are included under the comprehensive name of "properties." The bed-rooms were crowded with scenery, the kitchen was occupied by carpenters. Rehearsals took place every other night in the drawing-room, and every sofa in the house was more or less damaged by the perseverance and spirit with which Mr. Sempronius Gattleton and Miss Lucina rehearsed the smothering scene in "Othello"—it having been determined that that tragedy should form the first portion of the evening's entertainments.

"When we're a *leetle* more perfect, I think it will go off admirably," said Mr. Sempronius, addressing his *corps dramatique*, at the conclusion of the hundred and fiftieth rehearsal. In consideration of his sustaining the trifling inconvenience of bearing all the expenses of the play, Mr. Sempronius had been, in the most handsome manner, unanimously elected stage-manager "Evans," continued Mr. Gattleton, jun., addressing a tall, thin, pale young gentleman, with extensive whiskers—"Evans, upon my word, you play *Roderigo* beautifully."

"Beautifully!" echoed the three Miss Gattletons; for Mr. Evans was pronounced by all his lady friends to be "quite a dear." He looked so interesting, and had such lovely whiskers, to say nothing of his talent for writing verses in albums and playing the flute! The interesting *Roderigo* simpered and bowed.

"But I think," added the manager, "you are hardly perfect in the—fall—in the fencing-scene, where you are—you understand?"

"It's very difficult," said Mr. Evans, thoughtfully; "I've fallen about a good deal in our counting-house lately, for practice, only I find it hurts one so. Being obliged to fall backward, you see, it bruises one's head a good deal."

But you must take care you don't knock a wing down," said Mr. Gattleton, sen., who had been appointed prompter, and who took as much interest in the play as the youngest of the company. "The stage is very narrow, you know."

"Oh! don't be afraid," said Mr. Evans, with a very self-satisfied air: "I shall fall with my head 'off,' and then I can't do any harm."

"But, egad!" said the manager, rubbing his hands, "we shall make a decided hit in 'Masaniello.' Harleigh sings that music admirably."

Every body echoed the sentiment. Mr. Harleigh smiled, and looked foolish—not an unusual thing with him—hummed "Behold how brightly breaks the morning," and blushed as red as the fisherman's nightcap he was trying on.

"Let's see," resumed the manager, telling the number on his fingers, "we shall have three dancing female peasants, besides *Fenella*, and four fishermen. Then there's our man Tom, he can have a pair of ducks of mine, and a check shirt of Bob's, and a red nightcap, and he'll do for another—that's five. In the choruses, of course, we can sing at the sides, and in the market-scene, we can walk about in cloaks and things. When the revolt takes place, Tom must keep rushing in on one side and out on the other, with a pickaxe, as fast as he can. The effect will be electrical; 'twill look exactly as if there were a great number of 'em; and in the eruption scene, we must burn the red fire, and upset the tea-trays, and halloo, and make all sorts of noises—and it's sure to do."

"Sure! sure!" cried all the performers *unâ voce*—and away hurried Mr. Sempronius Gattleton to wash the burnt cork off his face, and superintend the "setting up" of some of the amateur-painted and never-sufficiently-to-be-admired scenery.

Mrs. Gattleton was a kind, good-tempered, vulgar soul, exceedingly fond of her husband and children, and entertaining only three dislikes. In the first place, she had a natural antipathy to any body else's unmarried daughters; and in the second, she was in bodily fear of any thing in the shape of ridicule; and, lastly—almost a necessary consequence of this feeling—she regarded with feelings of the utmost horror one Mrs. Joseph Porter, over the way. However, the good folks of Clapham and its vicinity stood very much in awe of scandal and sarcasm; and thus Mrs. Joseph Porter was courted, and flattered, and caressed, and invited, for very much the same reason that a poor author, without a farthing in his pocket, behaves with the most extraordinary civility to a twopenny-postman.

"Never mind, ma," said Miss Emma Porter, in colloquy with her respected relative, and trying to look unconcerned; "if they had invited me, you know that neither you nor pa would have allowed me to take part in such an exhibition."

"Just what I should have thought from your high sense of propriety," returned the mother. "I am glad to see, Emma, you know how to designate the proceeding." Miss P., by-the-by, had only the week before made "an exhibition" of herself, for four days, behind a counter at a fancy fair, to all and every of her Majesty's liege subjects who were disposed to pay a shilling each for the privilege of seeing some four dozen girls flirting with strangers, and playing at shop.

"There!" said Mrs. Porter, looking out of window; "there are two rounds of beef and a ham going in, clearly for sandwiches; and Thomas, the pastrycook, says there have been twelve dozen tarts ordered, besides blancmange and jellies. Upon my word! think of the Miss Gattletons in fancy dresses, too!"

"Oh, it's too ridiculous!" said Miss Porter, with a sort of hysterical chuckle.

"I'll manage to put them a little out of conceit with the business, however," said Mrs. Porter; and out she went on her charitable errand.

"Well, my dear Mrs. Gattleton," said Mrs. Joseph Porter—after they had been closeted for some time, and when, by dint of indefatigable pumping, she had managed to extract all the news about the play,—"well, my dear, people may say what they please; indeed we know they will, for some folks are *so* ill-natured. Ah, my dear Miss Lucina, how d'ye do?—I was just telling your mamma that I have heard it said, that——'

"What?"

"Mrs. Porter is alluding to the play, my dear," said Mrs. Gattleton; "she was, I am sorry to say, just informing me that——"

"Oh, now, pray don't mention it," interrupted Mrs. Porter; "it's most absurd—quite as absurd as young What's-his-name saying he wondered how Miss Caroline, with such a foot and ankle, could have the vanity to play *Fenella.*"

"Highly impertinent, whoever said it," said Mrs. Gattleton, bridling up.

"Certainly, my dear," chimed in the delighted Mrs. Porter; "most undoubtedly. Because, as I said, if Miss Caroline *does* play *Fenella,* it doesn't follow, as a matter of course, that she should think she has a pretty foot; and then—such puppies as these young men are—he had the impudence to say, that——"

How far the amiable Mrs. Porter might have succeeded in her pleasant purpose it is impossible to say, had not the entrance of Mr. Thomas Balderstone, Mrs. Gattleton's brother, familiarly called in the family "Uncle Tom," changed the course of conversation, and suggested to her mind an excellent plan of operation on the evening of the play.

Uncle Tom was very rich, and exceedingly fond of his nephews and nieces; as a matter of course, therefore, he was an object of great importance in his own family. He was one of the best hearted men in existence; always in a good temper, and always talking. It was his boast that he wore top-boots on all occasions, and had never worn a black-silk neckerchief; and it was his pride that he remembered all the principal plays of Shakspeare from beginning to end—and so he did. The result of this parrot-like accomplishment was, that he was not only perpetually quoting himself, but that he could never sit by and hear a misquotation from "The Swan of Avon," without setting the unfortunate delinquent right. He was also something of a wag; never missed an opportunity of saying what he considered a good thing, and invariably laughed till he cried at any thing that appeared to him mirth-moving or ridiculous

"Well, girls!" said Uncle Tom, after the preparatory ceremony of kissing and how-d'ye-do-ing had been gone through—"how d'ye get on? Know your parts, eh?—Lucina, my dear, act 2, scene 1—place, left—cue—'Unknown fate,'—What's next, ha?—Go on—'The heavens—' "

"Oh, yes," said Miss Lucina, "I recollect—"

"'The heavens forbid
But that our loves and comforts should increase
Even as our days do grow.' "

"Make a pause here and there,' said the old gentleman, who was a great critic in his own estimation. "'But that our loves and comforts should increase'—emphasis on the last syllable, 'crease,'—loud 'even,'—one, two, three, four; then loud again, 'as our days do grow;' emphasis on *days*. That's the way my dear; trust to your uncle for emphasis.—Ah! Sem, my boy, how are you?"

"Very well, thankee, uncle," returned Mr. Sempronius, who had just appeared, looking something like a ringdove, with a small circle round each eye, the result of his constant corking. "Of course we see you on Thursday."

"Of course, of course, my dear boy."

"What a pity it is your nephew didn't think of making you prompter, Mr. Balderstone," whispered Mrs. Joseph Porter; "you would have been invaluable."

"Well, I flatter myself, I *should* have been tolerably up to the thing," responded Uncle Tom.

"I must bespeak sitting next you on the night," resumed Mrs. Porter; "and then if our dear young friends here, should be at all wrong, you will be able to enlighten me. I shall be *so* interested."

"I am sure I shall be most happy to give you any assistance in my power."

"Mind, it's a bargain."

"Certainly."

"I don't know how it is," said Mrs. Gattleton to her daughters, as they were sitting round the fire in the evening, looking over their parts, "but I really very much wish Mrs. Joseph Porter wasn't coming on Thursday. I am sure she's scheming something."

"She can't make *us* ridiculous, however," observed Mr. Sempronius Gattleton, haughtily.

The long looked-for Thursday arrived in due course, and brought with it, as Mr. Gattleton, senior, philosophically observed, "no disappointments to speak of." True, it was yet a matter of doubt whether *Cassio* would be enabled to get into the dress which had been sent for him from the masquerade warehouse. It was equally uncertain whether the principal female singer would be sufficiently recovered from the influenza to make her appearance; Mr. Harleigh, the Masaniello of the night, was hoarse, and rather unwell, in consequence of the great quantity of lemon and sugar-candy he had eaten to improve his voice; and two flutes and a violoncello had pleaded severe colds. What of that? the audience were all coming. Every body knew his part; the dresses were covered with tinsel and spangles; the white plumes looked beautiful; Mr. Evans had practiced falling, till he was bruised from head to foot and quite perfect; and *Iago* was perfectly sure that, in the stabbing-scene, he should make "a decided hit." A self-taught deaf gentleman, who had kindly offered to bring his flute, would be a most valuable addition to the orchestra; Miss Jenkins's talent for the piano was too well known to be doubted for an instant; Mr. Cape had practiced the violin accompaniment with her frequently; and Mr. Brown, who had kindly undertaken at a few hours' notice, to bring his violoncello, would, no doubt, manage extremely well.

Seven o'clock came, and so did the audience; all the rank and fashion of Clapham and its vicinity was fast filling the theatre. There were the Smiths, the Gubbinses, the Nixons, the Dixons, the Hicksons, people with all sorts of names, two aldermen, a sheriff in perspective, Sir Thomas Glumper (who had been knighted in the last reign for carrying up an address on somebody's escaping from something); and last not least, there were Mrs. Joseph Porter and Uncle Tom, seated in the centre of the third row from the stage; Mrs. P. amusing Uncle Tom with all sorts of stories, and Uncle Tom amusing every one else by laughing most immoderately.

Ting, ting, ting! went the prompter's bell at eight o'clock precisely, and dash went the orchestra into the overture to "The Men of Prometheus." The pianoforte player hammered away with the most laudable perseverance; and the violoncello, which struck in at intervals, "sounded very well considering." The unfortunate individual, however, who had undertaken to play the flute accompaniment "at sight," found from fatal experience, the perfect truth of the old adage, "out of sight, out of mind;" for being very near-sighted, and being placed at a considerable distance from his music-book, all he had an opportunity of doing, was to play a bar now and then in the wrong place, and put the other performers out. It is, however, but justice to Mr. Brown to say that he did this to admiration. The overture, in fact, was not unlike a race between the different instruments; the piano came in first by several bars, and the violoncello next, quite distancing the poor flute; for the deaf gentleman too-too'd away, quite unconscious that he was at all wrong, until apprised by the applause of the audience, that the overture was concluded. A considerable bustle and shuffling of feet was then heard upon the stage, accompanied by whispers of "Here's a pretty go! —what's to be done?" &c. The audience applauded again, by way of raising the spirits of the performers; and then Mr. Sempronius desired the prompter, in a very audible voice to "clear the stage, and ring up."

Ting, ting, ting! went the bell again. Every body sat down; the curtain shook, rose sufficiently high to display several pair of yellow boots paddling about, and there it remained.

Ting, ting, ting! went the bell again. The curtain was violently convulsed, but rose no higher; the audience tittered; Mrs. Porter looked at Uncle Tom, and Uncle Tom looked at every body, rubbing his hands, and laughing with perfect rapture. After as much ringing with the little bell as a muffin-boy would make in going down a tolerably long street, and a vast deal of whispering, hammering, and calling for nails and cord, the curtain at length rose, and discovered Mr. Sempronius Gattleton *solus*, and decked for *Othello*. After three distinct rounds of applause, during which Mr. Sempronius applied his right hand to his left breast, and bowed in the most approved manner, the manager advanced and said—

"Ladies and gentlemen—I assure you it is with sincere regret that I regret to be compelled to inform you that *Iago* who was to have played Mr. Wilson—I beg your pardon, Ladies and Gentlemen, but I am naturally somewhat agitated (applause)—I mean Mr. Wilson, who was to have played *Iago*, is—that is, has been —or, in—in other words, Ladies and Gentlemen, the fact is, that I have just received a note, in which I am informed that *Iago* is unavoidably detained at the Post-office this evening. Under these circumstances, I trust—a—a—amateur performance—a—another gentleman undertaken to read the part—request indulgence for a short time—courtesy and kindness of a British audience" —(overwhelming applause). Exit Mr. Sempronius Gattleton, and curtain falls.

The audience were, of course, exceedingly good-humored; and the whole business was a joke; and accordingly they waited for an hour with the utmost patience, being enlivened by an interlude of route-cakes and lemonade. It appeared by Mr. Sempronius's subsequent explanation, that the delay would not have been so great, had it not so happened that when the substitute *Iago* had finished dressing, and just as the play was on the point of commencing, the original *Iago* unexpectedly arrived. The former was therefore compelled to undress, and the latter to dress for his part; which as he found some difficulty in getting into his clothes, occupied no inconsiderable time. At last the tragedy began in real earnest. It went off well enough, until the third scene of the first act, in which *Othello* addresses the Senate, the only remarkable circumstance being, that as *Iago* could not get on any of the stage boots, in consequence of his feet being violently swelled with the heat and excitement, he was under the necessity of playing the part in a pair of common hessians, which contrasted rather oddly with his richly embroidered pantaloons. When *Othello* started with his address to the senate (whose dignity was represented by the *Duke;* a carpenter, two men engaged on the recommendation of the gardener, and a boy) Mrs. Porter found the opportunity she so anxiously sought.

Mr. Sempronius proceeded—

"'Most potent, grave and reverend signiors,
My very noble and approved good masters,——
That I have ta'en away this old man's daughter,
It is most true;—rude am I in my speech——'"

"Is that right?" whispered Mrs. Porter to Uncle Tom.

"No."

"Tell him so, then."

"I will.—Sem!" called out Uncle Tom, "that's wrong, my boy."

"What's wrong, Uncle!" demanded *Othello,* quite forgetting the dignity of his situation.

"You've left out something. 'True I have married——'"

"Oh, ah!" said Mr. Sempronius, endeavoring to hide his confusion as much and as ineffectually as the audience attempted to conceal their half-suppressed tittering, by coughing with the most extraordinary violence—

'"————true I have married her;—
The very head and front of my offending
Hath this extent; no more."

(*Aside*) "Why don't you prompt, father?"

"Because I've mislaid my spectacles," said poor Mr. Gattleton, almost dead with the heat and bustle.

"There, now it's 'rude am I,'" said Uncle Tom.

"Yes, I know it is," returned the unfortunate manager, proceeding with his part.

It would be useless and tiresome to quote the number of instances in which Uncle Tom, now completely in his element, and instigated by the mischievous Mrs. Porter, corrected the mistakes of the performers; suffice it to say, that having mounted his hobby, nothing could induce him to dismount; so, during the whole remainder of the play, he performed a kind of running accompaniment, by muttering every body's part as it was being delivered in an under tone. The audience were highly amused, Mrs. Porter delighted, the performers embarrassed; Uncle Tom never was better pleased in all his life; and Uncle Tom's nephews and nieces had never, although the declared heirs to his large property, so heartily wished him gathered to his fathers as on that memorable occasion.

Several other minor causes, too, united to damp the ardor of the *dramatis personæ.* None of the performers could walk in their tights, or move their arms in their jackets; the pantaloons were too small, the boots too large, and the swords of all shapes and sizes. Mr. Evans, naturally too tall for the scenery, wore a black velvet hat with immense white plumes, the glory of which was lost in "the flies;" and the only other inconvenience of which was, that when it was off his head he could not put it on, and when it was on he could not take it off. Notwithstanding all his practice, too, he fell with his head and shoulders as neatly through one of the side scenes, as a harlequin would jump through a panel in a Christmas pantomime. The pianoforte player, overpowered by the extreme heat of the room, fainted away at the commencement of the entertainments, leaving the music of "Masaniello" to the flute and violoncello. The orchestra complained that Mr. Harleigh put them out, and Mr. Harleigh declared that the orchestra prevented his singing at all. The fishermen, who were hired for the occasion, revolted to the very life, positively refusing to play without an increased allowance of spirits; and their demand being complied with, they got drunk in the eruption scene as naturally as possible. The red fire, which was burnt at the conclusion of the second act, not only nearly suffocated the audience, but nearly set the house on fire into the bargain; and, as it was, the remainder of the piece was acted in a thick fog.

In short, the whole affair was, as Mrs. Joseph Porter triumphantly told every body, a "complete failure." The audience went home at four o'clock in the morning, exhausted with laughter, suffering from severe headaches, and smelling terribly of brimstone and gunpowder. The Messrs. Gattleton, senior and junior, retired to rest with the vague idea of emigrating to Swan River early in the ensuing week.

Rose villa has once again resumed its wonted appearance:

the dining-room furniture has been replaced; the tables are as nicely polished as formerly; the horsehair chairs are ranged against the wall as regularly as ever; Venetian blinds have been fitted to every window in the house, to intercept the prying gaze of Mrs. Joseph Porter. The subject of theatricals is now never mentioned in the Gattleton family, unless indeed, by Uncle Tom, who cannot refrain from sometimes expressing his surprise and regret at finding that his nephews and nieces appear to have lost the relish they once possessed for the beauties of Shakespeare, and quotations from the works of the immortal bard.

CHAPTER X.

PASSAGE IN THE LIFE OF MR. WATKINS TOTTLE.

CHAPTER THE FIRST.

MATRIMONY is proverbially a serious undertaking. Like an overweening predilection for brandy-and-water, it is a misfortune into which a man easily falls, and from which he finds it remarkably difficult to extricate himself. It is no use telling a man who is timorous on these points that it is but one plunge, and all is over. They say the same thing at the Old Bailey, and the unfortunate victims derive about as much comfort from the assurance in one case as in the other.

Mr. Watkins Tottle was a rather uncommon compound of strong uxorious inclinations, and an unparalleled degree of anti-connubial timidity. He was about fifty years of age; stood four feet six inches and three quarters in his socks—for he never stood in stockings at all—plump, clean and rosy. He looked something like a vignette to one of Richardson's novels, and had a clean-cravatish formality of manner, and kitchen-pokerness of carriage, which Sir Charles Grandison himself might have envied. He lived on an annuity, which was well adapted to the individual who received it, in one respect—it was rather small. He received it in periodical payments on every alternate Monday; but he ran himself out about a day after the expiration of the first week as regularly as an eight-day clock, and then to make the comparison complete, his landlady wound him up, and he went on with a regular tick.

Mr. Watkins Tottle had long lived in a state of single blessedness, as bachelors say, or single cursedness, as spinsters think; but the idea of matrimony had never ceased to haunt him. Wrapt in profound reveries on this never-failing theme, fancy transformed his small parlor in Cecil-street into a neat house in the suburbs—the half-hundredweight of coals under the kitchen-stairs suddenly sprang up into three tons of the best Walls-end—his small French bedstead was converted into a regular matrimonial four-poster—and on the empty chair on the opposite side of the fire-place, imagination seated a beautiful young lady with a very little independence or will of her own, and a very large independence under a will of her father's.

"Who's there?" inquired Mr. Watkins Tottle, as a gentle tap at his room-door disturbed these meditations one evening.

"Tottle, my dear fellow, how *do* you do?" said a short elderly gentleman with a gruffish voice, bursting into the room, and replying to the question by asking another; and then they shook hands with a great deal of solemnity.

"Told you I should drop in some evening," said the short gentleman, as he delivered his hat into Tottle's hand, after a little struggle and dodging.

"Delighted to see you, I'm sure," said Mr. Watkins Tottle, wishing internally, that his visitor had "dropped in" to the Thames at the bottom of the street, instead of dropping into his parlor. The fortnight was nearly up, and Watkins was hard up.

"How is Mrs. Gabriel Parsons?" inquired Tottle.

"Quite well, thank you," replied Mr. Gabriel Parsons, for that was the name the short gentleman revelled in. Here there was a pause; the short gentleman looked at the left hob of the fireplace, and Mr. Watkins Tottle stared vacancy out of countenance.

"Quite well," repeated the short gentleman, when five minutes had expired. "I may say remarkably well," and he rubbed the palms of his hands together as hard as if he was going to strike a light by friction.

"What will you take?" inquired Tottle, with the desperate suddenness of a man who knew that unless the visitor took his leave he stood very little chance of taking any thing else.

"Oh, I don't know.—Have you any whisky?"

"Why," replied Tottle very slowly, for all this was gaining time, "I *had* some capital and remarkably strong whisky last week; but it's all gone—and therefore its strength———"

"Is much beyond proof; or in other words, impossible to be proved," said the short gentleman; and he laughed very heartily, and seemed quite glad the whisky had been drank. Mr. Tottle smiled—but it was the smile of despair. When Mr. Gabriel Parsons had done laughing, he delicately insinuated that in the absence of whisky he would not be adverse to brandy. And Mr. Watkins Tottle, lighting a flat candle very ostentatiously, and displaying an immense key, which belonged to the street-door, but which for the sake of appearances, occasionally did duty in an imaginary wine-cellar, left the room to entreat his landlady to charge their glasses, and charge them in the bill. The application was successful—the spirits were speedily called; —not from "the vasty deep," but the adjacent wine-vaults. The two short gentlemen mixed their grog; and then sat cosily down before the fire—a pair of shorts, airing themselves.

"Tottle," said Mr. Gabriel Parsons, "you know my way—off-hand, open, say what I mean, mean what I say, damn reserve, and can't bear affectation. One is a bad domino which only hides what good people have about 'em, without making the bad look better; and the other is much about the same thing as pinking a white cotton stocking to make it look like a silk one. —Now listen to what I'm going to say."

Here the little gentleman paused, and took a long pull at his brandy-and-water. Mr. Watkins Tottle took a sip of his, stirred the fire, and assumed an air of profound attention.

"It's no use humming and ha'ing about the matter," resumed the short gentleman.—"You want to get married—don't you?"

"Why,"—replied Mr. Watkins Tottle, evasively; for he trembled violently, and felt a sudden tingling throughout his whole frame—"why—I should certainly—at least, I *think* I should like it."

"Won't do," said the short gentleman.—"Plain and free—or there's an end of the matter. Do you want money?"

"You know I do."

"You admire the sex?"

"I do."

"And you'd like to be married?'

"Certainly."

"Then you shall be.—There's an end of that." And thus saying, Mr. Gabriel Parsons took a pinch of snuff, and mixed another glass.

"Let me entreat you to be more explanatory," said Tottle.

"Really, as the party principally interested, I can not consent to be disposed of in this way."

"I'll tell you," replied Mr. Gabriel Parsons, warming with the subject, and the brandy-and-water. "I know a lady—she's stopping with my wife now—who is just the thing for you. Well educated; talks French; plays the piano; knows a good deal about flowers and shells, and all that sort of thing; and has five hundred a-year, with an uncontrolled power of disposing of it, by her last will and testament."

"I'll pay my addresses to her," said Mr. Watkins Tottle.—"She isn't *very* young—is she?"

'Not very; just the thing for you. I've said that already."

"What colored hair has the lady?" inquired Mr. Watkins Tottle.

"Egad! I hardly recollect," replied Gabriel, with great coolness. "Perhaps I ought to have observed, at first, she wears a front."

"A what!" ejaculated Tottle.

"One of those things which curls along here," said Parsons, drawing a straight line across his forehead, just over his eyes, in illustration of his meaning. "I know the front's black; I can't speak quite positively about her own hair; because, unless one walks behind her, and catches a glimpse of it under her bonnet, one seldom sees it; but I should say that it was *rather* lighter than the front—just a shade of a grayish tinge, perhaps."

Mr. Watkins Tottle looked as if he had certain misgivings of mind. Mr. Gabriel Parsons perceived it, and thought it would be safe to begin the next attack without delay.

"Now, were you ever in love, Tottle?" he inquired.

Mr. Watkins Tottle blushed up to the eyes, and down to the chin, and exhibited a most extensive combination of colors as he confessed the soft impeachment.

"I suppose you popped the question more than once, when you were a young—I beg your pardon—a younger—man," said Parsons.

"Never in my life," replied his friend, apparently indignant at being suspected of such an act. "Never! The fact is, that I entertain, as you know, peculiar opinions on these subjects. I am not afraid of ladies, young or old—far from it; but I think, that, in compliance with the custom of the present day, they allow too much freedom of speech and manner to marriageable men. Now, the fact is, that any thing like this easy freedom I never could acquire; and as I am always afraid of going too far, I am generally, I dare say, considered formal and cold."

"I shouldn't wonder if you were," replied Parsons, gravely; "I shouldn't wonder. However, you'll be all right in this case; for the strictness and delicacy of this lady's ideas greatly exceed your own. Lord bless you, why, when she came to our house, there was an old portrait of some man or other, with two large, black, staring eyes, hanging up in her bed-room; she positively refused to go to bed there till it was taken down, considering it decidedly improper.

"I think so, too," said Mr. Watkins Tottle; "certainly."

"And then the other night—I never laughed so much in my life," resumed Mr. Gabriel Parsons; "I had driven home in an easterly wind, and caught a devil of a face-ache. Well; as Fanny—that's Mrs. Parsons, you know—and this friend of hers, and I, and Frank Ross, were playing a rubber, I said, jokingly, that when I went to bed I should wrap my head in Fanny's flannel-petticoat. She instantly threw up her cards, and left the room."

"Quite right," said Mr. Watkins Tottle; "she could not possibly have behaved in a more dignified manner. What did you do?"

"Do?—Frank took Dummy; and I won sixpence."

"But didn't you apologize for hurting her feelings?"

"Devil a bit. Next morning, at breakfast, we talked it over. She contended that any reference to a flannel-petticoat was highly improper:—men ought not to be supposed to know that such things were. I pleaded my coverture; being a married man."

"And what did the lady say to that?" inquired Tottle, deeply interested.

"Changed her ground, and said that Frank being a single man, its impropriety was obvious."

"Noble-minded creature!" exclaimed the enraptured Tottle.

"Oh! both Fanny and I said at once, that she was reguıarly cut out for you."

A gleam of placid satisfaction shone on the circular face of Mr. Watkins Tottle, as he heard the prophecy.

"There's one thing I can't understand," said Mr. Gabriel Parsons, as he rose to depart, "I cannot for the life and soul of me imagine how the deuce you'll ever manage to come together. The lady would certainly go into convulsions if the subject were mentioned," and Mr. Gabriel Parsons sat down again, and laughed till he was weak. Tottle owed him money, so he had a perfect right to laugh at his expense.

Mr. Watkins Tottle feared in his own mind, that this was another characteristic which he had in common with this modern Lucretia. He, however, accepted the invitation to dine with the Parsonses on the next day but one, with great firmness; and looked forward to the introduction, when again left alone, with tolerable composure.

The sun that rose on the next day but one had never beheld a sprucer personage on the outside of the Norwood stage than Mr. Watkins Tottle, and when the coach drew up before a card-board looking house with disguised chimneys, and a lawn like a large sheet of green letter-paper, he certainly had never lighted to his place of destination a gentleman who felt more awkward or uncomfortable.

The coach stopped, and Mr. Watkins Tottle jumped—we beg his pardon—alighted with great dignity. "All right!" said he, and away went the coach up the hill with that beautiful equanimity of pace for which "short" stages are generally remarkable.

Mr. Watkins Tottle gave a faltering jerk to the handle of the garden-gate bell. He essayed a more energetic tug, and his previous nervousness was not at all diminished by hearing the bell ringing like a fire alarum.

"Is Mr. Parsons at home?" inquired Tottle of the man who opened the gate. He could hardly hear himself speak, for the bell had not yet done tolling.

"Here I am," shouted a voice on the lawn,—and there was Mr. Gabriel Parsons in a flannel-jacket, running backward and forward from a wicket to two hats piled on each other, and then from the two hats to the wicket, in the most violent manner, while another gentleman with his coat off was getting down the area of the house, after a ball. When the gentleman without the coat had found it—which he did in less than ten minutes—he ran back to the hats, and Gabriel Parsons pulled up. Then the gentleman without the coat called out "play" very loudly, and bowled: Mr. Gabriel Parsons knocked the ball several yards, and took another run. Then the other gentleman aimed at the wicket, and didn't hit it; and Mr. Gabriel Parsons, having finished running on his own account, laid down the bat and ran after the ball, which went into a neighboring field. They called this cricket.

"Tottle, will you 'go in'?" inquired Mr. Gabriel Parsons, as he approached him, wiping the perspiration off his face.

Mr. Watkins Tottle declined the offer, the bare idea of accepting which made him even warmer than his friend.

"Then we'll go into the house as it's past four, and I shall have to wash my hands before dinner," said Mr. Gabriel Parsons. "Here, I hate ceremony, you know—Timson, that is Tottle—Tottle, that's Timson, bred for the church, which I fear will never be bread for him;" and he chuckled at the old joke. Mr. Timson bowed carelessly. Mr. Watkins Tottle bowed stiffly, and Mr. Gabriel Parsons led the way to the house. He was a rich sugar-baker, and mistook rudeness for honesty, and abrupt bluntness for an open and candid manner; many besides Gabriel mistake bluntness for sincerity.

Mrs. Gabriel Parsons received the visitors most graciously on the steps, and preceded them to the drawing-room. On the sofa was seated a lady of very prim appearance, and remarkably inanimate. She was just one of those persons at whose age it is impossible to make any reasonable guess; her features might have been remarkably pretty when she was younger, and they might always have presented the same appearance. Her complexion—with a slight trace of powder here and there—was as clear as that of a well-made wax-doll, and her face as expressive. She was handsomely dressed, and was winding up a gold watch for effect.

"Miss Lillerton, my dear, this is our friend Mr. Watkins Tottle; a very old acquaintance I assure you," said Mrs. Parsons, presenting the Strephon of Cecil-street, Strand. The lady rose, and made a deep courtesy; Mr. Watkins Tottle made a serio-comic bow.

"Splendid, majestic creature!" thought Watkins Tottle. She was his *beau ideal* of a desirable female.

Mr. Timson advanced, and Mr. Watkins Tottle began to hate him. Men generally discover a rival instinctively, and Mr. Watkins Tottle felt that his hate was deserved.

"May I beg," said the reverend gentleman,—"May I beg to call upon you, Miss Lillerton, for some trifling donation to my soup, coals, and blanket distribution society?"

"Put my name down for two sovereigns, if you please," responded Miss Lillerton.

"You are truly charitable, madam," said the Reverend Mr. Timson, "and we know that charity will cover a multitude of sins. Let me beg you to understand that I do not say this from the supposition that you have many sins which require palliation: believe me when I say that I never yet met any one who had fewer to atone for than Miss Lillerton."

Something like a bad imitation of animation lighted up the lady's face, as she acknowledged the compliment. Watkins Tottle incurred the sin of wishing that the ashes of the Rev. Charles Timson were quietly deposited in the church-yard of his curacy, wherever it might be.

"I'll tell you what," interrupted Parsons, who had just appeared with clean hands, and a black coat, "it's my private opinion, Timson, that your 'distribution society' is rather a humbug."

"You are so severe," replied Timson, with a Christian smile; he disliked Parsons, but liked his dinners.

"So positively unjust," said Miss Lillerton.

"Certainly," observed Tottle. The lady looked up; her eyes met those of Mr. Watkins Tottle. She withdrew them in a sweet confusion, and Watkins Tottle did the same—the confusion was mutual.

"Why," urged Mr. Parsons, pursuing his objections, "what on earth is the use of giving a man coals who has nothing to cook, or giving him blankets when he hasn't a bed, or giving him soup, when he requires substantial food?—'like sending them ruffles when wanting a shirt.' Why not give 'em a trifle of money, as I do, when I think they deserve it, and let them purchase what they think best. Why?—because your subscribers wouldn't see their names flourishing in print on the church-door—that's the reason."

"Really, Mr. Parsons, I hope you don't mean to insinuate that I wish to see my name in print, on the church-door," interrupted Miss Lillerton.

"I hope not," said Mr. Watkins Tottle, putting in another word, and getting another glance.

"Certainly not," replied Parsons. "I dare say you wouldn't mind seeing it in writing, though, in the church-register—eh?"

"Register! What register?" inquired the lady, gravely.

"Why, the register of marriages, to be sure," replied Parsons, chuckling at the sally, and glancing at Tottle. Mr. Watkins Tottle thought he should have fainted for shame, and it is quite impossible to imagine what effect the joke would have had upon the lady, if dinner had not been that moment announced. Mr. Watkins Tottle, with an unprecedented effort of gallantry, offered the tip of his little finger; Miss Lillerton accepted it gracefully, with maiden modesty; and they proceeded in due state to the dinner-table, where they were soon deposited side by side. The room was very snug, the dinner very good, and the little party in tolerable spirits. The conversation became pretty general; and when Mr. Watkins Tottle had extracted one or two cold observations from his neighbor, and taken wine with her, he began to acquire confidence rapidly. The cloth was removed; Mrs. Gabriel Parsons drank four glasses of port on the plea of her being a nurse just then, and Miss Lillerton took about the same number of sips, on the plea of her not wanting any at all. At length the ladies retired, to the great gratification of Mr. Gabriel Parsons, who had been coughing and frowning at his wife, for half an hour previously—signals which Mrs. Parsons never happened to observe, until she had been pressed to take her ordinary quantum, which, to avoid giving trouble, she generally did at once.

"What do you think of her?" inquired Mr. Gabriel Parsons of Mr. Watkins Tottle, in an under tone.

"I dote on her with enthusiasm already," replied Mr. Watkins Tottle.

"Gentlemen, pray let us drink 'the ladies,'" said the Reverend Mr. Timson.

"The ladies!" said Mr. Watkins Tottle, emptying his glass. In the fullness of his confidence he felt as if he could make love to a dozen ladies, off hand.

"Ah!" said Mr. Gabriel Parsons, "I remember when I was a younger man—fill your glass, Timson."

"I have this moment emptied it."

"Then fill again."

"I will," said Timson, readily suiting the action to the word.

"I remember," resumed Mr. Gabriel Parsons, "when I was a younger man, with what a strange compound of feelings I used to drink that toast, and how I used to think that every woman was an angel—quite a superior being."

"Was that before you were married?" mildly inquired Mr. Watkins Tottle.

"Oh! certainly," replied Mr. Gabriel Parsons, "I have never thought so since; and a precious milksop I must have been, ever to have thought so at all. But, you know, I married Fanny under the oddest, and most ridiculous circumstances possible."

"What were they, if one may inquire?" asked Timson, who had heard the story, on an average twice a week for the last six months. Mr. Watkins Tottle listened attentively, in the hope of picking up some suggestion that might be useful to him in his new undertaking.

"I spent my wedding-night in a back-kitchen chimney," said Parsons, by way of a beginning.

"In a back-kitchen chimney!" ejaculated Watkins Tottle. "How dreadful!"

"Yes, it wasn't very pleasant," replied the small host. "The fact is, that Fanny's father and mother liked me well enough as an individual, but had a decided objection to my becoming a husband. You see I hadn't any money in those days, and they had; and so they wanted Fanny to pick up somebody else. However, we managed to discover the state of each other's affections somehow. I used to meet her at some mutual friends' parties; at first we danced together, and talked, and flirted, and all that sort of thing; then I used to like nothing so well as sitting by her side—we didn't talk so much then, but I remember I used to have a great notion of looking at her out of the extreme corner of my left eye, and then I got very miserable and sentimental, and began to write verses, and use Macassar. At last I couldn't bear it any longer, and after I had walked up and down the sunny side of Oxford-street in tight boots for a week—and a devilish hot summer it was, too—in the hope of meeting her, I sat down and wrote a letter, and begged her to manage to see me clandestinely, for I wanted to hear her decision from her own mouth. I said I had discovered, to my perfect satisfaction, that I couldn't live without her, and that if she didn't have me, I had made up my mind to take prussic acid, or take to drinking, or emigrate, so as to take myself off in some way or other. Well, I borrowed a pound, and bribed the housemaid to give her the note, which she did."

"And what was the reply?" inquired Timson, who had found before, that encouraging the repetition of old stories is sure to end in a general invitation.

"Oh, the usual one, you know—Fanny expressed herself very miserable; hinted at the possibility of an early grave; said that nothing should induce her to swerve from the duty she owed her parents; and implored me to forget her, and find out somebody more deserving, and all that sort of thing. She said she could on no account think of meeting me unknown to her pa and ma; and entreated me, as she should be in a particular part of Kensington Gardens at eleven o'clock next morning, not to attempt to meet her there."

"You didn't go, of course?" said Watkins Tottle.

"Didn't I?—Of course I did. There she was, with the identical housemaid in perspective, in order that there might be no interruption. We walked about for a couple of hours; made ourselves delightfully miserable; and were regularly engaged. Then we began to 'correspond'—that is to say, we used to exchange about four letters a day; what we used to say in 'em I can't imagine. And I used to have an interview in the kitchen, or in the cellar, or some such place, every evening. Well, things went on in this way for some time; and we got fonder of each other every day. At last, as our love was raised to such a pitch, and as my salary had been raised too, shortly before, we determined on a secret marriage. Fanny arranged to sleep at a friend's the previous night; we were to be married early in the morning, and then we were to return to her home and be pathetic. She was to fall at the old gentleman's feet and bathe his boots with her tears; and I was to hug the old lady and call her 'mother,' and use my pocket-handkerchief as much as possible. Married we were the next morning; two girls—friends of Fanny's—acting as bridesmaids, and a man, who was hired for five shillings and a pint of porter, officiating as father. Now, the old lady unfortunately put off her return from Ramsgate where she had been paying a visit, until the next morning; and as we placed great reliance upon her, we agreed to postpone our confession for four-and-twenty hours. My newly-made wife returned home, and I spent my wedding-day in strolling about Hampstead-heath and damning my father-in-law. Of course, I went to comfort my dear little wife at night as much as I could, with the assurance that our troubles would soon be over. I opened the garden-gate, of which I had a key, and was shown by the servant to our old place of meeting—a back kitchen, with a stone floor and a dresser, upon which, in the absence of chairs, we used to sit and make love."

"Make love upon a kitchen-dresser!" interrupted Mr. Watkins Tottle, whose ideas of decorum were greatly outraged.

"Ah!—on a kitchen-dresser!" replied Parsons.—"And let me tell you, old fellow, that, if you were really over head-and-ears in love, and had no other place to make love in, you'd be devilish glad to avail yourself of such an opportunity. However, let me see;—where was I?"

"On the dresser," suggested Timson.

"Oh—ah? Well, here I found poor Fanny, quite disconsolate and uncomfortable. The old boy had been very cross all day, which made her feel still more lonely; and she was quite out of spirits. So I put a good face on the matter, and laughed it off, and said we should enjoy the pleasures of a matrimonial life more by constrast; and at length, poor Fanny brightened up a little. I stopped there till about eleven o'clock, and, just as I was taking my leave for the fourteenth time, the girl came running down stairs, without her shoes, in a great fright, to tell us that the old villain—God forgive me for calling him so, for he is dead and gone now—prompted I suppose by the prince of darkness, was coming down to draw his own beer for supper—a thing he had not done before for six months, to my certain knowledge; for the cask stood in that very back kitchen. If he discovered me there, explanations would have been out of the question; for he was so outrageously violent, when at all excited, that he never would have listened to me. There was only one thing to be done.—The chimney was a very wide one: it had been originally built for an oven; went up perpendicularly for a few feet, and then shot backward and formed a sort of small cavern. My hopes and fortune—the means of our joint existence almost—were at stake. I scrambled in like a squirrel; coiled myself up in this recess; and, as Fanny and the girl replaced the deal chimney-board, I could see the light of the candle which my unconscious father-in-law carried in his hand. I heard him draw the beer; and I never heard beer run so slowly. He was just leaving the kitchen, and I was preparing to descend, when down came the infernal chimney-board with a tremendous crash. He stopped, and put down the candle and the jug of beer on the dresser; he was a nervous old fellow; and any unexpected noise annoyed him. He coolly observed that the fireplace was never used, and sending the frightened servant into the next kitchen for hammer and nails, actually nailed up the board, and locked the door on the outside. So there was I on my wedding-night, in the light kerseymere trousers fancy waistcoat and blue coat that I had been married in in the morning, in a back-kitchen chimney, the bottom of which was nailed up, and the top of which had been formerly raised some fifteen feet, to prevent the smoke from annoying the neighbors. And there," added Mr. Gabriel Parsons, as he passed the bottle—"there I remained till half-past seven the next morning, when the housemaid's sweetheart, who was a carpenter, unshelled me. The old dog had nailed me up so securely, that, to this very hour, I firmly believe that no one but a carpenter could ever have got me out."

"And what did Mrs. Parson's father say, when he found you were married?" inquired Watkins Tottle, who, although he never saw a joke, was not satisfied until he heard a story to the very end.

"Why the affair of the chimney so tickled his fancy that he pardoned us off-hand, and allowed us something to live upon till he went the way of all flesh. I spent the next night in his second-floor front much more comfortably than I had spent the preceding one; for, as you will probably-guess——"

"Please sir, missis has made tea," said a middle-aged female servant, bobbing into the room.

"That's the very housemaid that figures in my story," said Mr. Gabriel Parsons.—"She went into Fanny's service when we were first married, and has been with us ever since; but I don't think she has felt one atom of respect for me since the morning she saw me released, when she went into violent hysterics, to which she has been subject ever since. Now shall we join the ladies?"

"If you please," said Mr. Watkins Tottle.

"By all means," added the obsequious Mr. Timson; and the trio made for the drawing-room accordingly.

Tea being concluded, and the toast and cups having been duly handed, and occasionally upset, by Mr. Watkins Tottle, a rubber was proposed. They cut for partners—Mr. and Mrs. Parsons; and Mr. Watkins Tottle and Miss Lillerton. Mr. Timson being a clergyman, and having conscientious scruples on the subject of card-playing, drank brandy-and-water, and kept up a running spar with Mr. Watkins Tottle. The evening went off well; Mr. Watkins Tottle was in high spirits, having some reason to be gratified with his reception by Miss Lillerton; and before he left, a small party was made up to visit the Beulah Spa on the following Saturday.

"It's all right, I think," said Mr. Gabriel Parsons to Mr. Watkins Tottle, as he opened the garden-gate for him.

"I hope so," he replied squeezing his friend's hand.

"You'll be down by the first coach on Saturday," said Mr. Gabriel Parsons.

"Certainly," replied Mr. Watkins Tottle. "Undoubtedly."

But fortune had decreed that Mr. Watkins Tottle should not be down by the first coach on Saturday. His adventures on that day however, and the success of his wooing, are subjects for another chapter.

CHAPTER THE SECOND

"The first coach has not come in yet, has it, Tom?" inquired Mr. Gabriel Parsons, as he very complacently paced up and down the fourteen feet of gravel which bordered the "lawn" on the Saturday morning which had been fixed upon for the Beulah Spa jaunt.

"No, sir; I havn't seen it," replied a gardener in a blue apron, who let himself out to do the ornamental for half-a-crown a day and his "keep."

"Time Tottle was down," said Mr. Gabriel Parsons, ruminating—"Oh, here he is, no doubt," added Gabriel, as a cab drove rapidly up the hill; and he buttoned his dressing gown, and opened the gate to receive the expected visitor. The cab stopped, and out jumped a man in a coarse Petersham great-coat, whity-brown neckerchief, faded black suit, gamboge-colored top-boots, and one of those large crowned hats, formerly seldom met with, but now very generally patronized by gentlemen and costermongers.

"Mr. Parsons?" said the man, looking at the superscription of a note he held in his hand, and addressing Gabriel with an inquiring air.

"*My* name is Parsons," responded the sugar-baker.

"I've brought this here note," replied the individual in the painted tops, in a hoarse whisper; "I've brought this here note from a gen'lm'n as come to our house this mornin'."

"I expected the gentleman at my house," said Parsons, as he broke the seal, which bore the impression of her Majesty's profile, as it is seen on a sixpence.

"I've no doubt the gen'lm'n would ha' been here," replied the stranger, "if he hadn't happened to call at our house first; but we never trusts no gen'lm'n furder nor we can see him—no mistake about that there"—added the unknown, with a facetious grin; "beg yer pardon, sir, no offense meant, only—once in, and I wish you may—catch the idea, sir?"

Mr. Gabriel Parsons was not remarkable for catching any thing suddenly, but a cold. He therefore only bestowed a glance of profound astonishment on his mysterious companion, and proceeded to unfold the note of which he had been the bearer.

Once opened and the idea was caught with very little difficulty. Mr. Watkins Tottle had been suddenly arrested for 33*l.* 10*s.* 4*d.*, and dated his communication from a lock-up-house in the vicinity of Chancery-lane.

"Unfortunate affair, this!" said Parsons, refolding the note.

"Oh! nothin' ven you're used to it," coolly observed the man in the Petersham.

"Tom!" exclaimed Parsons, after a few minutes' consideration, "just put the horse in, will you?—Tell the gentleman that I shall be there almost as soon as you are," he continued, addressing the sheriff-officer's Mercury.

"Werry well," replied that important functionary; adding, in a confidential manner, "I'd adwise the gen'lm'n's friends to settle. You see it's a mere trifle, and, unless the gn'lm'n means to go up afore the court, it's hardly worth while waiting for detainers you know. Our governor's wide awake, he is. I'll never say nothin' agin him, nor no man; but he knows what's o'clock, he does, uncommon." Having delivered this eloquent, and, to Parsons, particularly intelligible harangue, the meaning of which was eked out by divers nods and winks, the gentleman in the boots reseated himself in the cab which went rapidly off, and was soon out of sight. Mr. Gabriel Parsons continued to pace up and down the pathway for some minutes, apparently absorbed in deep meditation. The result of his cogitations seemed to be perfectly satisfactory to himself, for he ran briskly into the house; said that business had suddenly summoned him to town; that he had desired the messenger to inform Mr. Watkins Tottle of the fact; and that they would return together to dinner. He then hastily equipped himself for a drive, and mounting his gig was soon on his way to the establishment of Mr. Solomon Jacobs, situate (as Mr. Watkins Tottle had informed him) in Cursitor-street, Chancery-lane.

When a man is in a violent hurry to get on, and has a specific object in view, the attainment of which depends on the completion of his journey, the difficulties which interpose themselves in his way appear not only to be innumerable, but to have been called into existence especially for the occasion. The remark is by no means a new one, and Mr. Gabriel Parsons had practical and painful experience of its justice in the course of his drive. There are three classes of animated objects which prevent your driving with any degree of comfort or celerity through the streets which are but little frequented—they are pigs, children, and old women. On the occasion we are describing, the pigs were luxuriating on cabbage-stalks, and the shuttlecocks fluttered from the little deal battledores, and the children played in the road; and women, with a basket in one hand and the street-door key in the other, *would* cross just before the horse's head, until Mr. Gabriel Parsons was perfectly savage with vexation, and quite hoarse with hoi-ing and imprecating. Then, when he got into Fleet-street, there was "a stoppage," in which people in vehicles have the satisfaction of remaining stationary for half an hour, and envying the slowest pedestrians: and where policemen rush about, and seize hold of horses' bridles, and back them into shop-windows, by way of clearing the road and preventing confusion. At length Mr. Gabriel Parsons turned into Chancery-lane, and having inquired for, and being directed to, Cursitor-street (for it was a locality of which he was quite ignorant), he soon found himself opposite the house of Mr. Solomon Jacobs. Confiding his horse and gig to the care of one of the fourteen boys who had followed him from the other side of Blackfriars-bridge on the chance of his requiring their services, Mr. Gabriel Parsons crossed the road and knocked at an inner door, the upper part of which was of glass, grated like the windows of this inviting mansion with iron bars—painted white to look comfortable.

The knock was answered by a sallow-faced, red-haired, sulky boy, who, after surveying Mr. Gabriel Parsons through the glass, applied a large key to an immense wooden excrescence, which was in reality a lock, but which, taken in conjunction with the iron nails with which the panels were studded, gave the door the appearance of being subject to warts.

"I want to see Mr. Watkins Tottle," said Parsons.

"It's the gentleman that come in this morning, Jem," screamed a voice from the top of the kitchen stairs, which belonged to a dirty woman who had just brought her chin to a level with the passage-floor. "The gentleman's in the coffee-room"

"Up stairs, sir," said the boy, just opening the door wide

enough to let Parsons in without squeezing him, and double-locking it the moment he had made his way through the aperture, "First floor—door on the left."

Mr. Gabriel Parsons, thus instructed, ascended the uncarpeted and ill-lighted staircase, and after giving several subdued taps at the before-mentioned "door on the left," which were rendered inaudible by the hum of voices within the room, and the hissing noise attendant on some frying operations which were carrying on below stairs, turned the handle, and entered the apartment. Being informed that the unfortunate object of his visit had just gone up stairs to write a letter, he had leisure to sit down and observe the scene before him.

The room—which was a small, confined den—was partitioned off into boxes, like the common room of some inferior eating-house. The dirty floor had evidently been as long a stranger to the scrubbing-brush as to carpet or floor-cloth; and the ceiling was completely blackened by the flare of the oil-lamp by which the room was lighted at night. The gray ashes on the edges of the tables, and the cigar ends which were plentifully scattered about the dusty grate, fully accounted for the intolerable smell of tobacco which pervaded the place; and the empty glasses and half-saturated slices of lemon on the tables, together with the porter-pots beneath them, bore testimony to the frequent libations which the individuals who honored Mr. Solomon Jacobs by a temporary residence in his house indulged. Over the mantel-shelf was a paltry looking-glass, extending about half the width of the chimney-piece; but, by way of counterpoise, the ashes were confined by a rusty fender about twice as long as the hearth.

From this cheerful room itself, the attention of Mr. Gabriel Parsons was naturally directed to its inmates. In one of the boxes, two men were playing at cribbage with a very dirty pack of cards, some with blue, some with green, and some with red backs—selections from decayed packs. The cribbage-board had been long ago formed on the table, by some ingenious visitor, with the assistance of a pocket-knife and a two-pronged fork, with which the necessary number of holes had been made in the table, at proper distances, for the reception of the wooden pegs. In another box, a stout, hearty-looking man, of about forty, was eating some dinner, which his wife—an equally comfortable-looking personage—had brought him in a basket; and in a third, a genteel-looking young man was talking earnestly, and in a low tone, to a young female, whose face was concealed by a thick vail, but whom Mr. Gabriel Parsons immediately set down in his own mind as the debtor's wife. A young fellow of vulgar manners, dressed in the very extreme of the prevailing fashion, was pacing up and down the room, with a lighted cigar in his mouth and his hands in his pockets, ever and anon puffing forth volumes of smoke, and occasionally applying, with much apparent relish, to a pint pot, the contents of which were "chilling" on the hob.

"Fourpence more, by gum!" exclaimed one of the cribbage-players, lighting a pipe, and addressing his adversary at the close of the game; "one 'ud think you'd got luck in a pepper-cruet, and shook it out when you wanted it."

"Well, that ain't a bad 'un," replied the other, who was a horse-dealer from Islington.

"No; I'm blessed if it is," interposed the jolly-looking fellow, who, having finished his dinner, was drinking out of the same glass as his wife, in truly conjugal harmony, some hot gin-and-water. The faithful partner of his cares had brought a plentiful supply of the anti-temperance fluid in a large flat stone bottle, which looked like a half-gallon jar that had been successfully tapped for the dropsy. "You're a rum chap, you are, Mr. Walker—will you dip your beak into this, sir?"

"Thank'ee, sir," replied Mr. Walker, leaving his box, and advancing to the other to accept the proffered glass. "Here's your health, sir, and your good 'ooman's, here. Gentlemen all—yours, and better luck still. Well, Mr. Willis," continued the facetious prisoner, addressing the young man with the cigar, you seem rather down, to-day—floored, as one may say. What's the matter, sir? Never say die, you know."

"Oh! I'm all right," replied the smoker. "I shall be bailed out to-morrow."

"Shall you, though?" inquired the other. "Damme, I wish I could say the same. I am as regularly over head and ears as the Royal George, and stand about as much chance of being *bailed out*. Ha! ha! ha!"

"Why," said the young man, stopping short, and speaking in a very loud key, "Look at me. What d'ye think I've stopped here two days for?"

"Cause you couldn't get out, I suppose," interrupted Mr. Walker, winking to the company. "Not that you're exactly obliged to stop here, only you can't help it. No compulsion, you know, only you must—eh?"

"A'n't he a rum un?" inquired the delighted individual, who had offered the gin-and-water, of his wife.

"Oh, he just is!" replied the lady, who was quite overcome by these flashes of imagination.

"Why, my case," frowned the victim, throwing the end of his cigar into the fire, and illustrating his argument by knocking the bottom of the pot on the table, at intervals,—"my case is a very singular one. My father's a man of large property, and I am his son."

"That's a very strange circumstance!" interrupted the jocose Mr. Walker, *en passant.*

"—I am his son, and have received a liberal education. I don't owe no man nothing—not the value of a farthing, but I was induced, you see, to put my name to some bills for a friend—bills to a large amount, I may say a very large amount, for which I didn't receive no consideration. What's the consequence?"

"Why, I suppose the bills went out, and you came in. The acceptances weren't taken up, and you were, eh?" inquired Walker.

"To be sure," replied the liberally-educated young gentleman. "To be sure; and so here I am, locked up for a matter of twelve hundred pound."

"Why don't you ask your old governor to stump-up!" inquired Walker, with a somewhat sceptical air.

"Oh! bless you, he'd never do it," replied the other, in a tone of expostulation—"Never!"

"Well, it is very odd to—be—sure," interposed the owner of the flat bottle, mixing another glass, "but I've been in difficulties, as one may say, now for thirty year. I went to pieces when I was in a milk-walk, thirty year ago; arterward, when I was a fruiterer, and kept a spring wan; and arter that again in the coal and 'tatur line—but all that time I never see a youngish chap come into a place of this kind, who wasn't going out again directly, and who hadn't been arrested on bills which he'd given a friend and for which he'd received nothing whatsomever—not a fraction."

"Oh! it's always the cry," said Walker. "I can't see the use on it; that's what makes me so wild. Why, I should have a much better opinion of an individual, if he'd say at once in an honorable and gentlemanly manner as he'd done every body he possible could."

"Ay, to be sure," interposed the horse-dealer, with whose notions of bargain and sale the axiom perfectly coincided, "so should I."

The young gentleman, who had given rise to these observations, was on the point of offering a rather angry reply to these sneers, but the rising of the young man before noticed, and of the female who had been sitting by him, to leave the room, interrupted the conversation. She had been weeping bitterly, and the noxious atmosphere of the room acting upon her excited feelings and delicate frame, rendered the support of her companion necessary as they quitted it together.

There was an air of superiority about them both, and something in their appearance so unusual in such a place, that a respectful silence was observed until the *whirr—r—bang* of the spring-door announced that they were out of hearing. It was broken by the wife of the ex-fruiterer.

"Poor creetur!" said she, quenching a sigh in a rivulet of gin-and-water. "She's very young."

"She's a nice-looking 'ooman too," added the horse-dealer.

"What's he in for, Ikey?" inquired Walker, of an individual who was spreading a cloth with numerous blotches of mustard upon it, on one of the tables, and whom Mr. Gabriel Parsons had no difficulty in recognizing as the man who had called upon him in the morning.

"Vy," responded the factotum, "it's one of the rummest rigs you ever heard on. He come in here last Vensday, which by-the-by he's going over the water to-night—hows'ever that's neither here nor there. You see I've been a going back'ard and for'ard about his business, and ha' managed to pick up some of his story from the servants and them; and so far as I can make it out, it seems to be summat to this here effect——"

"Cut it short, old fellow," interrupted Walker, who knew from former experience that he of the top-boots was neither very concise nor intelligible in his narratives.

"Let me alone," replied Ikey, "and I'll ha' vound up, and made my lucky in five seconds. This here young gen'lm'n's father so I'm told, mind ye—and the father o' the young voman, have always been on very bad, out-and-out, rig'lar knock-me-down sort o' terms; but somehow or another, when he was a wisitin' at some gentlefolk's house as he knowed at college, he come into contract with the young lady. He seed her several times, and then he up and said he'd keep company with her, if so be as she vos agreeable. Vell she vos as sweet upon him as he vos upon her, and so I s'pose they made it all right; for they got married 'bout six months arterward, unbeknown, mind ye, to the two fathers—leastways so I'm told. When they heard on it—my eyes, there was such a combustion! Starvation vos the very least that vos to be done to 'em. The young gen'lm'n's father cut him off vith a bob, 'cos he'd cut himself off vith a wife; and the young lady's father, he behaved even worser and more unnat'ral, for he not only blowed her up dreadful, and swore he'd never see her again, but he employed a chap as I knows—and as you knows, Mr. Valker, a precious sight too well—to go about and buy up the bills and them things on which the young husband, thinking his governor 'ud come round agin, had raised the vind just to blow himself on vith for a time; besides vich, he made all the interest he could to set other people agin him. Consequence vos that he paid as long as he could; but things he never expected to have to meet till he'd had time to turn himself round, come fast upon him, and he vos nabbed. He vos brought here, as I said afore, last Vensday, and I think there's about—ah, half-a-dozen detainers agin him down stairs now. I have been," added Ikey, "in the purfession these fifteen year, and I never met vith such windictiveness afore!"

"Poor creeturs!" exclaimed the coal-dealer's wife once more; again resorting to the same excellent prescription for nipping a sigh in the bud; "Ah! when they've seen as much trouble as

I and my old man here have, they'll be as comfortable under it as we are."

"The young lady's a pretty creature," said Walker, "only she's a little too delicate for my taste—there ain't enough of her. As to the young cove, he may be very respectable and what not, but he's too down the mouth for me—he ain't game."

"Game !" exclaimed Ikey, who had been altering the position of a green-handled knife and fork at least a dozen times, in order that he might remain in the room under the pretext of having something to do. "He's game enough ven there's any thing to be fierce about; but who could be game as you call it, Mr. Walker, with a pale young creetur like that, hanging about him ?—It's enough to drive any man's heart into his boots, to see 'em together—and no mistake at all about it. I never shall forget her first comin' here; he wrote to her on the Thursday to come—I know he did, 'cos I took the letter. Uncommon fidgety he was all day, to be sure, and in the evening he goes down into the office, and he says to Jacobs, says he, 'Sir, can I have the loan of a private room for a few minutes this evening, without incurring any additional expense—just to see my wife in ?' says he. Jacobs looked as much as to say—'Strike me bountiful if you ain't one of the modest sort !' but as the gen'lm'n who had been in the back parlor had just gone out, and had paid for it for that day, he says—werry grave—'Sir, says he, 'it's agin our rules to let private rooms to our lodgers on gratis terms, but,' says he, 'for a gentleman, I don't mind breaking through them for once.' So then he turns round to me, and says, 'Ikey, put two mould candles in the back parlor, and charge 'em to this gen'lm'n's account,' vich I did. Vel, by-and-by a hackney-coach comes up to the door, and there, sure enough, was the young lady, wrapped up in a hopera-cloak, as it might be, and all alone. I opened the gate that night, so I went up when the coach come, and he vos a waitin' at the parlor-door—and wasn't he a trembling, neither ? The poor creetur see him, and could hardly walk to meet him. 'Oh, Harry !" she says, 'that it should have come to this ! and all for my sake,' says she, putting her hand upon his shoulder. So he puts his arm round her pretty little waist, and leading her gently a little way into the room, so that he might be able to shut the door, he says, so kind and soft-like—' Why, Kate," says he——"

"Here's the gentleman you want," said Ikey, abruptly breaking off in his story, and introducing Mr. Gabriel Parsons to the crest-fallen Watkins Tottle, who at that moment entered the room. Watkins advanced with a wooden expression of passive endurance, and accepted the hand which Mr. Gabriel Parsons held out.

"I want to speak to you," said Gabriel, with a look strongly expressive of his dislike of the company.

"This way," replied the imprisoned one, leading the way to the front drawing-room, where rich debtors did the luxurious at the rate of a couple of guineas a day.

"Well, here I am," said Watkins, as he sat down on the sofa; and placing the palms of his hands on his knees, anxiously glanced at his friend's countenance.

"Yes; and here you're likely to be," said Gabriel, coolly, as he rattled the money in his unmentionable pockets, and looked out of the window.

"What's the amount with the costs?" inquired Parsons, after an awkward pause.

"37*l.* 3*s.* 10*d.*"

"Have you any money?'

"Nine and sixpence halfpenny."

Mr. Gabriel Parsons walked up and down the room for a few seconds, before he could make up his mind to disclose the plan he had formed; he was accustomed to drive hard bargains, but was always most anxious to conceal his avarice. At length he stopped short, and said,—"Tottle, you owe me fifty pounds."

"I do.

"And from all I see, I infer that you are likely to owe it me."

"I fear I am."

"Though you have every disposition to pay me if you could?"

"Certainly."

"Then," said Mr. Gabriel Parsons, "listen; here's my proposition. You know my way of old. Accept it—yes or no—I will or I won't. I'll pay the debt and costs, and I'll lend you 10*l.* more (which, added to your annuity, will enable you to carry on the war well), if you'll give me your note of hand to pay me one hundred and fifty pounds within six months after you are married to Miss Lillerton."

"My dear——"

"Stop a minute—on one condition; and that is, that you propose to Miss Lillerton at once."

"At once! My dear Parsons, consider."

"It's for you to consider, not me. She knows you well from reputation, though she did not know you personally until lately. Notwithstanding all her maiden modesty, I think she'd be devilish glad to get married out of hand, with as little delay as possible. My wife has sounded her on the subject, and she has confessed.

"What—what?" eagerly interrupted the enamored Watkins.

"Why," replied Parsons, "to say exactly what she has confessed, would be rather difficult, because they only spoke in hints, and so forth; but my wife, who is no bad judge in these cases, declared to me that what she had confessed was as good as to say, that she was not insensible of your merits—in fact, that no other man should have her."

Mr. Watkins Tottle rose hastily from his seat, and rang the bell.

"What's that for?" inquired Parsons.

"I want to send the man for the bill-stamp," replied Mr. Watkins Tottle.

"Then you've made up your mind?"

"I have,"—and they shook hands most cordially. The note of hand was given—the debt and costs were paid—Ikey was satisfied for his trouble, and the two friends soon found themselves on that side of Mr. Solomon Jacob's establishment, on which most of his visitors were very happy when they found themselves once again—to wit, the *out*side.

"Now," said Mr. Gabriel Parsons, as they drove to Norwood together—"you shall have an opportunity to make the disclosure to-night, and mind you speak out, Tottle."

"I will, I will!" replied Watkins, valorously.

"How I should like to see you together!" ejaculated Mr. Gabriel Parsons.—"What fun!"—and he laughed so long and so loudly, that he disconcerted Mr. Watkins Tottle, and frightened the horse.

"There's Fanny and your intended, walking about on the lawn," said Gabriel, as they approached the house—"Mind your eye, Tottle."

"Never fear," replied Watkins, resolutely, as he made his way to the spot where the ladies were walking.

"Here's Mr. Tottle, my dear," said Mrs. Parsons, addressing Miss Lillerton. The lady turned quickly round, and acknowledged his courteous salute with the same sort of confusion that Watkins had noticed on their first interview, but with something like a slight expression of disappointment or carelessness.

"Did you see how glad she was to see you?" whispered Parsons to his friend.

"Why I really thought she looked as if she would rather have seen somebody else," replied Tottle.

"Pooh, nonsense!" whispered Parsons again—"it's always the way with the women, young or old. They never show how delighted they are to see those whose presence makes their hearts beat. It's the way with the whole sex, and no man should have lived to your time of life without knowing it. Fanny confessed it to me, when we were first married, over and over again—see what it is to have a wife."

"Certainly," whispered Tottle, whose courage was vanishing fast.

"Well now, you'd better begin to pave the way," said Parsons, who, having invested some money in the speculation, assumed the office of director.

"Yes, yes, I will—presently," replied Tottle, greatly flurried.

"Say something to her, man," urged Parsons again. "Confound it! pay her a compliment, can't you?"

"No! not till after dinner," replied the bashful Tottle, anxious to postpone the evil moment.

"Well, gentlemen," said Mrs. Parsons, "you are really very polite; you stay away the whole morning, after promising to take us out, and when you do come home, you stand whispering together and take no notice of us."

"We were talking of the *business*, my dear, which detained

us this morning," replied Parsons, looking significantly at Tottle.

"Dear me! how very quickly the morning has gone," said Miss Lillerton, referring to the gold watch, which was wound up on state occasions, whether it required it or not.

"*I* think it has passed very slowly," mildly suggested Tottle.

("That's right—bravo!") whispered Parsons.

"Indeed!" said Miss Lillerton with an air of majestic surprise.

"I can only impute it to my unavoidable absence from your society, madam," said Watkins, "and that of Mrs. Parsons."

During this short dialogue, the ladies had been leading the way to the house.

"What the deuce did you stick Fanny into that last compliment for?" inquired Parsons, as they followed together; "it quite spoilt the effect."

"Oh! it really would have been too broad without," replied Watkins Tottle, "much too broad."

"He's mad!" Parsons whispered to his wife, as they entered the drawing-room, "mad from modesty."

"Dear me!" ejaculated the lady, "I never heard of such a thing."

"You'll find we have quite a family dinner, Mr. Tottle," said Mrs. Parsons, when the sat down to the table: "Miss Lillerton is one of us, and of course, we make no stranger of you."

Mr. Watkins Tottle expressed a hope that the Parsons family never would make a stranger of him; and wished internally that his bashfulness would allow him to feel a little less like a stranger himself.

"Take off the covers, Martha," said Mrs. Parsons, directing the shifting of the scenery with great anxiety. "The order was obeyed, and a pair of boiled fowls, with tongue and et ceteras, were displayed at the top, and a fillet of veal at the bottom. On one side of the table two green sauce-tureens, with ladles of the same, were setting to each other in a green dish; and on the other was a curried rabbit, in a brown suit, turned up with lemon.

"Miss Lillerton, my dear," said Mrs. Parsons, "shall I assist you?"

"Thank you, no ; I think I'll trouble Mr. Tottle."

Watkins started—trembled—helped the rabbit—and broke a tumbler. The countenance of the lady of the house, which had been all smiles previously, underwent an awful change.

"Extremely sorry," stammered Watkins, assisting himself to currie and parsley and butter, in the extremity of his confusion.

"Not the least consequence," replied Mrs. Parsons, in a tone which implied that it was of the greatest consequence possible,—directing aside the researches of the boy, who was groping under the table for the bits of broken glass.

"I presume," said Miss Lillerton, "that Mr. Tottle is aware of the interest which bachelors usually pay in such cases; a dozen glasses for one is the lowest penalty."

Mr. Gabriel Parsons gave his friend an admonitory tread on the toe. Here was a clear hint that the sooner he ceased to be a bachelor and emancipated himself from such penalties, the better. Mr. Watkins Tottle viewed the observation in the same light, and challenged Mrs. Parsons to take wine, with a degree of presence of mind, which, under all the circumstances, was really extraordinary.

"Miss Lillerton," said Gabriel, "may I have the pleasure?"

"I shall be most happy."

"Tottle, will you assist Miss Lillerton, and pass the decanter. Thank you." (The usual pantomimic ceremony of nodding and sipping gone through)—

"Tottle, were you ever in Suffolk?" inquired the master of the house, who was burning to tell one of his seven stock stories.

"No," responded Watkins, adding, by way of a saving clause, "but I've been in Devonshire."

"Ah!" replied Gabriel, "it was in Suffolk that a rather singular circumstance happened to me, many years ago. Did you ever happen to hear me mention it?"

Mr. Watkins Tottle *had* happened to hear his friend mention it some four hundred times. Of course he expressed great curiosity, and evinced the utmost impatience to hear the story again. Mr. Gabriel Parsons forthwith attempted to proceed, in spite of the interruptions to which, as our readers must frequently have observed, the master of the house is often exposed in such cases. We will attempt to give them an idea of our meaning.

"When I was in Suffolk," said Mr. Gabriel Parsons——

"Take off the fowls first, Martha," said Mrs. Parsons. "I beg your pardon, my dear."

"When I was in Suffolk," resumed Mr. Parsons, with an impatient glance at his wife, who pretended not to observe it, "which is now some years ago, business led me to the town of Bury St. Edmund's. I had to stop at the principal places in my way, and therefore, for the sake of convenience, I traveled in a gig. I left Sudbury one dark night—it was winter time—about nine o'clock; the rain poured in torrents, the wind howled among the trees that skirted the road-side, and I was obliged to proceed at a foot-pace, for I could hardly see my hand before me, it was so dark——"

"John," interrupted Mrs. Parsons, in a low, hollow voice, "don't spill that gravy."

"Fanny," said Parsons, impatiently, "I wish you'd defer these domestic reproofs to some more suitable time. Really, my dear, these constant interruptions are very annoying."

"My dear, I didn't interrupt you," said Mrs. Parsons.

"But, my dear, you did interrupt me," remonstrated Mr. Parsons.

"How very absurd you are, my love! I must give directions to the servants; I am quite sure that if I sat here and allowed John to spill the gravy over the new carpet, you'd be the first to find fault when you saw the stain to-morrow morning."

"Well," continued Gabriel, with a resigned air, as if he knew there was no getting over the point about the carpet. "I was just saying, it was so dark that I could hardly see my hand before me. The road was very lonely, and I assure you Tottle (this was a device to arrest the wandering attention of that individual, which was distracted by a confidential communication between Mrs. Parsons and Martha, accompanied by the delivery of a large bunch of keys), I assure you, Tottle, I became somehow impressed with a sense of the loneliness of my situation—"

"Pie to your master," interrupted Mrs. Parsons, again directing the servant.

"Now, pray, my dear," remonstrated Parsons, once more, very pettishly. Mrs. P. turned up her hands and eyebrows, and appealed in dumb show to Miss Lillerton. "As I turned a corner of the road," resumed Gabriel, "the horse stopped short, and reared tremendously. I pulled up, jumped out, ran to his head, and found a man lying on his back in the middle of the road, with his eyes fixed on the sky. I thought he was dead; but no, he was alive, and there appeared to be nothing the matter with him. He jumped up, and putting his hand to his chest, and fixing upon me the most earnest gaze you can imagine, exclaimed——"

"Pudding here," said Mrs. Parsons.

"Oh! it's no use," exclaimed the host, now rendered desperate. "Here, Tottle; a glass of wine. It's useless to attempt relating any thing when Mrs. Parsons is present."

This attack was received in the usual way. Mrs. Parsons talked *to* Miss Lillerton and *at* her better half; expatiated on the impatience of men generally; hinted that her husband was peculiarly vicious in this respect; and wound up by insinuating that she must be one of the best tempers that ever existed, or she never could put up with it. Really what she had to endure sometimes, was more than any one who saw her in every-day life could by possibility suppose.—The story was now a painful subject, and therefore Mr. Parsons declined entering into any details, and contented himself by stating that the man was a maniac, who had escaped from a neighboring mad-house.

The cloth was removed; the ladies soon afterward retired, and Miss Lillerton played the piano in the drawing-room overhead, very loudly, for the edification of the visitor. Mr. Watkins Tottle and Mr. Gabriel Parsons sat chatting comfortably enough, until the conclusion of the second bottle, when the latter, in proposing an adjournment to the drawing-room, informed Watkins that he had concerted a plan with his wife, for leaving him and Miss Lillerton alone, soon after tea.

"I say," said Tottle, as they went up stairs, "don't you think it would be better if we put it off till—till—to-morrow!"

"Don't *you* think it would have been much better if I had

left you in that wretched hole I found you in this morning!" retorted Parsons, bluntly.

"Well—well—I only made a suggestion," said poor Watkins Tottle, with a deep sigh.

Tea was soon concluded, and Miss Lillerton, drawing a small work-table on one side of the fire, and placing a little wooden frame upon it, something like a minature clay-mill without the horse, was soon busily engaged in making a watch-guard with brown silk.

"God bless me!" exclaimed Parsons, starting up with well-feigned surprise, "I've forgotten those confounded letters. Tottle, I know you'll excuse me."

If Tottle had been a free agent, he would have allowed no one to leave the room on any pretense, except himself. As it was, however, he was obliged to look cheerful when Parsons quitted the apartment.

He had scarcely left, when Martha put her head into the room, with—"Please, ma'am, you're wanted."

Mrs. Parsons left the room, shut the door carefully after her, and Mr. Watkins Tottle was left alone with Miss Lillerton.

For the first five minutes there was a dead silence.—Mr. Watkins Tottle was thinking how he should begin, and Miss Lillerton appeared to be thinking of nothing. The fire was burning low; Mr. Watkins Tottle stirred it and put some coals on.

"Hem!" coughed Miss Lillerton; Mr. Watkins Tottle thought the fair creature had spoken. "I beg your pardon," said he.

"Eh?"

"I thought you spoke."

"No."

"Oh!"

"There are some books on the sofa, Mr. Tottle, if you would like to look at them," said Miss Lillerton, after the lapse of another five minutes.

"No, thank you," returned Watkins: and then he added, with a courage which was perfectly astonishing, even to himself, "Madam, that is Miss Lillerton, I wish to speak to you."

"To me!" said Miss Lillerton, letting the silk drop from her hands, and sliding her chair back a few paces.—"Speak—to me!"

"To you, madam—and on the subject of the state of your affections." The lady hastily rose, and would have left the room; but Mr. Watkins Tottle gently detained her by the hand, and holding it as far from him as the joint length of their arms would permit, he thus proceeded: "Pray do not misunderstand me, or suppose that I am led to address you, after so short an acquaintance, by any feeling of my own merits—for merits I have none which could give me a claim to your hand. I hope you will acquit me of any presumption when I explain that I have been acquainted through Mrs. Parsons, with the state—that is, that Mrs. Parsons has told me—at least, not Mrs. Parsons, but——" here Watkins began to wander, but Miss Lillerton relieved him.

"Am I to understand, Mr. Tottle, that Mrs. Parsons has acquainted you with my feeling—my affection—I mean my respect, for an individual of the opposite sex?"

"She has."

"Then, what?" inquired Miss Lillerton, averting her face, with a girlish air, "what could induce *you* to seek such an interview as this? What can your object be? How can I promote your happiness, Mr. Tottle?"

Here was the time for a flourish. "By allowing me," replied Watkins, falling bump on his knees, and breaking two brace-buttons and a waistcoat-string in the act—"By allowing me to be your slave, your servant—in short, by unreservedly making me the confidant of your heart's feelings—may I say, for the promotion of your own happiness—may I say, in order that you may become the wife of a kind and affectionate husband?"

"Disinterested creature!" exclaimed Mrs. Lillerton, hiding her face in a white pocket-handkerchief with an eyelet-hole border.

Mr. Watkins Tottle thought that if the lady knew all, she might possibly alter her opinion on this last point. He raised the tip of her middle finger ceremoniously to his lips, and got off his knees as gracefully as he could. "My information was correct?" he tremulously inquired, when he was once more on his feet.

"It was." Watkins elevated his hands, and looked up to the

ornament in the centre of the ceiling, which had been made for a lamp, by way of expressing his rapture.

"Our situation, Mr. Tottle," resumed the lady, glancing at him through one of the eyelet-holes, "is a most peculiar and delicate one."

"It is," said Mr. Tottle.

"Our acquaintance has been of *so* short duration" said Miss Lillerton.

"Only a week," assented Watkins Tottle.

"Oh! more than that," exclaimed the lady, in a tone of surprise.

"Indeed!" said Tottle.

"More than a month—more than two months!" said Miss Lillerton.

"Rather odd, this," thought Watkins.

"Oh!" he said, recollecting Parsons's assurance that she had known him from report, "I understand. But, my dear madam, pray consider. The longer this acquaintance has existed, the less reason is there for delay now. Why not at once fix a period for gratifying the hopes of your devoted admirer?"

"It has been represented to me again and again that this is the course I ought to pursue," replied Miss Lillerton, "but pardon my feelings of delicacy, Mr. Tottle—pray excuse this embarrassment—I have peculiar ideas on such subjects, and I am quite sure that I never could summon up fortitude enough to name the day to my future husband."

"Then allow *me* to name it," said Tottle, eagerly.

"I should like to fix it myself," replied Miss Lillerton, bashfully, "but I can not do so without at once resorting to a third party."

"A third party!" thought Watkins Tottle; "who the dence is that to be, I wonder?"

"Mr. Tottle," continued Miss Lillerton, "you have made me a most disinterested and kind offer—that offer I accept. Will you, at once, be the bearer of a note from me—to Mr. Timson?"

"Mr. Timson!" said Watkins.

"After what has passed between us," responded Miss Lillerton, still averting her head, "you must understand whom I mean; Mr. Timson, the—the—clergyman."

"Mr. Timson, the clergyman!" ejaculated Watkins Tottle, in a state of inexpressible beatitude, and positive wonder at his own success. "Angel! Certainly—this moment!"

"I'll prepare it immediately," said Miss Lillerton, making for the door; the events of this day have flurried me so much, Mr. Tottle, that I shall not leave my room again this evening; I will send you the note by the servant."

"Stay—stay," cried Watkins Tottle, still keeping a most respectful distance from the lady; "when shall we meet again?"

"Oh! Mr. Tottle," replied Miss Lillerton, coquettishly, "when *we* are married, I can never see you too often, nor thank you too much;" and she left the room.

Mr. Watkins Tottle flung himself into an arm-chair, and indulged in the most delicious reveries of future bliss, in which the idea of "Five hundred pounds per annum, with an uncontrolled power of disposing of it by her last will and testament," was somehow or other the foremost. He had gone through the interview so well, and it had terminated so admirably, that he almost began to wish he had expressly stipulated for the settlement of the annual five hundred on himself.

"May I come in?" said Mr. Gabriel Parsons, peeping in at the door.

"You may," replied Watkins.

"Well, have you done it?" anxiously inquired Gabriel.

"Have I done it!" said Watkins Tottle, "Hush—I'm going to the clergyman."

"No!" said Parsons. "How well you have managed it!"

"Where does Timson live?" inquired Watkins.

"At his uncle's," replied Gabriel, "just round the lane. He's waiting for a living, and has been assisting his uncle here for the last two or three months. But how well you have done it—I didn't think you could have carried it off so!"

Mr. Watkins Tottle was proceeding to demonstrate that the Richardsonian principle was the best on which love could possibly be made, when he was interrupted by the entrance of Martha, with a little pink note folded like a fancy cocked-hat.

"Miss Lillerton's compliments," said Martha, as she delivered it into Tottle's hands, and vanished.

"Do you observe the delicacy?" said Tottle, appealing to Mr. Gabriel Parsons. "*Compliments* not *love*, by the servant, eh?"

Mr. Gabriel Parsons didn't exactly know what reply to make, so he poked the forefinger of his right hand between the third and fourth ribs of Mr. Watkins Tottle.

"Come," said Watkins, when the explosion of mirth consequent on this practical jest, had subsided, "we'll be off at once—let's lose no time."

"Capital!" echoed Gabriel Parsons; and in five minutes they were at the garden-gate of the villa tenanted by the uncle of Mr. Timson.

"Is Mr. Charles Timson at home?" inquired Mr. Watkins Tottle of Mr. Charles Timson's uncle's man.

"Mr. Charles *is* at home," replied the man, stammering; "but he desired me to say he couldn't be interrupted, sir, by any of the parishioners."

"*I* am not a parishioner," replied Watkins.

"Is Mr. Charles writing a sermon, Tom?" inquired Parsons, thrusting himself forward.

"No, Mr. Parsons, sir; he's not exactly writing a sermon, but he is practicing the violoncello in his own bed-room, and gave strict orders not to be disturbed."

"Say I'm here," replied Gabriel, leading the way across the garden; "Mr. Parsons and Mr. Tottle, on private and particular business."

They were shown into the parlor, and the servant departed to deliver his message. The distant groaning of the violoncello ceased; footsteps were heard on the stairs; and Mr. Timson presented himself, and shook hands with Parsons with the utmost cordiality.

"How do you do, sir?" said Watkins Tottle, with great solemnity.

"How do *you* do, sir?" replied Timson, with as much coldness as if it were a matter of perfect indifference to him how he did, as it very likely was.

"I beg to deliver this note to you," said Watkins Tottle, producing the cocked-hat.

"From Miss Lillerton!" said Timson, suddenly changing color. "Pray sit down."

Mr. Watkins Tottle sat down; and while Timson perused the note, fixed his eyes on an oyster-sauce-colored portrait of the Archbishop of Canterbury, which hung over the fireplace.

Mr. Timson rose from his seat when he had concluded the note, and looked dubiously at Parsons—"May I ask," he inquired, appealing to Watkins Tottle, "whether our friend here is acquainted with the object of your visit?"

"Our friend is in *my* confidence," replied Watkins, with considerable importance.

"Then, sir," said Timson, seizing both Tottle's hands, "allow me, in his presence, to thank you, most unfeignedly and cordially, for the noble part you have acted in this affair."

"He thinks I recommended him," thought Tottle. "Confound these fellows! they never think of any thing but their fees."

"I deeply regret having misunderstood your intentions, my dear sir," continued Timson. "Disinterested and manly indeed! There are very few men who would have acted as you have done."

Mr. Watkins Tottle could not help thinking that this last remark was any thing but complimentary. He therefore inquired, rather hastily, "When is it to be?"

"On Thursday," replied Timson—"on Thursday morning, at half-past eight."

"Uncommonly early," observed Watkins Tottle, with an air of triumphant self-denial. "I shall hardly be able to get down here by that hour." (This was intended for a joke.)

"Never mind, my dear fellow," replied Timson, all suavity, shaking hands with Tottle again most heartily; "so long as we see you to breakfast, you know——"

"Eh!" said Parsons, with one of the most extraordinary expressions of countenance that ever appeared in a human face.

"What?" ejaculated Watkins Tottle, at the same moment.

"I say, that so long as we see you to breakfast," repeated

Timson, "we will excuse your being absent from the ceremony, though of course your presence at it would give us the utmost pleasure."

Mr. Watkins Tottle staggered against the wall, and fixed his eyes on Timson with appalling perseverance.

"Timson," said Parsons, hurriedly brushing his hat with his left arm, "when you say 'us,' whom do you mean?"

Mr. Timson looked foolish in his turn, when he replied, "Why—Mrs. Timson that will be this day week: Miss Lillerton that is—"

"Now, don't stare at that idiot in the corner," angrily exclaimed Parsons, as the extraordinary convulsions of Watkins Tottle's countenance excited the wondering gaze of Timson,—"but have the goodness to tell me in three words the contents of that note."

"This note," replied Timson, "is from Miss Lillerton, to whom I have been for the last five weeks regularly engaged. Her singular scruples and strange feeling on some points have hitherto prevented my bringing the engagement to that termination which I so anxiously desire. She informs me here, that she sounded Mrs. Parsons with the view of making her her confidant and go-between, that Mrs. Parsons informed this elderly gentleman, Mr. Tottle, of the circumstance, and that he, in the most kind and delicate terms, offered to assist us in any way, and even undertook to convey this note, which contains the promise I have long sought in vain—an act of kindness for which I can never be sufficiently grateful."

"Good-night, Timson," said Parsons, hurrying off, and carrying the bewildered Tottle with him.

"Won't you stay—and have something?" said Timson.

"No, thank ye," replied Parsons, "I've had quite enough;" and away he went, followed by Watkins Tottle in a state of stupefaction.

Mr. Gabriel Parsons whistled until they had walked some quarter of a mile past his own gate, when he suddenly stopped, and said—

"You are a clever fellow, Tottle, ain't you?"

"I don't know," said the unfortunate Watkins.

"I suppose you'll say this is Fanny's fault, won't you?" inquired Gabriel.

"I don't know any thing about it," replied the bewildered Tottle.

"Well," said Parsons, turning on his heel to go home, "the next time you make an offer, you had better speak plainly, and don't throw a chance away. And the next time you're locked up in a spunging-house, just wait there till I come and take you out, there's a good fellow."

How, or at what hour, Mr. Watkins Tottle returned to Cecil-street is unknown. His boots were seen outside his bed-room-door next morning, but we have the authority of his landlady for stating that he neither emerged therefrom, nor accepted sustenance, for four-and-twenty hours. At the expiration of that period, and when a council of war was being held in the kitchen on the propriety of summoning the parochial beadle to break his door open, he rang his bell, and demanded a cup of milk-and-water. The next morning he went through the formalities of eating and drinking as usual, but a week afterward he was seized with a relapse, while perusing the list of marriages in a morning paper, from which he never perfectly recovered.

A few weeks after the last-named occurrence, the body of a gentlemen unknown, was found in the Regent's-canal. In the trousers-pockets were four shillings and threepence-halfpenny; a matrimonial advertisement from a lady which appeared to have been cut out of a Sunday paper; a toothpick, and a card-case, which it is confidently believed would have led to the identification of the unfortunate gentleman, but for the circumstance of there being none but blank cards in it. Mr. Watkins Tottle absented himself from his lodgings shortly before. A bill which has not been taken up was presented next morning; and a bill which has not been taken down was soon afterward affixed in his parlor window

CHAPTER XI.

THE BLOOMSBURY CHRISTENING.

[The Author may be permitted to observe that this sketch was published some time before the Farce entitled "The Christening" was first represented.]

MR. NICODEMUS DUMPS, or as his acquaintance called him, "long Dumps," was a bachelor, six feet high, and fifty years old; cross, cadaverous, odd, and ill-natured. He was never happy but when he was miserable; and always miserable when he had the best reason to be happy. The only real comfort of his existence was to make every body about him wretched—then he might be truly said to enjoy life. He was afflicted with a situation in the Bank worth five hundred a-year, and he rented a "first floor furnished," at Pentonville, which he originally took because it commanded a dismal prospect of an adjacent church-yard. He was familiar with the face of every tombstone, and the burial-service seemed to excite his strongest sympathy. His friends said he was surly—he insisted he was nervous; they thought him a lucky dog, but he protested that he was "the most unfortunate man in the world." Cold as he was, and wretched as he declared himself to be, he was not wholly unsusceptible of attachments. He revered the memory of Hoyle, as he was himself an admirable and imperturbable whist-player, and he chuckled with delight at a fretful and impatient adversary. He adored King Herod for his massacre of the Innocents; and if he hated one thing more than another, it was a child. However, he could hardly be said to hate any thing in particular, because he disliked every thing in general; but perhaps his greatest antipathies were cabs, old women, doors that would not shut, musical amateurs, and omnibus cads. He subscribed to the Socicty for the Suppression of Vice for the pleasure of putting a stop to any harmless amusements; and he contributed largely toward the support of two itinerant methodist parsons, in the amiable hope that if circumstances renderea any people happy in this world, they might perchance be rendered miserable by fears for the next.

Mr. Dumps had a nephew who had been married about a year, and who was somewhat of a favorite with his uncle, because he was an admirable subject for him to exercise his misery-creating powers upon. Mr. Charles Kitterbell was a small, sharp, spare man, with a very large head, and a broad, good-humored countenance. He looked like a faded giant with the head and face partially restored; and he had a cast in his eye which rendered it quite impossible for any one with whom he conversed to know where he was looking. His eyes appeared fixed on the wall, and he was staring you out of countenance; in short, there was no catching his eye, and perhaps it is a merciful dispensation of Providence that such eyes are not catching. In addition to these characteristics, it may be added that Mr. Charles Kitterbell was one of the most credulous and matter-of-fact little personages that ever took *to* himself a wife, and *for* himself a house in Great Russell-street, Bedford-square. (Uncle Dumps always dropped the "Bedford-square," and inserted in lieu thereof, the dreadful words "Tottenham-court-road.")

"No, but uncle, 'pon my life you must—you must promise to be godfather," said Mr. Kitterbell, as he sat in conversation with his respected relative one morning.

"I cannot, indeed I cannot," returned Dumps.

"Well, but why not? Jemima will think it very unkind. It's very little trouble."

"As to the trouble," rejoined the most unhappy man in existence, "I don't mind that; but my nerves are in that state—I cannot go through the ceremony. You know I don't like going out.—For God's sake, Charles, don't fidget with that stool so, you'll drive me mad." Mr. Kitterbell, quite regardless of his uncle's nerves, had occupied himself for some ten minutes in describing a circle on the floor with one leg of the office stool on which he was seated, keeping the other three up in the air, and holding fast on by the desk.

"I beg your pardon, uncle," said Kitterbell, quite abashed, suddenly releasing his hold of the desk, and bringing the three wandering legs back to the floor, with a force sufficient to drive them through it.

"But come, don't refuse. If it's a boy, you know, we must have two godfathers."

"*If* it's a boy!" said Dumps, "why can't you say at once, whether it *is* a boy or not?"

"I should be very happy to tell you, but it's impossible I can undertake to say whether it's a girl or a boy, if the child isn't born yet."

"Not born yet!" echoed Dumps, with a gleam of hope lighting up his lugubrious visage. "Oh, well, it *may* be a girl, and then you won't want me, or if it is a boy, it *may* die before it is christened."

"I hope not," said the father that expected to be, looking very grave.

"I hope not," acquiesced Dumps, evidently pleased with the subject. He was beginning to get happy. "*I* hope not, but distressing cases frequently occur during the first two or three days of a child's life; fits, I am told, are exceedingly common, and alarming convulsions are almost matters of course."

"Lord, uncle!" ejaculated little Kitterbell, gasping for breath.

"Yes; my landlady was confined—let me see—last Tuesday: an uncommonly fine boy. On the Thursday night the nurse was sitting with him upon her knee before the fire, and he was as well as possible. Suddenly he became black in the face, and alarmingly spasmodic. The medical man was instantly sent for, and every remedy was tried, but—"

"How frightful!" interrupted the horror-stricken Kitterbell.

"The child died of course. However your child *may* not die, and if it should be a boy, and should *live* to be christened, why I suppose I must be one of the sponsors." Dumps was evidently good-natured on the faith of his anticipations.

"Thank you, uncle," said his agitated nephew, grasping his hand as warmly as if he had done him some essential service. "Perhaps I had better not tell Mrs. K. what you have mentioned."

"Why, if she's low-spirited, perhaps you had better not mention the melancholy case to her," returned Dumps, who of course had invented the whole story, "though perhaps it would be but doing your duty as a husband to prepare her for the *worst.*"

A day or two afterward, as Dumps was perusing a morning paper at the chop-house which he regularly frequented, the following paragraph met his eye :

"*Births.*—On Saturday, the 18th inst., in Great Russell-street, the lady of Charles Kitterbell, Esq., of a son."

"It *is* a boy !" he exclaimed, dashing down the paper to the astonishment of the waiters. "It *is* a boy !" But he speedily regained his composure as his eye rested on a paragraph quoting the number of infant deaths from the bills of mortality.

Six weeks passed away, and as no communication had been received from the Kitterbells, Dumps was beginning to flatter himself that the child was dead, when the following note painfully resolved his doubts :

'*Great Russell-street,*
"*Monday morning.*

"DEAR UNCLE:

"You will be delighted to hear that my dear Jemima has left her room, and that your future godson is getting on capitally. He was very thin at first, but he is getting much larger, and nurse says he is filling-out every day. He cries a good deal, and is a very singular color, which made Jemima and me rather uncomfortable ; but as nurse says it's natural, and of course we know nothing about these things yet, we are quite satisfied with what nurse says. We think he will be a sharp child ; and nurse says she's sure he will, because he never goes to sleep. You will readily believe that we are all very happy, only we're a little worn out for want of rest, as he keeps us awake all night ; but this we must expect, nurse says, for the first six or eight months. He has been vaccinated, but in consequence of the operation being rather awkardly performed, some small particles of glass were introduced into the arm with the matter. Perhaps this may in some degree account for his being rather fractious ; at least, so nurse says. We propose to have him christened at twelve o'clock on Friday, at Saint George's church, in Hart-street, by the name of Frederick Charles William. Pray don't be later than a quarter before twelve. We shall have a very few friends in the evening, when of course, we shall see you. I am sorry to say that the dear boy appears rather restless and uneasy to-day; the cause, I fear, is fever.

"Believe me, dear Uncle,

"Yours affectionately,

"CHARLES KITTERBELL.

"P. S.—I open this note to say that we have just discovered the cause of little Frederick's restlessness. It is not fever, as I apprehended, but a small pin, which nurse accidentally stuck in his leg yesterday evening. We have taken it out, and he appears more composed, though he still sobs a good deal."

It is almost necessary to say that the perusal of the above interesting statement was no great relief to the mind of the hypochondriacal Dumps. It was impossible to recede, however, and so he put the best face—that is to say, an uncommonly miserable one—upon the matter; and purchased a handsome silver mug for the infant Kitterbell, upon which he ordered the initials "F. C. W. K.," with the customary untrained grape-vine-looking flourishes, and a large full stop to be engraved forthwith.

Monday was a fine day, Tuesday was delightful, Wednesday was equal to either, and Thursday was finer than ever; four successive fine days in London! Hackney-coachmen became revolutionary, and crossing-sweepers began to doubt the existence of a First Cause. The *Morning Herald* informed its readers that an old woman in Camden Town had been heard to say that the fineness of the season was "unprecedented in the memory of the oldest inhabitant;" and Islington clerks, with large families and small salaries, left off their black gaiters, disdained to carry their once green cotton umbrellas, and walked to town in the conscious pride of white stockings, and cleanly brushed Bluchers. Dumps beheld all this with an eye of supreme contempt—his triumph was at hand.—He knew that if it had been fine for four weeks instead of four days, it would rain when he went out: he was lugubriously happy in the conviction that Friday would be a wretched day—and so it was.

"I knew how it would be," said Dumps, as he turned round opposite the Mansion-house at half-past eleven o'clock on the Friday morning.—"I knew how it would be, *I* am concerned, and that's enough;"—and certainly the appearance of the day was sufficient to depress the spirits of a much more buoyant-hearted individual than himself. It had rained, without a moment's cessation, since eight o'clock; every body that passed up Cheapside, and down Cheapside, looked wet, cold, and dirty. All sorts of forgotten and long-concealed umbrellas had been put into requisition. Cabs whisked about, with the "fare" as carefully boxed up behind two glazed calico curtains as any mysterious picture in any one of Mrs. Radcliffe's castles; omnibus horses smoked like steam-engines; nobody thought of "standing up" under door-ways or arches; they were painfully convinced it was a hopeless case; and so every body went hastily along, jumbling and jostling, and swearing and perspiring, and slipping about, like amateur skaters behind wooden chairs on the Serpentine on a frosty Sunday.

Dumps paused; he could not think of walking, being rather smart for the christening. If he took a cab he was sure to be spilt, and a hackney-coach was too expensive for his economical ideas. An omnibus was waiting at the opposite corner—it was a desperate case—he had never heard of the omnibus upsetting or running away, and if the cad did knock him down, he could "pull him up," in return.

"Now, sir!" cried the young gentleman who officiated as "cad" to the "Lads of the Village," which was the name of the machine just noticed. Dumps crossed.

"This vay, sir!" shouted the driver of the "Hark-away," pulling up his vehicle immediately across the door of the opposition—"This vay, sir—he's full.'" Dumps hesitated, whereupon the "Lads of the Village" commenced pouring out a torrent of abuse against the "Hark-away;" but the conductor of the "Admiral Napier" settled the contest in a most satisfactory manner for all parties, by seizing Dumps round the waist, and thrusting him into the middle of his vehicle which had just come up and only wanted the sixteenth inside.

"All right," said the "Admiral," and off the thing thundered, like a fire-engine at full gallop, with the kidnapped customer inside, standing in the position of a half doubled-up boot-jack, and falling about with every jerk of the machine, first on the one side and then on the other, like a "Jack-in-the-green," on a May-day, setting to the lady with a brass ladle.

"For Heaven's sake, where am I to sit?" inquired the miserable man of an old gentleman, into whose stomach he had just fallen for the fourth time.

"Any where but on my *chest*, sir," replied the old gentleman, in a surly tone.

"Perhaps the box would suit the gentleman better," suggested a very damp lawyer's clerk, in a pink shirt, and a smirking countenance.

After a great deal of struggling and falling about, Dumps at last managed to squeeze himself into a seat, which, in addition to the slight disadvantage of being between a window that would not shut, and a door that must be open, placed him in close contact with a passenger, who had been walking about all the morning without an umbrella, and who looked as if he had spent the day in a full water-butt—only wetter.

"Don't bang the door so," said Dumps to the conductor, as he shut it, after letting out four of the passengers; "I am very nervous—it destroys me."

"Did any gen'lm'n say any think?" replied the cad, thrusting in his head, and trying to look as if he didn't understand the request.

"I told you not to bang the door so!" repeated Dumps, with an expression of countenance like the knave of clubs in convulsions.

"Oh! vy, it's rather a sing'ler circumstance about this here door, sir, that it von't shut without banging," replied the conductor; and he opened the door very wide, and shut it again with a terrific bang, in proof of the assertion.

"I beg your pardon, sir," said a little prim, wheezing old gentleman, sitting opposite Dumps, "I beg your pardon; but have you ever observed, when you have been in an omnibus on a wet day, that four people out of five always come in with large cotton umbrellas, without a handle at the top, or the brass spike at the bottom?"

"Why, sir," returned Dumps, as he heard the clock strike

twelve, "it never struck me before; but now you mention it, I—— Hollo! hollo!"—shouted the persecuted individual, as the omnibus dashed past Drury-lane, where he had directed to be set down.—"Where is the cad?"

"I think he's on the box, sir," said the young gentleman before noticed in the pink shirt, which looked like a white one ruled with red ink.

"I want to be set down!" said Dumps in a faint voice, overcome by his previous efforts.

"I think these cads want to be *set down*," returned the attorney's clerk, chuckling at his sally.

"Hollo!" cried Dumps again.

"Hollo!" echoed the passengers. The omnibus passed St. Giles's church.

"Hold hard!" said the conductor; "I'm blowed if we ha'n't forgot the gen'lm'n as vas to be set down at Doory-lane.—Now, sir, make haste, if you please," he added opening the door, and assisting Dumps out with as much coolness as if it was "all right." Dumps's indignation was for once getting the better of his cynical equanimity. "Drury-lane!" he gasped, with the voice of a boy in a cold bath for the first time.

"Doory-lane, sir?—yes, sir,—third turning on the right-hand side, sir."

Dumps's passion was paramount; he clutched his umbrella, and was striding off with the firm determination of not paying the fare. The cad, by a remarkable coincidence, happened to entertain a directly contrary opinion, and Heaven knows how far the altercation would have proceeded, if it had not been most ably and satisfactorily brought to a close by the driver.

"Hollo!" said that respectable person, standing up on the box, and leaning with one hand on the roof of the omnibus. "Hollo! Tom! tell the gentleman if so be as he feels aggrieved, we will take him up to the Edge-er (Edgeware) Road for nothing, and set him down at Doory-lane when we comes back. He can't reject that, anyhow."

The argument was irresistible: Dumps paid the disputed sixpence, and in a quarter of an hour was on the staircase of No. 14, Great Russell-street.

Every thing indicated that preparations were making for the

reception of "a few friends" in the evening. Two dozen extra tumblers, and four ditto wine-glasses—looking any thing but transparent, with little bits of straw in them—were on the slab in the passage, just arrived. There was a great smell of nutmeg, port wine and almonds on the staircase; the covers were taken off the stair-carpet, and the figure of Venus on the first landing looked as if she were ashamed of the composition-candle in her right hand, which contrasted beautifully with the lamp-blacked drapery of the goddess of love. The female servant (who looked very warm and bustling) ushered Dumps into a front drawing-room, very prettily furnished, with a plentiful sprinkling of little baskets, paper table-mats, china watchmen, pink and gold albums, and rainbow-bound little books on the different tables.

"Ah, uncle!" said Mr. Kitterbell, "how d'ye do? Allow me—Jemima, my dear—my uncle. I think you've seen Jemima before, sir?"

"Have had the *pleasure,*" returned big Dumps, his tone and look making it doubtful whether in his life he had ever experienced the sensation.

"I'm sure," said Mrs. Kitterbell with a languid smile, and a slight cough, "I'm sure—hem—any friend—of Charles's—hem—much less a relation, is——"

"I knew you'd say so, my love," said little Kitterbell, who, while he appeared to be gazing on the opposite houses, was looking at his wife with a most affectionate air; "bless you!" The last two words were accompanied with a simper, and a squeeze of the hand, which stirred up all Uncle Dumps's bile.

"Jane, tell nurse to bring down baby," said Mrs. Kitterbell, addressing the servant. Mrs. Kitterbell was a tall, thin young lady, with very light hair, and a particularly white face—one of those young women who almost invariably, though one hardly knows why, recall to one's mind the idea of a cold fillet of veal. Out went the servant, and in came the nurse, with a remarkably small parcel in her arms, packed up in a blue mantle trimmed with white fur.—This was the baby.

"Now, uncle," said Mr. Kitterbell, lifting up that part of the mantle which covered the infant's face, with an air of great triumph, "*Who* do you think he's like?"

"He! he! Yes, who?" said Mrs. K., putting her arm through

her husband's, and looking up into Dumps's face with an expression of as much interest as she was capable of displaying.

"Good God, how small he is!" cried the amiable uncle, starting back with a well-feigned surprise: "*remarkably* small indeed."

"Do you think so?" inquired poor little Kitterbell, rather alarmed. "He's a monster to what he was—ain't he nurse?"

"He's a dear," said the nurse, squeezing the child, and evading the question—not because she scrupled to disguise the fact, but because she couldn't afford to throw away the chance of Dumps's half-crown.

"Well, but who is he like?" inquired little Kitterbell.

Dumps looked at the little pink heap before him, and only thought at the moment of the best mode of mortifying the youthful parents.

"I really don't know *who* he's like," he answered, very well knowing the reply expected of him.

"Don't you think he's like *me*?" inquired his nephew, with a knowing air.

"Oh, *decidedly* not!" returned Dumps, with an emphasis not to be misunderstood. "Decidedly not like you. Oh, certainly not."

"Like Jemima?" asked Kitterbell, faintly

"Oh dear, no; not in the least. I'm no judge, of course, in such cases; but I really think he's more like one of those little carved representations that one sometimes sees blowing a trumpet on a tombstone!" The nurse stooped down over the child, and with great difficulty prevented an explosion of mirth. Pa and ma looked almost as miserable as their amiable uncle.

"Well!" said the disappointed little father, "you'll be better able to tell what he's like by-and-by. You shall see him this evening with his mantle off."

"Thank you," said Dumps, feeling particularly grateful.

"Now, my love," said Kitterbell to his wife, "its time we were off. We're to meet the other godfather and the godmother at the church, uncle,—Mr. and Mrs. Wilson from over the way—uncommonly nice people. My love, are you well wrapped up?"

"Yes, dear."

"Are you sure you won't have another shawl?" inquired the anxious husband.

"No, sweet," returned the charming mother, accepting Dumps's proffered arm; and the little party entered the hackney-coach that was to take them to the church; Dumps amusing Mrs. Kitterbell by expatiating largely on the danger of measles, thrush, teeth-cutting, and other interesting diseases to which children are subject.

The ceremony (which occupied about five minutes) passed off without any thing particular occurring. The clergyman had to dine some distance from town, and had two churchings, three christenings, and a funeral to perform in something less than an hour. The godfathers and godmothers, therefore, promised to renounce the devil and all his works—"and all that sort of thing"—as little Kitterbell said—"in less than no time;" and, with the exception of Dumps nearly letting the child fall into the font when he handed it to the clergyman, the whole affair went off in the usual business-like and matter-of-course manner, and Dumps re-entered the Bank-gates at two o'clock with a heavy heart, and the painful conviction that he was regularly booked for an evening party.

Evening came—and so did Dumps's pumps, black-silk stockings, and white cravat, which he had ordered to be forwarded, per boy, from Pentonville. The depressed godfather dressed himself at a friend's counting-house, from whence, with his spirits fifty degrees below proof, he sallied forth—as the weather had cleared up, and the evening was tolerably fine—to walk to Great Russell-street. Slowly he paced up Cheapside, Newgate-street, down Snow-hill, and up Holborn ditto, looking as grim as the figure-head of a man-of-war, and finding out fresh causes of misery at every step. As he was crossing the corner of Hatton-garden, a man apparently intoxicated, rushed against him, and would have knocked him down, had he not been providentially caught by a very genteel young man who happened to be close to him at the time. The shock so disarranged Dumps's nerves, as well as his dress, that he could hardly stand. The gentleman took his arm, and in the kindest manner walked with him as far as Furnival's Inn. Dumps, for about the first time in his life, felt grateful and polite; and he and the gentlemanly-looking young man parted with mutual expressions of good-will.

"There are at least some well-disposed men in the world," ruminated the misanthropical Dumps, as he proceeded toward his destination.

Rat—tat—ta-ra-ra-ra-ra-rat—knocked a hackney-coachman at Kitterbell's door, in imitation of a gentleman's servant, just as Dumps reached it; and out came an old lady in a large toque, and an old gentleman in a blue coat, and three female copies of the old lady in pink dresses, and shoes to match.

"It's a large party," sighed the unhappy godfather, wiping the perspiration from his forehead, and leaning against the area-railings. It was some time before the miserable man could muster up courage to knock at the door, and when he did, the smart appearance of a neighboring greengrocer (who had been hired to wait for seven and sixpence, and whose calves alone were worth double the money), the lamp in the passage, and the Venus on the landing, added to the hum of many voices, and the sound of a harp and two violins, painfully convinced him that his surmises were but too well founded.

"How are you?" said little Kitterbell, in a greater bustle than ever, bolting out of the little back parlor with a corkscrew in his hand, and various particles of sawdust, looking like so many inverted commas, on his inexpressibles.

"Good God!" said Dumps, turning into the aforesaid parlor to put his shoes on which he had brought in his coat-pocket, and still more appalled by the sight of seven fresh-drawn corks, and a corresponding number of decanters. "How many people are there up-stairs?"

"Oh, not above thirty-five. We've had the carpet taken up in the back drawing-room, and the piano and the card-tables are in the front. Jemima thought we'd better have a regular sit-down supper, in the front parlor, because of the speechifying, and all that. But, Lord! uncle, what's the matter?" continued the excited little man, as Dumps stood with one shoe on, rummaging his pockets with the most frightful distortion of visage. "What have you lost? Your pocket-book?"

"No," returned Dumps, diving first into one pocket and

then into the other, and speaking in a voice like Desdemona with the pillow over her mouth.

"Your card-case? snuff-box? the key of your lodgings?" continued Kitterbell, pouring question on question with the rapidity of lightning.

"No! no!" ejaculated Dumps, still diving eagerly into his empty pocket.

"Not—not—the mug you spoke of this morning?"

"Yes, the mug!" replied Dumps, sinking into a chair.

"How *could* you have done it?" inquired Kitterbell. "Are you sure you brought it out?"

"Yes! yes! I see it all," said Dumps, starting up as the idea flashed across his mind; "miserable dog that I am—I was born to suffer. I see it all; it was the gentlemanly-looking young man!"

"Mr. Dumps!" shouted the greengrocer in a stentorian voice, as he ushered the somewhat recovered godfather into the drawing-room half an hour after the above declaration. "Mr. Dumps!"—every body looked at the door, and in came Dumps, feeling about as much out of place as a salmon might be supposed to be on a gravel-walk.

"Happy to see you again," said Mrs. Kitterbell, quite unconscious of the unfortunate man's confusion and misery; "you must allow me to introduce you to a few of our friends:—my mamma, Mr. Dumps—my papa and sisters." Dumps seized the hand of the mother as warmly as if she was his own parent, bowed to the young ladies, and against a gentleman behind him, and took no notice whatever of the father, who had been bowing incessantly for three minutes and a quarter.

"Uncle," said little Kitterbell, after Dumps had been introduced to a select dozen or two, "you must let me lead you to the other end of the room, to introduce you to my friend Danton. Such a splendid fellow!—I'm sure you'll like him—this way,"—Dumps followed as tractably as a tame bear.

Mr. Danton was a young man of about five-and-twenty, with a considerable stock of impudence, and a very small share of ideas: he was a great favorite, especially with young ladies of from sixteen to twenty-six years of age, both inclusive. He could imitate the French-horn to admiration, sang comic songs most inimitably, and had the most insinuating way of saying impertinent nothings to his doting female admirers. He had acquired, somehow or other, the reputation of being a great wit, and, accordingly, whenever he opened his mouth, every body who knew him laughed very heartily.

The introduction took place in due form. Mr. Danton bowed and twirled a lady's handkerchief, which he held in his hand, in a most comic way. Every body smiled.

"Very warm," said Dumps, feeling it necessary to say something.

"Yes. It was warmer yesterday," returned the brilliant Mr. Danton.—A general laugh.

"I have great pleasure in congratulating you on your first appearance in the character of a father, sir," he continued, addressing Dumps—"godfather, I mean."—The young ladies were convulsed, and the gentlemen in ecstacies.

A general hum of admiration interrupted the conversation, and announced the entrance of nurse with the baby. An universal rush of the young ladies immediately took place. (Girls are always *so* fond of babies in company.)

"Oh, you dear!" said one.

"How sweet!" cried another, in a low tone of the most enthusiastic admiration.

"Heavenly!" added a third.

"Oh! what dear little arms!" said a fourth, holding up an arm and fist about the size and shape of the leg of a fowl cleanly picked.

"Did you ever"—said a little coquette with a large bustle. who looked like a French lithograph, appealing to a gentleman in three waistcoats—"Did you ever!"

"Never, in my life," returned her admirer, pulling up his collar.

"Oh! *do* let me take it, nurse," cried another young lady. "The love!"

"Can it open its eyes, nurse?" inquired another, affecting the utmost innocence. Suffice it to say, that the single ladies unanimously voted him an angel, and that the married ones, *nem. con.*, agreed that he was decidedly the finest baby they had ever beheld—except their own.

The quadrilles were resumed with great spirit. Mr. Danton was universally admitted to be beyond himself, several young ladies enchanted the company and gained admirers by singing "We met"—"I saw her at the Fancy Fair"—and other equally sentimental and interesting ballads. "The young men," as Mrs. Kitterbell said, "made themselves very agreeable;" the girls did not lose their opportunity; and the evening promised to go off excellently. Dumps didn't mind it; he had devised a plan for himself—a little bit of fun in his own way—and he was almost happy! He played a rubber and lost every point. Mr. Danton said he could not have lost every point, because he made a point of losing:—every body laughed tremendously. Dumps retorted with a better joke, and nobody smiled, with the exception of the host, who seemed to consider it his duty to laugh till he was black in the face, at every thing. There was only one drawback—the musicians did not play with quite as much spirit as could have been wished. The cause, however, was satisfactorily explained; for it appeared, on the testimony of a gentleman who had come up from Gravesend in the afternoon, that they had been engaged on board a steamer all day, and had played almost without cessation all the way to Gravesend, and all the way back again.

The "sit-down supper" was excellent; there were four barley-sugar temples on the table, which would have looked beautiful if they had not melted away when the supper began; and a water-mill, whose only fault was that instead of going round, it ran over the table-cloth. Then there were fowls, and tongue, and trifle, and sweets, and lobster-salad, and potted beef—and every thing. And little Kitterbell kept calling out for clean plates, and the clean plates did not come; and then the gentlemen who wanted the plates said they didn't mind, they'd take a lady's; and then Mrs. Kitterbell applauded their gallantry, and the greengrocer ran about till he thought his seven and sixpence was very hardly earned; and the young ladies didn't eat much for fear it shouldn't look romantic, and the married ladies eat as much as possible, for fear they shouldn't have enough; and a great deal of wine was drank, and every body talked and laughed considerably.

"Hush! hush!" said Mr. Kitterbell, rising and looking very

important. "My love (this was addressed to his wife at the other end of the table), take care of Mrs. Maxwell, and your mamma, and the rest of the married ladies ; the gentlemen will persuade the young ladies to fill their glasses, I am sure."

"Ladies and gentlemen," said long Dumps, in a very sepulchral voice and rueful accent, rising from his chair like the ghost in Don Juan, "will you have the kindness to charge your glasses? I am desirous of proposing a toast."

A dead silence ensued, and the glasses were filled—every body looked serious.

"Ladies and gentlemen," slowly continued the ominous Dumps, "I"—(here Mr. Danton imitated two notes from the French-horn in a very loud key, which electrified the nervous toast-proposer, and convulsed his audience).

"Order! order!" said little Kitterbell, endeavoring to suppress his laughter.

"Order!" said the gentlemen.

"Danton, be quiet," said a particular friend on the opposite side of the table.

"Ladies and gentlemen," resumed Dumps, somewhat recovered, and not much disconcerted, for he was always a pretty good hand at a speech—"In accordance with what is, I believe, the established usage on these occasions, I as one of the godfathers of Master Frederick Charles William Kitterbell—(here the speaker's voice faltered, for he remembered the mug)—venture to rise to propose a toast. I need hardly say that it is the health and prosperity of that young gentleman, the particular event of whose early life we have met here to celebrate—(applause). Ladies and gentlemen, it is impossible to suppose that our friends here, whose sincere well-wishers we all are, can pass through life without some trials, considerable suffering, severe affliction, and heavy losses?"—Here the arch-traitor paused, and slowly drew forth a long, white pocket-handkerchief—his example was followed by several ladies. "That these trials may be long spared them, is my most earnest prayer, my most fervent wish (a distinct sob from the grandmother). I hope and trust, ladies and gentlemen, that the infant whose christening we have this evening met to celebrate, may not be removed from the arms of his parents by premature decay (several cambrics were in requisition) ; that his young and now *apparently* healthy form may not be wasted by lingering disease. (Here Dumps cast a sardonic glance around, for a great sensation was manifest among the married ladies.) You, I am sure will concur with me in wishing that he may live to be a comfort and blessing to his parents. ("Hear, hear!" and an audible sob from Mr. Kitterbell.) But should he not be what we could wish—should he forget in after times, the duty which he owes to them—should they unhappily experience that distracting truth, 'how sharper than a serpent's tooth it is to have a thankless child.'"—Here Mrs. Kitterbell, with her handkerchief to her eyes, and accompanied by several ladies, rushed from the room, and went into violent hysterics in the passage, leaving her better half in almost as bad a condition, and a general impression in Dumps's favor; for people like sentiment after all.

It need hardly be said that this occurrence quite put a stop to the harmony of the evening. Vinegar, hartshorn, and cold water, were now about as much in request as negus, rout-cakes, and *bon-bons* had been a short time before. Mrs. Kitterbell was immediately conveyed to her apartment, the musicians were silenced, flirting ceased, and the company slowly departed. Dumps left the house at the commencement of the bustle, and walked home with a light step, and (for him) a cheerful heart. His landlady, who slept in the next room, has offered to make oath, that she heard him laugh in his peculiar manner, after he had locked his door. The assertion, however, is so improbable, and bears on the face of it such strong evidence of untruth, that it has never obtained credence to this hour.

The family of Mr. Kitterbell has considerably increased since the period to which we have referred ; he has now two sons and a daughter : and as he expects at no distant period, to have another addition to his blooming progeny, he is anxious to secure an eligible godfather for the occasion. He is determined, however, to impose upon him two conditions. He must bind himself by a solemn obligation, not to make any speech after supper; and it is indispensable that he should be in no way connected with the most miserable man in the world."

CHAPTER XII.

THE DRUNKARD'S DEATH.

We will be bold to say, that there is scarcely a man in the constant habit of walking, day after day, through any of the crowded thoroughfares of London, who cannot recollect among the people whom he "knows by sight," to use a familiar phrase, some being of abject and wretched appearance whom he remembers to have seen in a very different condition, whom he has observed sinking lower and lower by almost imperceptible degrees, and the shabbiness and utter destitution of whose appearance, at last, strike forcibly and painfully upon him, as he passes by. Is there any man who has mixed much with society, or whose avocations have caused him to mingle, at one time or other, with a great number of people, who cannot call to mind the time when some shabby, miserable wretch, in rags and filth, who shuffles past him now in all the squalor of disease and poverty, was a respectable tradesman, or a clerk, or a man following some thriving pursuit, with good prospects, and decent means;—or cannot any of our readers call to mind from among the list of their *quondam* acquaintance, some fallen and degraded man, who lingers about the pavement in hungry misery—from whom every one turns coldly away, and who preserves himself from sheer starvation nobody knows how? Alas! such cases are of too frequent occurrence to be rare items in any man's experience; and but too often arise from one cause—drunkenness,—that fierce rage for the slow, sure poison, that oversteps every other consideration: that casts aside wife, children, friends, happiness, and station; and hurries its victims madly on to degradation and death.

Some of these men have been impelled by misfortune and misery to the vice that has degraded them. The ruin of worldly expectations, the death of those they loved, the sorrow that slowly consumes, but will not break the heart, has driven them wild; and they present the hideous spectacle of madmen, slowly dying by their own hands. But, by far the greater part have willfully, and with open eyes, plunged into the gulf from which the man who once enters it never rises more, but into which he sinks deeper and deeper down, until recovery is hopeless.

Such a man as this, once stood by the bed-side of his dying wife, while his children knelt around, and mingled low bursts of grief with their innocent prayers. The room was scantily and meanly furnished; and it needed but a glance at the pale form from which the light of life was fast passing away, to know that grief, and want, and anxious care, had been busy at the heart for many a weary year. An elderly female, with her face bathed in tears, was supporting the head of the dying woman—her daughter—on her arm. But it was not toward her that the wan face turned; it was not her hand that the cold and trembling fingers clasped; they pressed the husband's arm; the eyes so soon to be closed in death rested on his face; and the man shook beneath their gaze. His dress was slovenly and disordered, his face inflamed, his eyes bloodshot and heavy. He had been summoned from some wild debauch to the bed of sorrow and death.

A shaded lamp by the bed-side cast a dim light on the figures around, and left the remainder of the room in thick, deep shadow. The silence of night prevailed without the house, and the stillness of death was in the chamber. A watch hung over the mantle-shelf; its low ticking was the only sound that broke the profound quiet, but it was a solemn one, for well they knew, who heard it, that before it had recorded the passing of another hour, it would beat the knell of a departed spirit.

It is a dreadful thing to wait and watch for the approach of death; to know that hope is gone, and recovery impossible; and to sit and count the dreary hours through long, long, nights—such nights as only watchers by the bed of sickness know. It chills the blood to hear the dearest secrets of the heart, the pent-up, hidden secrets of many years, poured forth by the unconscious helpless being before you; and to think how little the reserve, and cunning of a whole life will avail, when fever and delirium tear off the mask at last. Strange tales have been told in the wanderings of dying men; tales so full of guilt and crime, that those who stood by the sick person's couch have fled in horror and affright, lest they should be scared to madness by what they heard and saw; and many a wretch has died alone, raving of deeds, the very name of which, has driven the boldest man away.

But no such ravings were to be heard at the bed-side by which the children knelt. Their half-stifled sobs and moanings alone broke the silence of the lonely chamber. And when at last the mother's grasp relaxed; and turning one look from the children to their father, she vainly strove to speak, and fell backward on the pillow, all was so calm and tranquil that she seemed to sink to sleep. They leant over her; they called upon her name, softly at first, and then in the loud and piercing tones of desperation. But there was no reply. They listened for her breath, but no sound came. They felt for the palpitation of the heart, but no faint throb responded to the touch. That heart was broken, and she was dead!

The husband sank into a chair by the bed-side, and clasped his hands upon his burning forehead. He gazed from child to child, but when a weeping eye met his, he quailed beneath its look. No word of comfort was whispered in his ear, no look of kindness lighted on his face. All shrunk from, and avoided him; and when at last he staggered from the room, no one sought to follow or console the widower.

The time had been, when many a friend would have crowded round him in his affliction, and many a heartfelt condolence would have met him in his grief. Where were they now? One by one, friends, relations, the commonest acquaintance even, had fallen off from and deserted the drunkard. His wife alone had clung to him in good and evil, in sickness and poverty; and how had he rewarded her? He had reeled from the tavern to her bed-side, in time to see her die.

He rushed from the house and walked swiftly through the streets. Remorse, fear shame, all crowded on his mind. Stupefied with drink, and bewildered by the scene he had just witnessed, he re-entered the tavern he had quitted shortly before. Glass succeeded glass. His blood mounted, and his brain whirled round. Death! Every one must die, and why not *she*. She was too good for him; her relations had often told him so.

Curses on them! Had they not deserted her, and left her to whine away the time at home? Well; she was dead, and happy perhaps. It was better as it was. Another glass—one more! Hurrah! It was a merry life while it lasted; and he would make the most of it.

Time went on; the three children who were left to him, grew up, and were children no longer;—the father remained the same —poorer, shabbier, and more dissolute looking, but the same confirmed and irreclaimable drunkard. The boys had, long ago, run wild in the streets, and left him; the girl alone remained, but she worked hard, and words or blows could always procure him something for the tavern. So he went on in the old course, and a merry life he led.

One night, as early as ten o'clock—for the girl had been sick for many days, and there was, consequently, little to spend at the public-house—he bent his steps homeward, bethinking himself that if he would have her able to earn money, it would be as well to apply to the parish surgeon, or, at all events, to take the trouble of inquiring what ailed her, which he had not yet thought it worth while to do. It was a wet December night; the wind blew piercing cold, and the rain poured heavily down. He begged a few halfpence from a passer by, and having bought a small loaf (for it was his interest to keep the girl alive, if he could) he shuffled onward, as fast as the wind and rain would let him.

At the back of Fleet-street, and lying between it and the water-side, are several mean and narrow courts, which form a portion of White-friars; it was to one of these that he directed his steps.

The alley into which he turned, might, for filth and misery, have competed with the darkest corner of this ancient sanctuary in its dirtiest and most lawless time. The houses, varying from two stories in height to four, were stained with every indescribable hue that long exposure to the weather, damp, and rottenness can impart to tenements composed originally of the roughest and coarsest materials. The windows were patched with paper, and stuffed with the foulest rags; the doors were falling from their hinges; poles with lines on which to dry clothes, projected from every casement, and sounds of quarreling or drunkenness issued from every room.

The solitary oil lamp in the centre of the court had been blown out, either by the violence of the wind or the act of some inhabitant, who had excellent reasons for objecting to his residence being rendered too conspicuous : and the only light which fell upon the broken and uneven pavement was derived from the miserable candles that here and there twinkled in the rooms of such of the more fortunate residents as could afford to indulge in so expensive a luxury. A gutter ran down the centre of the alley—all the sluggish odors of which had been called forth by the rain ; and as the wind whistled through the old houses, the doors and shutters creaked upon their hinges, and the windows shook in their frames, with a violence which every moment seemed to threaten the destruction of the whole place.

The man whom we have followed into this den, walked on in the darkness, sometimes stumbling into the main gutter, and at others into some branch repositories of garbage which had been formed by the rain, until he reached the last house in the court. The door, or rather what was left of it, stood ajar, for the convenience of the numerous lodgers ; and he proceeded to grope his way up the old and broken stair, to the attic story.

He was within a step or two of his room door, when it opened, and a girl, whose miserable and emaciated appearance was only to be equaled by that of the candle which she shaded with her hand, peeped anxiously out.

"Is that you, father ?" said the girl.

"Who else should it be ?" replied the man gruffly. "What are you trembling at ? It's little enough that I've had to drink to-day, for there's no drink without money, and no money without work. What the devil's the matter with the girl ?"

"I am not well father—not at all well," said the girl, bursting into tears.

"Ah !" replied the man, in the tone of a person who is compelled to admit a very unpleasant fact, to which he would rather remain blind, if he could. "You must get better somehow, for we must have money. You must go to the parish doctor, and make him give you some medicine. They're paid for it, damn 'em. What are you standing before the door, for? Let me come in, can't you?"

"Father," whispered the girl, shutting the door behind her, and placing herself before it; "William has come back."

"Who!" said the man, with a start.

"Hush," replied the girl, "William; brother William."

"And what does he want?" said the man, with an effort at composure—"money? meat? drink? He's come to the wrong shop for that, if he does. Give me the candle—give me the candle, fool—I ain't going to hurt him." He snatched the candle from her hand, and walked into the room.

Sitting on an old box, with his head resting on his hand, and his eyes fixed on a wretched cinder fire that was smoldering on the hearth, was a young man of about two-and-twenty, miserably clad in an old coarse jacket and trousers. He started up when his father entered.

"Fasten the door, Mary," said the young man hastily—"Fasten the door. You look as if you didn't know me, father. It's long enough, since you drove me from home; you may well forget me."

"And what do you want here, now?" said the father, seating himself on a stool, on the other side of the fireplace. "What do you want here, now?"

"Shelter," replied the son. "I'm in trouble; that's enough. If I'm caught I shall swing; that's certain. Caught I shall be, unless I stop here; that's as certain. And there's an end of it."

"You mean to say, you've been robbing or murdering, then?" said the father.

"Yes, I do," replied the son. "Does it surprise you, father?" He looked steadily in the man's face, but he withdrew his eyes, and bent them on the ground.

"Where's your brothers?" he said, after a long pause.

"Where they'll never trouble you," replied his son; "John's gone to America, and Henry's dead."

"Dead!" said the father, with a shudder, which even he could not repress.

"Dead," replied the young man. "He died in my arms—shot like a dog, by a game-keeper. He staggered back, I caught him, and his blood trickled down my hands. It poured out from his side like water. He was weak, and it blinded him, but he threw himself down on his knees, on the grass, and prayed to God, that if his mother was in Heaven, He would hear her prayers for pardon for her youngest son. 'I was her favorite boy, Will,' he said, 'and I am glad to think, now, that when she was dying, though I was a very young child then, and my little heart was almost bursting, I knelt down at the foot of the bed, and thanked God for having made me so fond of her as to have never once done any thing to bring the tears into her eyes. Oh, Will, why was she taken away, and father left!' There's his dying words, father," said the young man; "make the best you can of 'em. You struck him across the face, in a drunken fit, the morning we ran away; and here's the end of it."

The girl wept aloud; and the father, sinking his head upon his knees, rocked himself to and fro.

"If I am taken," said the young man, "I shall be carried back into the country, and hung for that man's murder. They can not trace me here, without your assistance, father. For aught I know, you may give me up to justice; but unless you do, here I stop, until I can venture to escape abroad."

For two whole days all three remained in the wretched room, without stirring out. On the third evening, however, the girl was worse than she had been yet, and the few scraps of food they had were gone. It was indispensably necessary that somebody should go out; and as the girl was too weak and ill, the father went, just at nightfall.

He got some medicine for the girl, and a trifle in the way of pecuniary assistance. On his way back, he earned sixpence by holding a horse; and he turned homeward with enough money to supply their most pressing wants for two or three days to come. He had to pass the public-house. He lingered for an instant, walked past it, turned back again, lingered once more, and finally slunk in. Two men whom he had not observed, were on the watch. They were on the point of giving up their search in despair, when his loitering attracted their attention; and when he entered the public-house, they followed him.

"You'll drink with me, master," said one of them, proffering him a glass of liquor.

"And me too," said the other, replenishing the glass as soon as it was drained of its contents.

The man thought of his hungry children, and his son's danger. But they were nothing to the drunkard. He *did* drink; and his reason left him.

"A wet night, Warden," whispered one of the men in his ear, as he at length turned to go away, after spending in liquor one-half of the money on which, perhaps, his daughter's life depended.

"The right sort of night for our friends in hiding, Master Warden," whispered the other.

"Sit down here," said the one who had spoken first, drawing him into a corner. "We have been looking arter the young 'un. We came to tell him it's all right now, but we couldn't find him 'cause we hadn't got the precise direction. But that ain't strange, for I don't think he know'd it himself, when he come to London, did he?"

"No, he didn't," replied the father.

The two men exchanged glances.

"There's a vessel down at the docks, to sail at midnight, when it's high water," resumed the first speaker, "and we'll put him on board. His passage is taken in another name, and what's better than that, it's paid for. It's lucky we met you."

"Very," said the second.

"Capital luck," said the first, with a wink to his companion.

"Great," replied the second, with a slight nod of intelligence.

"Another glass here; quick"—said the first speaker. And in five minutes more, the father had unconsciously yielded up his own son into the hangman's hands.

Slowly and heavily the time dragged along, as the brother and sister, in their miserable hiding-place, listened in anxious suspense to the slightest sound. At length a heavy footstep was heard upon the stair; it approached nearer; it reached the landing; and the father staggered into the room.

The girl saw that he was intoxicated, and advanced with the

candle in her hand to meet him; she stopped short, gave a loud scream, and fell senseless on the ground. She had caught sight of the shadow of a man, reflected on the floor. They both rushed in, and in another instant the young man was a prisoner, and handcuffed.

"Very quietly done," said one of the men to his companion, "thanks to the old man. Lift up the girl, Tom—come, come, it's no use crying, young woman. It's all over now, and can't be helped."

The young man stooped for an instant over the girl, and then turned fiercely round upon his father, who had reeled against the wall, and was gazing on the group with drunken stupidity.

"Listen to me, father," he said, in a tone that made the drunkard's flesh creep. "My brother's blood, and mine, is on your head: I never had kind look, or word, or care, from you, and, alive or dead, I never will forgive you. Die when you will, or how, I will be with you. I speak as a dead man now, and I warn you, father, that as surely as you must one day stand before your Maker, so surely shall your children be there, hand in hand, to cry for judgment against you." He raised his manacled hands in a threatening attitude, fixed his eyes on his shrinking parent, and slowly left the room; and neither father nor sister ever beheld him more, on this side of the grave.

When the dim and misty light of a winter's morning penetrated into the narrow court, and struggled through the begrimed window of the wretched room, Warden awoke from his heavy sleep, and found himself alone. He rose, and looked round him; the old flock mattress on the floor was undisturbed; every thing was just as he remembered to have seen it last; and there were no signs of any one, save himself, having occupied the room during the night. He inquired of the other lodgers, and of the neighbors; but his daughter had not been seen or heard of. He rambled through the streets, and scrutinized each wretched face among the crowds that thronged them, with anxious eyes. But his search was fruitless, and he returned to his garret when night came on, desolate and weary.

For many days he occupied himself in the same manner, but no trace of his daughter did he meet with, and no word of her reached his ears. At length he gave up the pursuit as hopeless. He had long thought of the probability of her leaving him, and endeavoring to gain her bread in quiet, elsewhere. She had left him, at last, to starve alone. He ground his teeth, and cursed her!

He begged his bread from door to door. Every halfpenny he could wring from the pity or credulity of those to whom he addressed himself, was spent in the old way. A year passed over his head; the roof of a jail was the only one that had sheltered him for many months. He slept under archways, and in brick-fields—any where, where there was some warmth or shelter from the cold and rain. But in the last stage of poverty, disease, and houseless want, he was a drunkard still.

At last, one bitter night, he sunk down on a door-step, faint and ill. The premature decay of vice and profligacy had worn him to the bone. His cheeks were hollow and livid; his eyes were sunken, and their sight was dim. His legs trembled beneath his weight, and a cold shiver ran through every limb.

And now the long-forgotten scenes of a misspent life crowded thick and fast upon him. He thought of the time when he had a home—a happy, cheerful home—and of those who peopled it, and flocked about him then, until the forms of his elder children seemed to rise from the grave, and stand about him—so plain, so clear, and so distinct they were that he could touch and feel them. Looks that he had long forgotten were fixed upon him once more; voices long since hushed in death sounded in his ears like the music of village bells. But it was only for an instant. The rain beat heavily upon him; and cold and hunger were gnawing at his heart again.

He rose, and dragged his feeble limbs a few paces further. The street was silent and empty; the few passengers who passed by, at that late hour, hurried quickly on, and his tremulous voice was lost in the violence of the storm. Again that heavy chill struck through his frame, and his blood seemed to stagnate beneath it. He coiled himself up in a projecting doorway, and tried to sleep.

But sleep had fled from his dull and glazed eyes. His mind wandered strangely, but he was awake, and conscious. The well-known shout of drunken mirth sounded in his ear, the glass was at his lips, the board was covered with choice rich food—they were before him: he could see them all, he had but to reach out his hand and take them—and, though the illusion was reality itself, he knew that he was sitting alone in the deserted street, watching the rain-drops as they pattered on the stones; that death was coming upon him by inches—and that there were none to care for or help him.

Suddenly, he started up, in the extremity of terror. He had heard his own voice shouting in the night air, he knew not what, or why. Hark! A groan!—another! His senses were leaving him: half-formed and incoherent words burst from his lips; and his hands sought to tear and lacerate his flesh. He was going mad, and he shrieked for help till his voice failed him.

He raised his head, and looked up the long dismal street. He recollected that outcasts like himself, condemned, to wander day and night in those dreadful streets, had sometimes gone distracted with their own loneliness. He remembered to have heard many years before that a homeless wretch had once been found in a solitary corner, sharpening a rusty knife to plunge into his own heart, preferring death to that endless, weary, wandering to and fro. In an instant his resolve was taken, his limbs received new life; he ran quickly from the spot, and paused not for breadth until he reached the riverside.

He crept softly down the steep stone stairs that lead from the commencement of Waterloo Bridge, down to the water's level. He crouched into a corner, and held his breath, as the patrol passed. Never did prisoner's heart throb with the hope of liberty and life half so eagerly as did that of the wretched man at the prospect of death. The watch passed close to him, but he remained unobserved; and after waiting till the sound of footsteps had died away in the distance, he cautiously descended, and stood beneath the gloomy arch that forms the landing-place from the river.

The tide was in, and the water flowed at his feet. The rain had ceased, the wind was lulled, and all was, for the moment, still and quiet—so quiet that the slightest sound on the opposite bank, even the rippling of the water against the barges that were moored there, was distinctly audible to his ear. The stream stole languidly and sluggishly on. Strange and fantastic forms rose to the surface, and beckoned him to approach; dark gleaming eyes peered from the water, and seemed to mock his hesitation, while hollow murmurs from behind urged him onward. He retreated a few paces, took a short run, desperate leap, and plunged into the river.

Not five seconds had passed when he rose to the water's surface—but what a change had taken place in that short time, in all his thoughts and feelings! Life—life—in any form, poverty, misery, starvation—any thing but death. He fought and struggled with the water that closed over his head, and screamed in agonies of terror. The curse of his own son rang in his ears. The shore—but one foot of dry ground—he could almost touch the step. One hand's-breadth nearer, and he was saved—but the tide bore him onward, under the dark arches of the bridge, and he sank to the bottom.

Again he rose, and struggled for life. For one instant—for one brief instant—the buildings on the river's banks, the lights on the bridge through which the current had borne him, the black water, and the fast flying clouds, were distinctly visible—once more he sunk, and once again he arose. Bright flames of fire shot up from earth to heaven, and reeled before his eyes, while the water thundered in his ears, and stunned him with its furious roar.

A week afterward the body was washed ashore, some miles down the river, a swollen and disfigured mass. Unrecognized and unpitied, it was borne to the grave; and there it has long since mouldered away!

CHAPTER XIII.

PUBLIC LIFE OF MR. TULRUMBLE—ONCE MAYOR OF MUDFOG.

Mudfog is a pleasant town—a remarkably pleasant town—situated in a charming hollow by the side of a river, from which river Mudfog derives an agreeable scent of pitch, tar, coals, and rope-yarn, a roving population in oil-skin hats, a pretty steady influx of drunken bargemen, and a great many other maritime advantages. There is a good deal of water about Mudfog, and yet it is not exactly the sort of town for a watering-place, either. Water is a perverse sort of element at the best of times, and in Mudfog it is particularly so. In winter it comes oozing down the streets and tumbling over the fields—nay, rushes into the very cellars and kitchens of the houses, with a lavish prodigality that might well be dispensed with; but in the hot summer weather it will dry up, and turn green; and although green is a very good color in its way, especially in grass, still it certainly is not becoming to water; and it can not be denied that the beauty of Mudfog is rather impaired, even by this trifling circumstance. Mudfog is a healthy place—very healthy;—damp, perhaps, but none the worse for that. It's quite a mistake to suppose that damp is unwholesome: plants thrive best in damp situations, and why shouldn't men! The inhabitants of Mudfog are unanimous in asserting that there exists not a finer race of people on the face of the earth; here we have an indisputable and veracious contradiction of the vulgar error at once. So, admitting Mudfog to be damp, we distinctly state that it is salubrious.

The town of Mudfog is extremely picturesque. Limehouse and Ratcliffe Highway are both something like it, but they give you a very faint idea of Mudfog. There are a great many more public-houses in Mudfog,—more than in Ratcliffe Highway and Limehouse put together. The public buildings, too, are very imposing. We consider the town-hall one of the finest specimens of shed-architecture extant; it is a combination of tne pig-sty and tea-garden-box orders; and the simplicity of its design is of surpassing beauty. The idea of placing a large window on one side of the door, and a small one on the other, is particularly happy. There is a fine bold Doric beauty, too, about the padlock and scraper, which is strictly in keeping with the general effect.

In this room do the mayor and corporation of Mudfog assemble together in solemn council for the public weal. Seated on the massive wooden benches, which, with the table in the centre, form the only furniture of the whitewashed apartment, the sage men of Mudfog spend hour after hour in grave deliberation. Here they settle at what hour of the night the public-houses shall be closed, at what hour of the morning they shall be permitted to open; how soon it shall be lawful for people to eat their dinner on church-days, and other great political questions; and sometimes, long after a silence has fallen on the town, and the distant lights from the shops and houses have ceased to twinkle, like far-off stars, to the sight of the boatmen on the river, the illumination in the two unequal-sized windows of the Town-hall, warns the inhabitants of Mudfog that its little body of legislators, like a larger and better-known body of the same genus, a great deal more noisy, and not a whit more profound, are patriotically dozing away in company, far into the night, for their country's good.

Among this knot of sage and learned men, no one was so eminently distinguished, during many years, for the quiet modesty of his appearance and demeanor, as Nicholas Tulrumble, the well-known coal-dealer. However exciting the subject of discussion, however animated the tone of the debate, or however warm the personalities exchanged, (and even in Mudfog we get personal sometimes,) Nicholas Tulrumble was always the same. To say truth, Nicholas, being an industrious man, and always up betimes, was apt to fall asleep when a debate began, and to remain asleep till it was over, when he would wake up very much refreshed, and give his vote with the greatest complacency. The fact was, that Nicholas Tulrumble, knowing that every body there had made up his mind beforehand, considered the talking as just a long botheration about nothing at all; and to the present hour it remains a question whether, on this point at all events, Nicholas Tulrumble was not pretty near right.

Time, which strews a man's head with silver, sometimes fills his pockets with gold. As he gradually performed one good office for Nicholas Tulrumble, he was obliging enough not to omit the other. Nicholas began life in a wooden tenement of four feet square, with a capital of two-and-ninepence, and a stock-in-trade of three bushels and a half of coals, exclusive of the large lump which hung by way of sign-board outside. Then he enlarged the shed, and kept a truck; then he left the shed, and the truck too, and started a donkey and a Mrs. Tulrumble; then he moved again, and set up a cart; the cart was soon afterward exchanged for a wagon; and so he went on, like his great predecessor Whittington—only without a cat for a partner—increasing in wealth and fame, until at last he gave up business altogether, and retired with Mrs. Tulrumble and family to Mudfog Hall, which he had himself erected, on something which he had endeavored to delude himself into the belief was a hill, about a quarter of a mile distant from the town of Mudfog.

About this time, it began to be murmured in Mudfog that Nicholas Tulrumble was growing vain and haughty; that prosperity and success had corrupted the simplicity of his manners, and tainted the natural goodness of his heart; in short, that he was setting up for a public character, and a great gentleman, and affected to look down upon his old companions with compassion and contempt. Whether these reports were at the time well-founded, or not, certain it is that Mrs. Tulrumble very shortly afterward started a four-wheeled chaise, driven by a tall postillion in a yellow cap,—that Mr. Tulrumble, junior, took to smoking cigars, and calling the footman a "feller,"—and that Mr. Tulrumble, from that time forth, was no more seen in his old seat in the chimney-corner of the Lighterman's Arms at night. This looked bad; but, more than this, it began to be observed that Mr. Nicholas Tulrumble attended the corporation meetings more frequently than heretofore; that he no longer went to sleep as he had done for so many years, but propped his eyelids open with his two forefingers; that he read the newspapers by himself at home; and that he was in the habit of indulging abroad in distant and mysterious allusions to "masses of people," and "the property of the country," and "productive power," and "the moneyed interest:" all of which denoted and proved that Nicholas Tulrumble was either mad, or worse; and it puzzled the good people of Mudfog amazingly.

At length, about the middle of the month of October, Mr. Tulrumble and family went up to London; the middle of October being, as Mrs. Tulrumble informed her acquaintance in Mudfog, the very height of the fashionable season.

Somehow or other, just about this time, despite the health-preserving air of Mudfog, the Mayor died. It was a most extraordinary circumstance; he had lived in Mudfog for eighty-five years; the corporation didn't understand it at all; indeed, it was with great difficulty that one old gentleman, who was a great stickler for forms, was dissuaded from proposing a vote of censure on such unaccountable conduct. Strange as it was, however, die he did, without taking the slightest notice of the corporation; and the corporation were imperatively called upon to elect his successor. So, they met for the purpose; and being very full of Nicholas Tulrumble just then, and Nicholas Tulrumble being a very important man, they elected him, and wrote off to London by the very next post to acquaint Nicholas Tulrumble with his new elevation.

Now, it being November time, and Mr. Nicholas Tulrumble being in the capital, it fell out that he was present at the Lord Mayor's show and dinner, at sight of the glory and splendor whereof, he, Mr. Tulrumble, was greatly mortified, inasmuch as the reflection would force itself on his mind, that, had he been born in London instead of in Mudfog, he might have been a Lord Mayor too, and have patronized the judges, and been affable to the Lord Chancellor, and friendly with the Premier, and coldly condescending to the Secretary to the Treasury, and have dined with a flag behind his back, and done a great many other acts and deeds which unto Lord Mayors of London peculiarly appertain. The more he thought of the Lord Mayor, the more enviable a personage he seemed. To be a King was all very well; but what was the King to the Lord Mayor! When the King made a speech, every body knew it was somebody else's writing; whereas, here was the Lord Mayor, talking away for half an hour—all out of his own head—amidst the enthusiastic applause of the whole company, while it was notorious that the King might talk to his parliament till he was black in the face, without getting so much as a single cheer. As all these reflections passed through the mind of Mr. Nicholas Tulrumble, the Lord Mayor of London appeared to him the greatest sovereign on the face of the earth, beating the Emperor of Russia all to nothing, and leaving the Great Mogul immeasurably behind.

Mr. Nicholas Tulrumble was pondering over these things, and inwardly cursing the fate which had pitched his coal-shed in Mudfog, when the letter of the corporation was put into his hand. A crimson flush mantled over his face as he read it, for visions of brightness were already dancing before his imagination.

"My dear," said Mr. Tulrumble to his wife, "they have elected me Mayor of Mudfog."

"Lor-a-mussy!" said Mrs. Tulrumble; "why, what's become of old Sniggs?"

"The late Mr. Sniggs, Mrs. Tulrumble," said Mr. Tulrumble, sharply, for he by no means approved of the notion of unceremoniously designating a gentleman who had filled the high office of Mayor as "old Sniggs,"—"The late Mr. Sniggs, Mrs. Tulrumble, is dead."

This communication was very unexpected; but Mrs. Tulrumble only ejaculated "Lor-a-mussy" once again, as if a Mayor were a mere ordinary Christian, at which Mr. Tulrumble frowned gloomily.

"What a pity 'tan't in London, ain't it?" said Mrs. Tulrumble, after a short pause; "what a pity 'tan't in London, where you might have had a show."

"I *might* have a show in Mudfog, if I thought proper, I apprehend," said Mr. Tulrumble, mysteriously.

"Lor! so you might, I declare," replied Mrs. Tulrumble.

"And a good one, too," said Mr. Tulrumble.

"Delightful!" exclaimed Mrs. Tulrumble.

"One which would rather astonish the ignorant people down there," said Mr. Tulrumble.

"It would kill them with envy," said Mrs. Tulrumble.

So it was agreed that his Majesty's lieges in Mudfog should be astonished with splendor, and slaughtered with envy, and that such a show should take place as had never been seen in that town or in any other town before,—no, not even in London itself.

On the very next day after the receipt of the letter, down came the tall postillion in a post-chaise, not upon one of the horses, but inside—actually inside the chaise,—and, driving up to the very door of the town-hall, where the corporation were assembled, delivered a letter, written by the Lord knows who, and signed by Nicholas Tulrumble, in which Nicholas said, all through four sides of closely-written, gilt-edged, hot-pressed, Bath-post, letter-paper, that he responded to the call of his fellow-townsmen with feelings of heartfelt delight; that he accepted the arduous office which their confidence had imposed upon him; that they would never find him shrinking from the discharge of his duty; that he would endeavor to execute his functions with all that dignity which their magnitude and importance demanded; and a great deal more to the same effect. But even this was not all. The tall postillion produced from his right-hand top-boot a damp copy of that afternoon's number of the county paper; and there, in large type, running the whole length of the very first column, was a long address from Nicholas Tulrumble to the inhabitants of Mudfog, in which he said that he cheerfully complied with their requisition; and, in short, as if to prevent any mistake about the matter, told them over again what a grand fellow he meant to be, in very much the same terms as those in which he had already told them all about the matter in his letter.

The corporation stared at one another very hard at all this, and then looked as if for an explanation to the tall postillion, but as the tall postillion was intently contemplating the gold tassel on the top of his yellow cap, and could have afforded no explanation whatever, even if his thoughts had been entirely disengaged, they contented themselves with coughing very dubiously, and looking very grave. The tall postillion then delivered another letter, in which Nicholas Tulrumble informed the corporation, that he intended repairing to the town-hall, in grand state and gorgeous procession, on the Monday afternoon then next ensuing. At this the corporation looked still more solemn; but, as the epistle wound up with a formal invitation to the whole body to dine with the Mayor on that day, at Mudfog Hall, Mudfog Hill, Mudfog, they began to see the fun of the thing directly, and sent back their compliments, and they'd be sure to come.

Now, there happened to be in Mudfog, as somehow or other there does happen to be in almost every town in the British dominions, and perhaps in foreign dominions too—we think it very likely, but, being no great traveler, cannot distinctly say—there happened to be, in Mudfog, a merry-tempered, pleasant-faced, good-for-nothing sort of vagabond, with an invincible dislike to manual labor, and an unconquerable attachment to strong beer and spirits, whom every body knew, and nobody, except his wife, took the trouble to quarrel with, who inherited from his ancestors the appellation of Edward Twigger, and rejoiced in the *sobriquet* of Bottle-nosed Ned. He was drunk, upon the average, once a day, and penitent, upon an equally fair calculation, once a month; and when he was penitent, he was invariably in the very last stage of maudlin intoxication. He was a ragged, roving, soaring kind of fellow, with a burly form, a sharp wit, and a ready head, and could turn his hand to any thing when he chose to do it. He was by no means opposed to hard labor on principle, for he would work away at a cricket-match by the day together,—running, and catching, and batting, and bowling, and reveling in toil which would exhaust a galley-slave. He would have been invaluable to a fire-office; never was a man with such natural taste for pumping engines, running up ladders, and throwing furniture out of two-pair-of-stairs' windows: nor was this the only element in which he was at home; he was a humane society in himself, a portable drag, an animated life-preserver, and had saved more people, in his time, from drowning, than the Plymouth light-boat or Captain Manby's apparatus. With all these qualifications, notwithstanding his dissipation, Bottle-nosed Ned was a general favorite; and the authorities of Mudfog, remembering his numerous services to the population, allowed him, in return, to get drunk in his own way, without the fear of stocks, fine, or imprisonment.

He had a general license, and he showed his sense of the compliment by making the most of it.

We have been thus particular in describing Bottle-nosed Ned. because it enables us to introduce a fact politely, without hauling it into the reader's presence, with indecent haste, by the head and shoulders, and brings us very naturally to relate, that on the very same evening on which Mr. Nicholas Tulrumble and family returned to Mudfog, Mr. Tulrumble's new secretary, just imported from London, with a pale face and light whiskers, thrust his head down to the very bottom of his neckcloth-tie, in at the tap-room door of the Lighterman's Arms, and inquiring whether one Ned Twigger was luxuriating within, announced himself as the bearer of a message from Nicholas Tulrumble, Esquire, requiring Mr. Twigger's immediate presence at the hall, on private and particular business. It being by no means Mr. Twigger's interest to affront the Mayor, he rose from the fire-place with a slight sigh, and followed the light-whiskered secretary through the dirt and wet of Mudfog streets, up to Mudfog Hall, without further ado.

Mr. Nicholas Tulrumble was seated in a small cavern with a skylight, which he called his library, sketching out a plan of the procession on a large sheet of paper; and into the cavern the secretary ushered Ned Twigger.

"Well, Twigger!" said Nicholas Tulrumble, condescendingly.

There was a time when Twigger would have replied, "Well, Nick!" but that was in the days of the truck, and a couple of years before the donkey; so he only bowed.

"I want you to go into training, Twigger," said Mr. Tulrumble.

"What for, sir?" inquired Ned, with a stare.

"Hush, hush, Twigger!" said the Mayor. "Shut the door, Mr. Jennings. Look here, Twigger."

As the Mayor said this, he unlocked a high closet, and disclosed a complete suit of brass armor, of gigantic dimensions.

"I want you to wear this, next Monday, Twigger," said the Mayor.

"Bless your heart and soul, sir," replied Ned, "you might as well ask me to wear a seventy-four pounder, or a cast-iron boiler."

"Nonsense, Twigger! nonsense!" said the Mayor.

"I couldn't stand under it, sir," said Twigger; "it would make mashed potatoes of me, if I attempted it."

"Pooh, pooh, Twigger!" returned the Mayor. "I tell you I have seen it done with my own eyes, in London, and the man wasn't half such a man as you are, either."

"I should have as soon thought of a man's wearing the case of an eight-day clock to save his linen," said Twigger, casting a look of apprehension at the brass suit.

"It's the easiest thing in the world," rejoined the Mayor.

"It's nothing," said Mr. Jennings.

"When your used to it," added Ned.

"You do it by degrees," said the Mayor. "You would begin with one piece to-morrow, and two the next day, and so on, till you have got it all on. Mr. Jennings, give Twigger a glass of rum. Just try the breast-plate, Twigger. Stay; take another glass of rum first. Help me to lift it, Mr. Jennings. Stand firm, Twigger! There!—it isn't half as heavy as it looks, is it?"

Twigger was a good strong, stout fellow; so after a great deal of staggering, he managed to keep himself up, under the breast-plate, and even contrived with the aid of another glass of rum to walk about in it, and the gauntlets into the bargain. He made a trial of the hemlet, but was not equally successful, inasmuch as he tipped over instantly,—an accident which Mr. Tulrumble clearly demonstrated to be occasioned by his not having a counteracting weight of brass on his legs.

"Now, wear that with grace and propriety on Monday next," said Tulrumble, "and I'll make your fortune."

"I'll try what I can do, sir," said Twigger.

"It must be kept a profound secret," said Tulrumble.

"Of course, sir," replied Twigger.

"And you must be sober," said Tulrumble; "perfectly sober."

Mr. Twigger at once solemnly pledged himself to be as sober as a judge, and Nicholas Tulrumble was satisfied, although had we been Nicholas, we should certainly have exacted some promise of a more specific nature; inasmuch as, having attended the Mudfog assizes in the evening more than once, we can solemnly testify to having seen the judges with very strong symptoms of dinner under their wigs. However, that's neither here nor there.

The next day, and the day following, and the day after that, Ned Twigger was securely locked up in the small cavern with the skylight, hard at work at the armor. With every additional piece he could manage to stand upright in, he had an additional glass of rum: and at last, after many partial suffocations, he contrived to get on the whole suit, and to stagger up and down the room in it, like an intoxicated effigy from Westminster Abbey.

" Never was man so delighted as Nicholas Tulrumble; never was woman so charmed as Nicholas Tulrumble's wife. Here was a sight for the common people of Mudfog! A live man in brass armor! Why, they would grow wild with wonder!

The day—*the* Monday—arrived.

If the morning had been made to order, it couldn't have been better adapted to the purpose. They never showed a better fog in London on Lord Mayor's day, than enwrapped the town of Mudfog on that eventful occasion. It had risen slowly and surely from the green and stagnant water with the first light of morning, until it reached a little above the lamp-post tops; and there it had stopped, with a sluggish obstinacy, which bade defiance to the sun, who had got up very blood-shot about the eyes, as if he had been at a drinking party over night, and was doing his day's work with the worst possible grace. The thick damp mist hung over the town like a huge gauze curtain. All was dim and dismal. The church-steeples had bidden a temporary adieu to the world below; and every object of lesser importance—houses, barns, hedges, trees, and barges—had all taken the vail.

The church-clock struck one. A cracked trumpet from the front-garden of Mudfog Hall produced a feeble flourish, as if some asthmatic person had coughed into it accidentally; the gate flew open, and out came a gentleman in a moist-sugar colored charger, intended to represent a herald, but bearing a much stronger resemblance to a court-card on horseback. This was one of the Circus people, who always came down to Mudfog at that time of the year, and who had been engaged by Nicholas Tulrumble expressly for the occasion. There was the horse, whisking his tail about, balancing himself on his hind-legs, and flourishing away with his fore-feet, in a manner which would have gone to the hearts and souls of any reasonable crowd. But a Mudfog crowd never was a reasonable one, and in all probability never will be. Instead of scattering the very fog with their shouts, as they ought most indubitably to have done, and were fully intended to do, by Nicholas Tulrumble, they no sooner recognized the herald, then they began to growl forth the most unqualified disapprobation at the bare notion of his riding like any other man. If he had come out on his head indeed, or jumping through a hoop, or flying through a red-hot drum, or even standing on one leg with his other foot in his mouth, they might have had something to say to him; but for a professional gentleman to sit astride in the saddle, with his feet in the stirrups, was rather too good a joke. So the herald was a decided failure, and the crowd hooted with great energy, as he pranced ingloriously away.

On the procession came. We are afraid to say how many supernumeraries there were, in striped shirts and black velvet raps to imitate the London watermen, or how many base imitations of running-footmen, or how many banners, which owing to the heaviness of the atmosphere, could by no means be prevailed on to display their inscriptions; still less do we feel disposed to relate how the men who played the wind instruments, looking up into the sky (we mean the fog) with musical fervor, walked through pools of water and hillocks of mud, till they covered the powdered heads of the running-footmen aforesaid, with splashes that looked curious, but not ornamental; or how the barrel-organ performer put on the wrong stop, and played one tune while the band played another; or how the horses being used to the arena and not the streets, would stand still and dance, instead of going on and prancing;—all of which are matters which might be dilated upon to great advantage, but which we have not the least intention of dilating upon, notwithstanding.

Oh! it was a grand and beautiful sight to behold the corporation in glass coaches, provided at the sole cost and charge of Nicholas Tulrumble, coming rolling along, like a funeral out of mourning, and to watch the attempts the corporation made to look great and solemn, when Nicholas Tulrumble himself, in the four-wheel chaise, with the tall postillion, rolled out after them, with Mr. Jennings on one side to look like the chaplain, and a supernumerary on the other, with an old life-guardsman's sabre, to imitate the sword-bearer; and to see the tears rolling down the faces of the mob as they screamed with merriment. This was beautiful! and so was the appearance of Mrs. Tulrumble and son, as they bowed with grave dignity out of their coach-window to all the dirty faces that were laughing around them; but it is not even with this that we have to do, but with the sudden stopping of the procession at another blast of the trumpet, whereat, and whereupon, a profound silence ensued, and all eyes were turned toward Mudfog Hall, in the confident anticipation of some new wonder.

"They won't laugh now, Mr. Jennings," said Nicholas Tulrumble.

"I think not, sir," said Mr. Jennings.

"See how eager they look," said Nicholas Tulrumble. "Aha! the laugh will be on our side now; eh, Mr. Jennings?"

"No doubt of that, sir," replied Mr. Jennings; and Nicholas Tulrumble, in a state of pleasurable excitement, stood up in the four-wheel chaise, and telegraphed gratification to the Mayoress behind.

While all this w is going forward, Ned Twigger had descended into the kitchen of Mudfog Hall, for the purpose of indulging the servants with a private view of the curiosity that was to burst upon the town; and, somehow or other, the footman was so companionable, and the housemaid so kind, and the cook so friendly, that he could not resist the offer of the first-mentioned to sit down and take something—just to drink success to master in.

So, down Ned Twigger sat himself in his brass livery on the top of the kitchen-table; and in a mug of something strong, paid for by the unconscious Nicholas Tulrumble, and provided by the companionable footman, drank success to the Mayor and his procession; and, as Ned laid by his helmet to imbibe the something strong, the companionable footman put it on his own head, to the immeasurable and unrecordable delight of the cook and house-maid. The companionable footman was very facetious to Ned, and Ned was very gallant to the cook and housemaid by turns. They were all very cosy and comfortable; and the something strong went briskly round.

At last Ned Twigger was loudly called for, by the procession people; and, having had his helmet fixed on, in a very complicated manner, by the companionable footman, and the kind housemaid, and the friendly cook, he walked gravely forth, and appeared before the multitude.

The crowd roared—it was not with wonder, it was not with surprise; it was most decidedly and unquestionably with laughter.

"What!" said Mr. Tulrumble, starting up in the four-wheel chaise. "Laughing? If they laugh at a man in real brass armor, they'd laugh when their own fathers were dying. Why doesn't he go into his place, Mr. Jennings? What's he rolling down toward us for?—he has no business here!"

"I am afraid, sir——" faltered Mr. Jennings.

"Afraid of what, sir?" said Nicholas Tulrumble, looking up in the Secretary's face.

"I am afraid he's drunk, sir;" replied Mr. Jennings.

Nicholas Tulrumble took one look at the extraordinary figure that was bearing down upon them; and then, clasping his secretary by the arm, uttered an audible groan in anguish of spirit.

It is a melancholy fact that Mr. Twigger having full license to demand a single glass of rum on the putting on of every piece of the armor, got by some means or other, rather out in his calculation in the hurry and confusion of preparation, and drank about four glasses to a piece instead of one, not to mention the something strong which went on the top of it. Whether the brass armor checked the natural flow of perspiration, and thus prevented the spirit from evaporating, we are not scientific enough to know; but, whatever the cause was, Mr. Twigger no sooner found himself outside the gate of Mudfog Hall, than he also found himself in a very considerable state of intoxication, and hence his extraordinary style of progressing. This was bad enough, but, as if fate and fortune had conspired against Nicholas Tulrumble, Mr. Twigger, not having been penitent for a good calendar month, took it into his head to be most especially and particularly sentimental, just when his repentance could have been most conveniently dispensed with. Immense tears were rolling down his cheeks, and he was vainly endeavoring to conceal his grief by applying to his eyes a blue cotton pocket-handkerchief with white spots,—an article not strictly in keeping with a suit of armor some three hundred years old, or thereabouts.

"Twigger, you villain!" said Nicholas Tulrumble, quite forgetting his dignity, "go back!"

"Never," said Ned. "I'm a miserable wretch. I'll never leave you."

The by-standers of course received this declaration with acclamations of "That's right, Ned; don't!"

"I don't intend it," said Ned, with all the obstinacy of a very tipsy man. "I'm very unhappy. I'm the wretched father of an unfortunate family; but I am very faithful, sir. I'll never leave you." Having reiterated this obliging promise, Ned proceeded in broken words to harangue the crowd upon the number of years he had lived in Mudfog, the excessive respectability of his character, and other topics of the like nature.

"Here! will any body lead him away?" said Nicholas: "if they'll call on me afterward, I'll reward them well."

Two or three men stepped forward, with the view of bearing Ned off, when the secretary interposed.

"Take care! take care!" said Mr. Jennings. "I beg your pardon, sir; but they'd better not go too near him, because, if he falls over, he'll certainly crush somebody."

At this hint the crowd retired on all sides to a very respectful distance, and left Ned, like the Duke of Devonshire, in a little circle of his own.

"But Mr. Jennings," said Nicholas Tulrumble, "he'll be suffocated."

"I'm very sorry for it, sir," replied Mr. Jennings; "but nobody can get that armor off, without his own assistance. I'm quite certain of it, from the way he put it on."

Here Ned wept dolefully, and shook his helmeted head, in a manner that might have touched a heart of stone; but the crowd had not hearts of stone, and they laughed heartily.

"Dear me, Mr. Jennings," said Nicholas, turning pale at the possibility of Ned's being smothered in his antique costume—"Dear me, Mr. Jennings, can nothing be done with him?"

"Nothing at all," replied Ned, "nothing at all. Gentlemen,

I'm an unhappy wretch. I'm a body, gentleman, in a brass coffin." At this poetical idea of his own conjuring up, Ned cried so much that the people began to get sympathetic, and to ask what Nicholas Tulrumble meant by putting a man into such a machine as that, and one individual in a hairy waistcoat like the top of a trunk, who had previously expressed his opinion that if Ned hadn't been a poor man, Nicholas wouldn't have dared to do it, hinted at the propriety of breaking the four-wheel chaise, or Nicholas's head, or both, which last compound proposition the crowd seemed to consider a very good notion.

It was not acted upon, however, for it had hardly been broached, when Ned Twigger's wife made her appearance abruptly in the little circle before noticed, and Ned no sooner caught a glimpse of her face and form, than from the mere force of habit he set off toward his home just as fast as his legs would carry him; and that was not very quick in the present instance either, for, however ready they might have been to carry *him*, they couldn't get on very well under the brass armor. So, Mrs. Twigger had plenty of time to denounce Nicholas Tulrumble to his face: to express her opinion that he was a decided monster; and to intimate that, if her ill-used husband sustained any personal damage from the brass armor, she would have the law of Nicholas Tulrumble for manslaughter. When she had said all this with due vehemence, she posted after Ned, who was dragging himself along as best he could, and deploring his unhappiness in most dismal tones.

What a wailing and screaming Ned's children raised when he got home at last! Mrs. Twigger tried to undo the armor, first in one place, and then in another, but she couldn't manage it; so she tumbled Ned into bed, helmet, armor, gauntlets, and all. Such a creaking as the bedstead made, under Ned's weight in his new suit! It didn't break down though; and there Ned lay, like the anonymous vessel in the Bay of Biscay, till next day, drinking barley-water, and looking miserable; and every time he groaned, his good lady said it served him right, which was all the consolation Ned Twigger got.

Nicholas Tulrumble and the gorgeous procession went on together to the town-hall, amid the hisses and groans of all the spectators, who had suddenly taken it into their heads to consider poor Ned a martyr. Nicholas was formally installed in his new office, in acknowledgment of which ceremony he delivered himself of a speech, composed by the secretary, which was very long, and no doubt very good, only the noise of the people outside prevented anybody from hearing it, but Nicholas Tulrumble himself. After which, the procession got back to Mudfog Hall any how it could; and Nicholas and the corporation sat down to dinner.

But the dinner was flat, and Nicholas was disappointed. They were such dull sleepy old fellows, that corporation. Nicholas made quite as long speeches as the Lord Mayor of London had done, nay, he said the very same things that the Lord Mayor of London had said, and the deuce a cheer the corporation gave him. There was only one man in the party who was thoroughly awake; and he was insolent, and called him Nick. Nick! What would be the consequence, thought Nicholas, of any body presuming to call the Lord Mayor of London "Nick!" He should like to know what the sword-bearer would say to that; or the recorder, or the toast-maker, or any other of the great officers of the city. They'd nick him.

But these were not the worst of Nicholas Tulrumble's doings; if they had been, he might have remained a Mayor to this day, and have talked till he lost his voice. He contracted a relish for statistics, and got philosophical; and the statistics and philosophy together, led him into an act which increased his unpopularity and hastened his downfall.

At the very end of the Mudfog High-street, and abutting on the river-side, stands the Jolly Boatmen, an old-fashioned, low-roofed, bay-windowed house, with a bar, kitchen, and tap-room, all in one, and a large fire-place with a kettle to correspond, round which the working-men have congregated time out of mind on a winter's night, refreshed by draughts of good strong beer, and cheered by the sounds of a fiddle and tambourine; the Jolly Boatmen have been duly licensed by the Mayor and corporation, to scrape the fiddle and thumb the tambourine from time, whereof the memory of the oldest inhabitants goeth not to the contrary. Now Nicholas Tulrumble had been reading pamphlets on crime, and parliamentary reports,—or had made the secretary read them to him, which is the same thing in effect,—and he at once perceived that this fiddle and tambourine must have done more to demoralize Mudfog, than any other operating causes that ingenuity could imagine. So he read up for the subject and determined to come out on the corporation with a burst, the very next time the license was applied for.

The licensing day came, and the red-faced landlord of the Jolly Boatmen walked into the town-hall, looking as jolly as need be, having actually put on an extra fiddle for that night, to commemorate the anniversary of the Jolly Boatmen's music license. It was applied for in due form, and was just about to be granted, as a matter of course, when up rose Nicholas Tulrumble, and drowned the astonished corporation in a torrent of eloquence. He descanted in glowing terms upon the increasing depravity of his native town of Mudfog, and the excesses committed by its population. Then he related how shocked he had been to see barrels of beer sliding down into the cellar of the Jolly Boatmen week after week; and how he had sat at a window opposite the Jolly Boatmen for two days together, to count the people who went in for beer between the hours of twelve and one o'clock alone—which, by-the-by, was the time at which the great majority of the Mudfog people dined. Then he went on to state how the number of people who came out with beer-jugs, averaged twenty-one in five minutes, which, being multiplied by twelve, gave two hundred and fifty-two people with beer-jugs in an hour, and multiplied again by fifteen (the number of hours during which the house was open daily), yielded three thousand seven hundred and eighty people with beer-jugs per day, or twenty-six thousand four hundred and sixty people with beer-jugs per week. Then he proceeded to show that a tambourine and moral degradation were synonymous terms, and a fiddle and vicious propensities wholly inseparable. All these arguments he strengthened and demonstrated by frequent references to a large book with a blue cover, and sundry quotations from the Middlesex magistrates; and in the end, the corporation, who were posed with the figures, and sleepy with the speech, and sadly in want of dinner into the bargain, yielded the palm to Nicholas Tulrumble, and refused the music license to the Jolly Boatmen.

But although Nicholas triumphed, his triumph was short.

He carried on the war against beer-jugs and fiddles, forgetting the time when he was glad to drink out of the one, and to dance to the other, till the people hated, and his old friends shunned him. He grew tired of the lonely magnificence of Mudfog Hall, and his heart yearned toward the Lighterman's Arms. He wished he had never set up as a public man, and sighed for the good old times of the coal-shop, and the chimney-corner.

At length old Nicholas, being thoroughly miserable, took heart of grace, paid the secretary a quarter's wages in advance, and packed him off to London by the next coach. Having taken this step, he put his hat on his head, and his pride in his pocket, and walked down to the old room at the Lighterman's Arms. There were only two of the old fellows there, and they looked coldly on Nicholas as he proferred his hand.

"Are you going to put down pipes, Mr. Tulrumble?" said one.

"Or trace the progress of crime to 'baccer?" growled the other.

"Neither," replied Nicholas Tulrumble, shaking hands with them both, whether they would or not. "I've come down to say that I'm very sorry for having made a fool of myself, and that I hope you'll give me up the old chair again."

The old fellows opened their eyes, and three or four more old fellows opened the door, to whom Nicholas, with tears in his eyes, thrust out his hand to, and told the same story. They raised a shout of joy, that made the bells in the ancient church-tower vibrate again, and wheeling the old chair into the warm corner, thrust old Nicholas down into it, and ordered in the very largest-sized bowl of hot punch, with an unlimited number of pipes, directly.

The next day, the Jolly Boatmen got the license, and the next night, old Nicholas and Ned Twigger's wife led off a dance to the music of the fiddle and tambourine, the tone of which seemed mightily improved by a little rest, for they never had played so merrily before. Ned Twigger was in the very height of his glory, and he danced hornpipes, and balanced chairs on his chin, and straws on his nose, till the whole company, including the corporation, were in raptures of admiration at the brilliancy of his acquirements.

Mr. Tulrumble, junior, couldn't make up his mind to be any thing but magnificent, so he went up to London and drew bills on his father ; and when he had overdrawn, and got into debt, he grew penitent and came home again.

As to old Nicholas, he kept his word, and having had six weeks of public life, he never tried it any more. He went to sleep in the town-hall at the very next meeting ; and, in full proof of his sincerity, has requested us to write this faithful narrative. We wish it could have the effect of reminding the Tulrumbles of another sphere, that puffed-up conceit is not dignity, and that snarling at the little pleasures they were once glad to enjoy, because they would rather forget the times when they were of lower station, renders them objects of contempt and ridicule.

This is the first time we have published any of our gleanings from this particular source. Perhaps, at some future period, we may venture to open the chronicles of Mudfog.

CHAPTER XIV.

THE PANTOMIME OF LIFE.

Before we plunge headlong into this paper, let us at once confess to a fondness for pantomimes—to a gentle sympathy with clowns and pantaloons—to an unqualified admiration of harlequins and columbines—to a chaste delight in every action of their brief existence, varied and many colored as those actions are, and inconsistent though they occasionally be with those rigid and formal rules of propriety which regulate the proceedings of meaner and less comprehensive minds. We revel in pantomimes—not because they dazzle one's eyes with tinsel and gold leaf; not because they present to us, once again, the well-beloved chalked faces and goggle eyes of our childhood; not even because, like Christmas-day, and Twelfth-night, and Shrove Tuesday, and one's own birthday, they come to us but once a-year;—our attachment is founded on a graver and very different reason. A pantomime is, to us, a mirror of life; nay more, we maintain that it is to audiences generally, although they are not aware of it; and that this very circumstance is the secret cause of their amusement and delight.

Let us take a slight example. The scene is a street; an elderly gentleman, with a large face, and strongly marked features, appears. His countenance beams with a sunny smile, and a perpetual dimple is on his broad red cheek. He is evidently an opulent elderly gentleman, comfortable in circumstances, and well to do in the world. He is not unmindful of the adornment of his person, for he is richly, not to say gaudily dressed; and that he indulges to a reasonable extent in the pleasures of the table, may be inferred from the joyous and oily manner in which he rubs his stomach, by way of informing the audience that he is going home to dinner. In the fullness of his heart, in the fancied security of wealth, in the possession and enjoyment of all the good things of life, the elderly gentleman suddenly loses his footing and stumbles. How the audience roar! He is set upon by a noisy and officious crowd, who buffet and cuff him unmercifully. They scream with delight! Every time the elderly gentleman struggles to get up, his relentless persecutors knock him down again. The spectators are convulsed with merriment! And when at last the elderly gentleman does get up, and staggers away, despoiled of hat, wig, and clothing, himself battered to pieces, and his watch and money gone, they are exhausted with laughter, and express their merriment and admiration in rounds of applause.

Is this like life? Change the scene to any real street;—to the Stock Exchange, or the City banker's; the merchant's counting-house, or even the tradesman's shop. See any one of these men fall,—the more suddenly, and the nearer the zenith of his pride and riches, the better. What a wild halloo is raised over his prostrate carcass by the shouting mob; how they whoop and yell as he lies humbled beneath them! Mark how eagerly they set upon him when he is down; and how they mock and deride him as he slinks away. Why, it is the pantomine to the very letter.

Of all the pantomimic *dramatis personæ*, we consider the pantaloon the most worthless and debauched. Independent of the dislike one naturally feels at seeing a gentleman of his years engaged in pursuits highly unbecoming his gravity and time of life, we cannot conceal from ourselves the fact that he is a treacherous, worldly-minded old villain, constantly enticing his younger companion, the clown, into acts of fraud or petty larceny, and generally standing aside to watch the result of the enterprise: if it be successful, he never forgets to return for his share of the spoil; but if it turn out a failure, he generally retires with remarkable caution and expedition, and keeps carefully aloof until the affair has blown over. His amorous propensities, too, are eminently disagreeable; and his mode of addressing ladies in the open street at noon-day is downright improper, being usually neither more nor less than a perceptible tickling of the aforesaid ladies in the waist, after committing which, he starts back, manifestly ashamed (as well he may be) of his own indecorum and temerity; continuing, nevertheless to ogle and beckon to them from a distance in a very unpleasant and immoral manner.

Is there any man who cannot count a dozen pantaloons in his own social circle? Is there any man who has not seen them swarming at the west end of the town on a sunshiny day or a summer's evening, going through the last-named pantomimic feats with as much liquorish energy, and as total an absence of reserve, as if they were on the very stage itself? We can tell upon our fingers a dozen pantaloons of our acquaintance at this moment—capital pantaloons, who have been performing all kinds of strange freaks, to the great amusement of their friends and acquaintance, for years past; and who to this day are making such comical and ineffectual attempts to be young and dissolute, that all beholders are like to die with laughter.

Take that old gentleman who has just emerged from the *Café de l'Europe* in the Haymarket, where he has been dining at the expense of the young man upon town with whom he shakes hands as they part at the door of the tavern. The affected warmth of that shake of the hand, the courteous nod, the obvious recollection of the dinner, the savory flavor of which still hangs upon his lips, are all characteristics of his great prototype. He hobbles away humming an opera tune, and twirling his cane to and fro, with affected carelessness. Suddenly he stops—'tis at the milliner's window. He peeps through one of the large panes of glass; and, his view of the ladies within being obstructed by the India shawls, directs his attentions to the young girl with the bandbox in her hand, who is gazing in at the window also. See! he draws beside her. He coughs, she turns away from him. He draws near her again; she disregards him. He gleefully chucks her under the chin, and retreating a few steps nods and beckons with fantastic grimaces, while the girl bestows a contemptuous and supercilious look upon his wrinkled visage. She turns away with a flounce, and the old gentleman trots after her with a toothless chuckle. The pantaloon to the life!

But the close resemblance which the clowns of the stage bear to those of every-day life, is perfectly extraordinary. Some people talk with a sigh of the decline of pantomime, and mur-

mur in low and dismal tones the name of Grimaldi. We mean no disparagement to the worthy and excellent old man when we say, that this is downright nonsense. Clowns that beat Grimaldi all to nothing turn up every day, and nobody patronizes them—more's the pity!

"I know who you mean," says some dirty-faced patron of Mr. Osbaldistone's, laying down the Miscellany when he has got thus far; and bestowing upon vacancy a most knowing glance: "You mean C. J. Smith as did Guy Fawkes, and George Barnwell, at the Garden." The dirty-faced gentleman has hardly uttered the words when he is interrupted by a young gentleman in no shirt-collar and a Petersham coat. "No, no," says the young gentleman; "he means Brown, King, and Gibson, at the 'Delphi." Now, with great deference both to the first-named gentleman with the dirty face, and the last-named gentleman in the non-existing shirt collar, we do *not* mean, either the performer who so grotesquely burlesqued the Popish conspirator, or the three unchangeables who have been dancing the same dance under different imposing titles, and doing the same thing under various high-sounding names, for some five or six years last past. We have no sooner made this avowal than the public, who have hitherto been silent witnesses of the dispute, inquire what on earth it is we *do* mean; and with becoming respect, we proceed to tell them.

It is very well known to all play-goers and pantomime-seers, that the scenes in which a theatrical clown is at the very height of his glory are those which are described in the playbills as "Cheesemonger's shop, and Crockery warehouse," or "Tailor's shop and Mrs. Queertable's boarding-house," or places bearing some such title, where the great fun of the thing consists in the hero's taking lodgings which he has not the slightest intention of paying for, or obtaining goods under false pretenses, or abstracting the stock-in-trade of the respectable shopkeeper next door, or robbing warehouse-porters as they pass under his window, or, to shorten the catalogue, in his swindling everybody he possibly can; it only remaining to be observed, that the more extensive the swindling is, and the more barefaced the impudence of the swindler, the greater the rapture and ecstasy of the audience. Now it is a most remarkable fact that pre cisely this sort of thing occurs in real life day after day, and nobody sees the humor of it. Let us illustrate our position by detailing the plot of this portion of the pantomime—not of the theatre, but of life.

The Honorable Captain Fitz-Whisker Fiercy, attended by his livery-servant Do'em,—a most respectable servant to look at, who has grown gray in the service of the captain's family,—views, treats for, and ultimately obtains possession of, the unfurnished house, such a number, such a street. All the tradesmen in the neighborhood are in agonies of competition for the captain's custom; the captain is a good-natured, kind-hearted, easy man, and to avoid being the cause of disappointment to any, he most handsomely gives orders to all. Hampers of wine, baskets of provisions, cart-loads of furniture, boxes of jewelry, supplies of luxuries of the costliest description, flock to the house of the Honorable Captain Fitz-whisker Fiercy, where they are received with the utmost readiness by the highly respectable Do'em; while the captain himself struts and swaggers about with that compound air of conscious superiority, and generous blood-thirstiness, which a military captain should always, and does most times wear, to the admiration and terror of plebeian men. But the tradesmen's backs are no sooner turned than the captain, with all the eccentricity of a mighty mind, and assisted by the faithful Do'em, whose devoted fidelity is not the least touching part of his character, disposes of every thing to great advantage; for, although the articles fetch small sums, still they are sold considerably above cost price, the cost to the captain being nothing at all. After various maneuvres, the imposture is discovered, Fitz-Fiercy and Do'em are recognized as confederates, and the police-office, to which they are both taken, is thronged with their dupes.

Who can fail to recognize in this, the exact counterpart of the best portion of a theatrical pantomime—Fitz-whisker Fiercy by the clown; Do'em by the pantaloon; and supernumaries by the tradesmen? The best of the joke too, is, that the very coal-merchant who is loudest in his complaints against the person who defrauded him, is the identical man who sat in the centre of the very front row of the pit last night and laughed the most boisterously at this very same thing,—and not so well done either. Talk of Grimaldi, we say again! Did Grimaldi, in his best days, ever do any thing in this way equal to Da Costa?

The mention of this latter justly-celebrated clown reminds us of his last piece of humor, the fraudulently obtaining certain stamped acceptances from a young gentleman in the army. We had scarcely laid down our pen to contemplate for a few moments this admirable actor's performance of that exquisite practical joke, than a new branch of our subject flashed suddenly upon us. So we take it up again at once.

All people that have been behind the scenes, and most people who have been before them, know, that in the representation of a pantomime, a good many men are sent upon the stage for the express purpose of being cheated, or knocked down, or both. Now, down to a moment ago, we had never been able to understand for what possible purpose a great number of odd, lazy, large-headed men, whom one is in the habit of meeting here, and there, and everywhere, could ever have been created. We see it all, now. They are the supernumeraries in the pantomime of life; the men who have been thrust into it, with no other view, than to be constantly tumbling over each other, and running their heads against all sorts of strange things. We sat opposite to one of these men at a supper-table, only last week. Now we think of it, he was exactly like the gentleman with the paste-board heads and faces, who do the corresponding business in the theatrical pantomime; there was the same broad, stolid simper—the same dull, leaden eye—the same unmeaning, vacant stare; and whatever was said or whatever was done, he always came in at precisely the wrong place, or jostled against something that he had not the slightest business with. We looked at the man across the table, again and again; and could not satisfy ourselves what race of beings to class him with. How very odd that this never occurred to us before!

We will frankly own that we have been much troubled with the harlequin. We see harlequins of so many kinds in the real living pantomime, that we hardly know which to select as the proper fellow of him of the theatres. At one time we were disposed to think that the harlequin was neither more nor less than a young man of family and independent property, who had run away with an opera dancer, and was fooling his life and means away in light and trivial amusements. On reflection, however, we remembered that harlequins are occasionally guilty of witty, and even clever acts, and we are rather disposed to acquit our young men of family and independent property, generally speaking, of any such misdemeanors. On a more mature consideration of the subject, we have arrived at the conclusion, that the harlequins of life are just ordinary men, to be found in no particular walk or degree, on whom a certain station, or particular conjunction of circumstances, confers the magic wand; and this brings us to a few words on the pantomime of public and political life, which we shall say at once, and then conclude; merely premising in this place, that we decline any reference whatever to the columbine, being in no wise satisfied of the nature of her connection with her parti-colored lover, and not feeling by any means clear that we should be justified in introducing her to the virtuous and respectable ladies who peruse our lucubrations.

We take it that the commencement of a session of parliament is neither more or less than the drawing up of the curtain for a grand comic pantomime; and that his Majesty's most gracious speech on the opening thereof, may be not inaptly compared to the clown's opening speech of "Here we are!" "My lords and gentlemen, here we are!" appears to our mind at least, to be a very good abstract of the point and meaning of the propitiatory address of the ministry. When we remember how frequently this speech is made, immediately after the change too, the parallel is perfect and still more singular.

Perhaps the cast of our political pantomime never was richer than at this day. We are particularly strong in clowns. At no former time, we should say, have we had such astonishing tumblers, or performers so ready to go through the whole of their feats for the amusement of an admiring throng. The extreme readiness to exhibit, indeed, has given rise to some ill-natured reflections; it having been objected that by exhibiting gratuitously through the country when the theatre is closed, they reduce themselves to the level of mountebanks, and thereby tend to degrade the respectability of the profession. Certainly Grimaldi never did this sort of thing; and though Brown, King and Gibson have gone to the Surrey in vacation-time, and Mr. C. J. Smith has ruralized at Saddler's Wells, we find no theatrical precedent for a general tumbling through the country except in the gentleman, name unknown, who threw somersets in behalf of the late Mr. Richardson, and who is no authority either, because he has never been on the regular boards.

But laying aside this question, which after all is a mere matter of taste, we may reflect with pride and gratification of heart on the proficiency of our clowns as exhibited in the season. Night after night will they twist and tumble about, till two, three and four o'clock in the morning; playing the strangest antics, and giving each other the funniest slaps on the face that can possibly be imagined, without evincing the smallest tokens of fatigue. The strange noises, the confusion, the shouting and roaring amid which this is done, too, would pnt to shame the most turbulent six-penny gallery that ever yelled through a boxing-night.

It is especially curious to behold one of these clowns compelled to go through the most surprising contortions by the irresistible influence of the wand of office, which his leader or harlequin holds above his head. Acted upon by the wonderful charm, he will become perfectly motionless, moving neither hand, foot, or finger, and will even lose the faculty of speech at an instant's notice; or on the other hand, he will become all life and animation if required, pouring forth a torrent of words without sense or meaning, throwing himself into the wildest and most fantastic contortions, and even groveling on the earth and licking up the dust. These exhibitions are more curious than pleasing; indeed they are rather disgusting than otherwise, except to the admirers of such things, with whom we confess to have no fellow-feeling.

Strange tricks—very strange tricks—are also performed by the harlequin who holds, for the time being, the magic wand we have just mentioned. The mere waving it before a man's eyes will dispossess his brain of all the notions previously stored there, and fill it with an entirely new set of ideas; one gentle tap on the back will alter the color of a man's coat completely; and there are some expert performers, who having this wand held first on the one side, and then on the other, will change from side to side, turning their coats at every evolution, with so much rapidity and dexterity, that the quickest eye can scarcely detect their motions. Occasionally, the genius who confers the wand, wrests it from the hand of the temporary possesssor, and consigns it to some new performer ; on which occasion all the characters change sides, and then the race and the hard knocks begin anew.

We might have extended this chapter to a much greater length—we might have carried the comparison into the liberal professions—we might have shown, as was in fact our original purpose, that each is in itself a little pantomime with scenes and characters of its own, complete; but, as we fear we have been quite lengthy enough already, we shall leave the chapter just where it is. A gentleman, not altogether unknown as a dramatic poet, wrote thus a year or two ago——

> "All the world's a stage,
> And all the men and women merely players ;"

and we, tracking out his footsteps at the scarcely-worth-mentioning little distance of a few millions of leagues behind, venturing to add, by way of new reading, that he meant a Pantomime, and that we are all actors in The Pantomime of Life.

THE END.

www.ingramcontent.com/pod-product-compliance
Lightning Source LLC
LaVergne TN
LVHW010220110826
845151LV00004B/1156

* 9 7 8 1 4 2 5 5 2 6 9 5 5 *